ECONOMY AND ARCHITECTURE

Economy and Architecture addresses a timely, critical and much-debated topic in both its historical and contemporary dimensions. From the Apple Store in New York City to the street markets of the Pan-American Highway, from commercial Dubai to the public schools of Australia, this book takes a critical look at contemporary architecture from across the globe, whilst extending its range back in history as far as the Homeric epics of ancient Greece.

The book addresses the challenges of practising architecture within the strictures of contemporary economies, grounded on the fundamental definition of 'economy' as the well managed household – derived from the Greek *oikonomia* – *oikos* (house) and *nemein* (manage). The diverse enquiries of the study are structured around the following key questions:

- How do we define our economies?
- How are the values of architecture negotiated among the various actors involved?
- How do we manage the production of a good architecture within any particular system?
- How does political economy frame and influence architecture?

The majority of examples are taken from current or recent architectural practice; historical examples, which include John Evelyn's villa, Blenheim Palace, John Ruskin's Venice and early twentieth century Paris, place the debates within an extended critical perspective.

Juliet Odgers is Lecturer at the WSA, Cardiff University. Her research relates architecture and landscape design to conceptions of nature, with a particular focus on seventeenth-century Europe.

Mhairi McVicar is Senior Lecturer and Director of Engagement at the WSA, Cardiff University. Her research investigates the processes of architectural practice, with a particular emphasis on the pursuit of precision through written and drawn communications.

Stephen Kite a Professor at the WSA, Cardiff University. His research examines the history, theory and aesthetics of architecture and its wider links to visual culture.

ECONOMY AND ARCHITECTURE

Edited by Juliet Odgers, Mhairi McVicar and Stephen Kite

LONDON AND NEW YORK

First published 2015
by Routledge
2 Park Square, Milton Park, Abingdon, Oxon OX14 4RN

and by Routledge
711 Third Avenue, New York, NY 10017

Routledge is an imprint of the Taylor & Francis Group, an informa business

© 2015 Juliet Odgers, Mhairi McVicar and Stephen Kite

The right of the editors to be identified as the authors of the editorial material, and of the authors for their individual chapters, has been asserted in accordance with sections 77 and 78 of the Copyright, Designs and Patents Act 1988.

All rights reserved. No part of this book may be reprinted or reproduced or utilised in any form or by any electronic, mechanical, or other means, now known or hereafter invented, including photocopying and recording, or in any information storage or retrieval system, without permission in writing from the publishers.

Trademark notice: Product or corporate names may be trademarks or registered trademarks, and are used only for identification and explanation without intent to infringe.

British Library Cataloguing-in-Publication Data
A catalogue record for this book is available from the British Library

Library of Congress Cataloging-in-Publication Data
Economy and architecture / [edited by] Juliet Odgers, Mhairi McVicar and Stephen Kite.
  pages cm
Includes bibliographical references and index.
1. Architecture and society. 2. Architecture--Economic aspects. I. Odgers, Jo, editor. II. McVicar, Mhairi, editor. III. Kite, Stephen, editor.
 NA2543.S6E29 2015
 720.1'03--dc23
 2015003733

ISBN: 978-1-138-02547-9 (hbk)
ISBN: 978-1-138-02548-6 (pbk)
ISBN: 978-1-315-71466-0 (ebk)

Typeset in Bembo and ITC Stone Sans
by GreenGate Publishing Services, Tonbridge, Kent

Printed and bound in Great Britain by
TJ International Ltd, Padstow, Cornwall

In memory of Diana Odgers, 1936–2012

CONTENTS

List of illustrations x
Contributors xiii
Acknowledgements xvii
Foreword by David Leatherbarrow xviii

Editors' introduction 1
Juliet Odgers, Mhairi McVicar and Stephen Kite

PART 1
Defining household 9

1 Equalitarianism 13
   Simon Sadler

2 The earthly paradise of *économie sociale* 27
   Diana Periton

3 Parker Morris and the economies of the Fordist house 38
   Gary A. Boyd

4 Care of commons: exploring questions of care, gifts and reciprocity
   in making new commons 49
   Kim Trogal

5 John Evelyn's villa at Sayes Court: a microcosm of labour and love 59
   Juliet Odgers

PART 2
Negotiating value   69

6 Architectural husbandry   73
   Christine Stevenson

7 Home economics   86
   Flora Samuel

8 Four economies of architecture   99
   Adam Sharr

9 The libidinal economy of architecture: skin, membranes and
   other surfaces of desire   108
   Chris L. Smith

10 Architectural renewal and poetic persistence: investing in
   an economy of stories   118
   Lisa Landrum

PART 3
Managing production   127

11 Scarcity constructs   131
   Jeremy Till

12 Economy of means   143
   Jonathan Sergison, Sergison Bates architects LLP

13 An optional extra: valuing architecture at the Brompton Boilers   151
   Mhairi McVicar

14 The architect: a disappearing species in a financialized space?   162
   Silke Ötsch

15 The Pan-American Highway: informal urbanism in
   Latin-American border cities   175
   Cristian Suau

PART 4
Politics and economy 187

16 The death and life of PFI urbanism: vagaries of style and politics
  in British Cities, 2009–present 191
  Owen Hatherley

17 A stimulus for education: global economic events and the design
  of Australian schools 204
  Hannah Lewi and Cameron Logan

18 Restricted by scarcity, striving for greater bounty: the role of
  architecture in making Dubai 216
  Kevin Mitchell

19 Designing public space in Austerity Britain 226
  Suzanne Hall

20 The bricks of Venice: material and craft in John Ruskin's
  political economy 237
  Stephen Kite

  List of illustration credits 248
  Select bibliography 250
  Index 257

ILLUSTRATIONS

Figures

0.1	The Heroines Pyxis in the British Museum	xx
1.1	Bernard Maybeck, First Church of Christ Scientist, Berkeley, California, 1910	14
1.2	Joseph Esherick, Hedgerow House 1, the Sea Ranch, California, 1966-1967	16
1.3	Sim van der Ryn and the Office of Alternative Technology, Bateson Building, Sacramento, California, 1977	19
1.4	Apple Store, Fifth Avenue, Manhattan, 2009	21
2.1	*Cité-jardin de Suresnes*	28
2.2	*Palais d'économie sociale*, Paris Exposition: Paris, France, 1900	30
2.3	*Cité-jardin de Suresnes*, avenue Edouard Vaillant	35
3.1	Diagram by Gordon Cullen, from *Homes for Today and Tomorrow*	41
3.2	'Examples of Meal Services Arrangements' from *Meals in Modern Homes*	42
3.3	The promiscuous arrow, from *Homes for Today and Tomorrow*	43
3.4	Wall-less electrical services, from *Homes for Today and Tomorrow*	46
4.1	Gifted produce: outside the college, Todmorden, March 2011	50
4.2	Gifted produce: Propaganda Garden, Todmorden, March 2011	54
4.3	Invisible labour: fifty new fruit trees, March 2011	55
5.1	The plan of Sayes Court house and garden, by John Evelyn, c. 1652	60
6.1	Blenheim Palace, Oxfordshire	75
6.2	Burley-on-the-Hill, Rutland, 1694–1700	76

6.3	Blenheim Kitchen Court, designed 1707–1708, built 1716	77
6.4	St Luke's Hospital, Old Street, London	82
7.1	Architect types	90
8.1	'One foot in the past'	100
9.1	'Membrane Interaction'	113
9.2	'Membrane Arrays'	113
9.3	'Membrane Interaction'	115
12.1	Bricklayer, Crediton Road	143
13.1	Exterior view of the South Kensington Museum (the 'Brompton Boilers') under construction	153
13.2	Exterior view of the south front entrance of the South Kensington Museum (the 'Brompton Boilers')	155
14.1	Power Tower, Linz	167
14.2	Betham Tower, Manchester	168
14.3	Centre Commercial Euralille, Lille	168
15.1	Comparative maps of borderlands, edge cities and mega-cities	178
15.2	Distribution of household income in Santiago and sequence of informal commerce along the *Panamericana* in Santiago	180
15.3	Informal settlement: immigrants dwelling outside the urban limit of Arica, Chile, 2014	183
15.4	Informal commerce: the Fox Flea Market is an illicit marquee in El Paso, USA, 2014	184
16.1	Exurbanism and PFI: Darent Valley Hospital, Dartford	193
16.2	Regeneration, pre-crash: Manchester skyline	196
16.3	Regeneration, post-crash: Kings Cross	202
17.1	Cartoon showing economic stimulus building in the likeness of former Prime Minister Kevin Rudd with chimney styled as Deputy Prime Minister and Education Minister at the time, Julia Gillard	207
17.2	Example template designs by Hayball and Gray Puksand Architects for the Victorian Education Department	209
17.3	Building the Education Revolution billboard outside the newly completed multi-purpose hall for Fairfield Primary School, Victoria	211
18.1	Apartment blocks in the China cluster in International City, Dubai	221
18.2	Model of the Burj Khalifa on display in Dubai Mall	222
18.3	The Burj Khalifa shown in the context of Dubai's skyline	223
19.1	Seeds of the Urban Forest	231

19.2	Maturing the Forest	233
20.1	Window 'at the Tana', Corte Contarina	241
20.2	John Ruskin, window 'at the Tana'	243
20.3	Detail of *The Granary*, Bristol	245

Table

14.1	Architects' strategies and earnings	170

CONTRIBUTORS

Gary A. Boyd is Reader in Architecture at Queen's University, Belfast. In 2014, he was joint commissioner/curator of *Infra-Éireann: Making Ireland Modern*, the Irish Pavilion for the Venice Architectural Biennale 2014 and co-edited *Infrastructure and the Architectures of Modernity in Ireland 1916–2016* (2015). Other books include *Ordnance: War + Architecture & Space* (co-editor, 2013) and *Dublin 1745–1922: Hospitals, Spectacles* (author, 2006). He has contributed chapters and essays to many other publications including *Architecture 1600–2000: Volume IV of the Art and Architecture of Ireland* (2014).

Suzanne Hall is an urban ethnographer and has practised as an architect in South Africa. She teaches in the Cities programme at the London School of Economics and Political Science, and her research focuses on socio-spatial elaborations of urban migration. Her monograph, *City, Street and Citizen*, was published in 2012.

Owen Hatherley was born in Southampton, England, in 1981, and divides his time between Woolwich and Warsaw. He works as a freelance writer on architecture and cultural politics, writing regularly for *Architects Journal*, *Architectural Review*, *Icon*, *The Guardian* and *New Humanist*. He is the author of five books: *Militant Modernism* (2009), *A Guide to the New Ruins of Great Britain* (2010), *Uncommon*, on the pop group Pulp (2011), *A New Kind of Bleak: Journeys Through Urban Britain* (2012) and *Across the Plaza*, on squares in Eastern Europe (2012). Most recently, he edited and updated Ian Nairn's *Towns* (2013). He received a PhD in 2011 from Birkbeck College, London, for a thesis on 'The Political Aesthetics of Americanism in Weimar Germany and the Soviet Union, 1919–34', and is currently working on two books, one on architecture and communism, and another on austerity nostalgia.

Stephen Kite is Professor at the Welsh School of Architecture, Cardiff University, Wales, UK. His research explores the history and theory of architecture and its wider connections to visual culture. His recent books are a study of the critical writings on architecture and art of Adrian Stokes – *Adrian Stokes: An Architectonic Eye* (2009), and an examination of the evolution of Ruskin's observation of architecture – *Building Ruskin's Italy: Watching Architecture* (2012). His current book project is *Shadow Makers: A Cultural History of Shadows in Architecture* (forthcoming). He is an editor of *Architectural Research Quarterly*.

Lisa Landrum is an architect and Associate Professor in the Department of Architecture at the University of Manitoba in Winnipeg, Canada. Her primary research explores dramatic agencies of architecture and architectural theory. She has contributed book chapters to *Architecture as a Performing Art* (2013), *Architecture and Justice: Judicial Meanings in the Public Realm* (2013) and *Architecture's Appeal: How Theory Informs Praxis* (2015).

Hannah Lewi is Associate Professor and Associate Dean in the Faculty of Architecture, Building and Planning at the University of Melbourne. She is the vice-chair of Docomomo Australia, a past president of SAHANZ and co-editor and author of the book *Community: Building Modern Australia* (2010).

Cameron Logan is Senior Lecturer and Director of Heritage Conservation in the Faculty of Architecture, Design and Planning at the University of Sydney. He is the author of *Historic Capital: Preservation, Race and Real Estate in Washington, DC* (forthcoming).

Mhairi McVicar is Senior Lecturer at the Welsh School of Architecture. Her research investigates the pursuit of precision and its consequences in architectural practice. Recent publications include 'Specifying intent at the Museum of Childhood' in *Architectural Research Quarterly* (2012), 'God is in the details/The detail is moot: A meeting between Koolhaas and Mies' in *Reading Architecture and Culture: Researching Buildings, Spaces and Documents* (2012) and 'Passion and control: Lewerentz and a mortar joint' in *Quality out of Control: Standards for Measuring Architecture* (2010).

Kevin Mitchell has taught at the American University of Sharjah since 1999 and currently serves as Interim Provost. Recent work includes an issue of *Architectural Design (AD)* focused on architecture and urbanism in the Gulf (co-edited with George Katodrytis) and essays in *The Superlative City: Dubai and the Urban Condition in the Early Twenty-First Century* (2013) and *Architecture and Globalisation in the Persian Gulf Region* (2013).

Juliet Odgers is Lecturer in Architecture at the Welsh School of Architecture, Cardiff University. This is the third in a series of edited books by Routledge to which she has contributed as editor. The others are *Primitive: Original Matters in Architecture* (2008) and *Quality out of Control: Standards for Measuring Architecture*

(2010). Her primary research field is in early modern garden design and visions of nature, on which see 'Gaffarel's influence on John Evelyn' in *Jacques Gaffarel: Between Magic and Science* (2014). She is an editor of *Architectural Research Quarterly*.

Silke Ötsch has been a postdoctoral researcher at the Department of Sociology at the University of Innsbruck (Austria) since 2009. Her main field of research is financialised capitalism from the perspective of political and cultural economy, transformation and the sociology of the profession of the architect.

Diana Periton is Senior Lecturer in Architecture at De Montfort University, Leicester. Her research focuses on the development of urbanism as an explicit discipline in the early twentieth century, and its relationship to social policy, housing and landscape design, particularly in France. Recent publications include contributions to two books published by Routledge: *Reading Architecture and Culture*, ed. Adam Sharr (2012); and *Intimate Metropolis: Urban Subjects in the Modern City*, eds Vittoria Di Palma, Diana Periton and Marina Lathouri (2009). She is founding co-editor of the new journal *Architecture and Culture*, launched in 2013.

Simon Sadler is Professor in the Department of Design at the University of California, Davis. A key theme of his publications, which include *Archigram: Architecture without Architecture* (2005) and *The Situationist City* (1998), is the deployment of design as a way to reimagine political economy.

Flora Samuel is Professor of Architecture at the University of Sheffield. She has published very extensively on Le Corbusier but is now focusing on what the architecture profession needs to do better to demonstrate its value – namely develop practice-based research. She is now working very hard from within RIBA to develop the research culture within the profession and is writing a book called *Why Architects Matter*.

Jonathan Sergison established Sergison Bates architects in 1996 together with Stephen Bates. The practice has been awarded the Heinrich Tessenow and Erich Schelling medals and many of their buildings have won international recognition. Jonathan Sergison has taught at a number of prestigious schools of architecture and is currently Professor of Architectural Design at the Accademia di Architettura, Mendrisio, Switzerland. His publications include *Papers* (2001), *Brick-work: Thinking and Making* (2005), *Papers 2* (2007) and *Buildings* (2012).

Adam Sharr is Professor of Architecture at Newcastle University, Editor-in-Chief of *arq: Architectural Research Quarterly*, Principal of Adam Sharr Architects and Series Editor of *Thinkers for Architects* (Routledge). His books include *Heidegger's Hut* (2006), *Reading Architecture and Culture* (2012) and *Demolishing Whitehall* (2013).

Chris L. Smith is Associate Professor in Architectural Design and Technê in the Faculty of Architecture at the University of Sydney. His research is concerned with the interdisciplinary nexus of philosophy, biology and architectural theory.

He is presently concentrating upon an Australian Research Council Grant project focused on architectural expression and bio-medicine.

Christine Stevenson is Professor at The Courtauld Institute of Art, University of London. Economy is a major theme in her first book, *Medicine and Magnificence: British Hospital and Asylum Architecture 1660–1815* (2000). How buildings and monuments are granted value is the subject of her most recent book, *The City and the King: Architecture and Politics in Restoration London* (2013).

Cristian Suau holds a PhD in Architecture and a Masters in Urban Design. He has taught architectural design at the Welsh School of Architecture and in various international design workshops. Currently he is Senior Lecturer and Director of the Glasgow Project Office at Strathclyde University, Department of Architecture.

Jeremy Till is Head of Central Saint Martins and Pro Vice-Chancellor, University of the Arts London. His extensive written work includes the books *Flexible Housing* (2007), *Architecture Depends* (2009) and *Spatial Agency* (2011), all three of which won the RIBA President's Award for Research. As an architect, he worked with Sarah Wigglesworth Architects.

Kim Trogal is a postdoctoral Research Fellow at Central Saint Martins and post-doctoral Research Assistant at the Sheffield School of Architecture. She has a PhD in architecture, for which she was awarded the RIBA LKE Ozolins Studentship. She is co-editor, with Doina Petrescu, of *The Social (Re)Production of Architecture: Politics, Economies and Actions in Contemporary Practice* (2015).

ACKNOWLEDGEMENTS

The editors would like to acknowledge a number of people for their help and inspiration in creating the international conference, held at the Welsh School of Architecture, Cardiff University, from which this book derives: Katrina Lewis; David Leatherbarrow and Adam Sharr; Phil Jones and Chris Tweed; Heidi Day; Charles Drozynski; Marie-Cécile Embleton; Shiyu Jiang; Matthew Jones; and Gabriela Zapata-Lancaster. We are grateful to all the participants for their contributions, notably those whose work we have not been able to include here, and particularly our keynote speakers who established formidable agendas for the different strands of debate: Owen Hatherley, Simon Sadler, Flora Samuel, Jonathan Sergison, Christine Stevenson and Jeremy Till.

FOREWORD

Economy: what gives the theme its urgency in architecture today?

Is it a desire for an alternative to wasteful construction methods and settlement patterns, the feeling that now is the time to recalibrate spending and saving, that the only defensible responses to the increasing scarcity of resources are practices that are less profligate and more economical? Or does the topic's currency result from developments within the architecture discipline itself: that today's critics see significant accomplishment and elegance in solutions that are internally coherent and sparing? Is there something both timely and good about designs that are both lean and resource conserving? Much of this book says yes to these questions. And it says more: the concern for economy has been on the minds of architects for centuries, and this history gives greater amplitude, even richness, to current conceptions.

For the ancient Greeks the topic's importance was obvious: the more perfect the economy the more complete the self-sufficiency, independence and leisure it allowed; the fuller the sense of *freedom*. Saving and spending were not central to ancient accounts of economical living; instead, ideas of place, which is to say, definite locations for all the equipment, furnishings and settings that comprised the house, its gardens, out-buildings and fields (the entire estate took precedence). For the modern reader this seems odd, not only the connection between economy and freedom, but their dependence on spatial configuration and topography. *Oeconomicus*, Xenophon's fourth century BCE treatise on estate management, presented the *oikos* as an ensemble of places, a network of receptacles, variously sized and shaped, but tailored so closely to their contents, glove-like, that they seemed incomplete without them: 'The place itself will miss whatever is not in it.' Like Aristotle, he thought that being in a place was natural to things. Many modern thinkers have argued similarly. This conception explains why return is what things desire most when not serving their purpose. The same was true for people, as the story of Odysseus' longing for Ithaca revealed. Tidiness was not the most important result of domestic economy; instead, beauty. And that, like freedom, was no small outcome, not for the house, estate, village or town.

The wider horizon of economical arrangements is captured rather well by a modern term, ecology, which not only derives from the same stem, but likewise prescribes places for things, although at a larger scale: organisms in their native habitats. In the eighteenth and nineteenth centuries writers such as Linnaeus, Darwin and Haeckel tried to explain the 'economy of nature' with concepts of habitat in mind. Haeckel criticized earlier studies for their neglect of 'the place each organism takes in the household of nature, in the economy of all nature'. Once again, the matters of spending and saving, surplus and scarcity were not decisive; rather, congeniality between forms of existence and their locations, enmeshed in a web of interdependencies.

When twentieth-century figures such as Adolf Loos, Le Corbusier and Frank Lloyd Wright invoked the idea of economy they too envisaged a structure of mutualities: the order of the *Raumplan*, forms determined by the 'engineer's aesthetic' and elements that express 'plasticity'. When figures today speak of 'resolving the most material problems with the greatest amount of elegance' (Nouvel), or 'engaging circumstances in order to be free from them' (Siza), or architecture responding 'with absolute clarity to the fundamental situations that sustain human life' (Mendes da Rocha), they invoke dimensions of economic thinking that have informed architecture for centuries. It is hardly surprising, and entirely encouraging, that it attracts so much attention today.

David Leatherbarrow

FIGURE 0.1 The Heroines Pyxis in the British Museum

EDITORS' INTRODUCTION

Juliet Odgers, Mhairi McVicar and Stephen Kite

In recent years the Director of the British Museum, Neil MacGregor, has caught the imagination of many with his BBC Radio talks, and subsequent book – *A History of the World in 100 Objects*.[1] In each of his talks MacGregor weaves a narrative around one artefact from the Museum's vast collections. In organizing the international conference on *Economy and Architecture* (Welsh School of Architecture, Cardiff University, July 2011) and this resulting collection of essays, one British Museum artefact in particular – an object not discussed by MacGregor – became *our* logo and touchstone. It is a fifth century BCE Attic red-figure pyxis (a box for cosmetics or jewellery) which shows six women engaged in activities of domestic life, set in an architecturally articulated frame.[2] Moving from left to right, a seated woman works wool, whilst, facing her, another holds a vessel; a Doric column, supporting an entablature, frames the scene and separates it from the ensuing pairing where one woman proffers a basket to another; in the final scene a woman emerges from a double door, decorated with bosses and with triglyphs above, to greet another woman bearing a jewellery box. This sequence of images vividly portrays some of the practices entailed in running a home – practices that engage personal relationships between the members of the household, their labours, their exchange of products and fruits, their shared values and, crucially, their spatial setting. We take this image as a starting point to lead us into a definition of economy.

In a story from two millennia ago, the Athenian estate owner Ischomachos brought his bride into his *oikos* and, entering the house, he said: 'This household is what is common [*koinos*] to us'.[3] The word 'economy' is derived from the Greek *oikonomia* (*oikos*/house and *nemein*/manage). In its original formulation, then, 'economy' means the management of a 'household', an idea that we interpret broadly as the place that is common to us. The collection of essays contained in this book is neither ignorant nor dismissive of the very different current understanding of 'economy' – the market economy of modern liberal economics. Indeed we are all too aware, as any practising architect must be, that a skilful engagement with the exigencies of markets, money and price are necessary not only in running a successful practice, but also in 'procuring' a building.[4] However, as the economic historian Karl Polanyi elaborates in his study *The Livelihood of Man*, 'formal' ways of analysing, constructing and running economies through abstract systems, such as those exemplified by liberal economics, are neither a universal nor a necessary part of 'substantial economy' – that is to say the production and distribution of those material things that are needful for life, and for the cultural articulation and enjoyment of life.[5] Furthermore an excessive reliance on the mechanics of 'formal' economics as the mechanism of social 'good' all too often leads in the opposite direction, towards a degradation of the social, cultural and physical dimensions of the *oikos*.

These then are the two poles of our understanding of 'economy' – the 'formal' systematics of liberal economics and a more ancient understanding of household as 'communities of persons that bind individuals in their association and that define the moral location of their community in a wider array of goods'[6] – a dense matrix of human relationships towards common ends. The pyxis image serves as an evocation of the latter – potent, if lightly sketched. But if the vision of harmonious domestic life offered by this ancient Greek image still has resonance for us, we might well ask if it is merely nostalgia to make it an emblem of our concerns? Notwithstanding its charm, the image illustrates an elite dwelling wherein some of the household 'members' were slaves and in which women were, without exception, confined to subordinate positions. Issues of ethical engagement, social justice and politics necessarily inform the conversation carried out in the pages of this volume. We see this as all the more necessary in a time of austerity politics and financial crisis, where many already face the constant challenge of living without any stable and secure house to manage.

We have included studies from a long time span – the earliest engaging with ancient Greece, the latest treating contemporary architectural practice. As introduction, we offer the following briefest sketch of the changes wrought during this long period.

In the ancient *oikos* and *polis*, the production of space, the good communal life and participation in the city was hierarchical; in many of its aspects this model was not successfully challenged until the Enlightenment. In the eighteenth century, a more abstracted conception of economy was conceived and instituted, one that sought to spread the freedoms traditionally enjoyed only by a limited patriarchal elite to a greater section of society. In this modern conception of economy, hierarchical systems were loosened and relations modelled more as networks and ecologies than as privileged arborescent structures. On the one hand, this delivered a more functionally sophisticated knowledge of the interconnectedness of goods, labour and exchange; on the other, the networks themselves started to occupy a privileged position as the mechanism of 'freedom' and 'efficiency', thus usurping the place of ethical action as a way of attaining the 'goods' of life. As political economy evolved as a science of the networked flow of capital, it lost its connections to those peoples and places so visible in the household models of the polity, and the capacity to value crucial common goods such as social relationships or beautiful environments.

This however is not the whole story. Even the most stringently market-oriented economies are pervaded by places where more traditional models of economy continue to hold sway – the family is the most obvious locus of this phenomenon. Here it is acknowledged that non-market, non-contracted, non-commodified economic relationships predominate, despite the incursions of consumables into our modern domestic spheres, despite wi-fi, and despite increasing institutional protection of the autonomous rights of its constituent members. The family is far from being the only such organized community – but it is paradigmatic.[7] Our lived experience of such common familial situations remains potent and through it we still know and instinctively respond to the arena of familial mutuality presented by our ancient Greek illustration. Add to this continuity another; that modern economies, like their traditional predecessors, remain predicated on the hope of facilitating a 'good life' – though we may question for which sectors of society, and how those 'goods' are conceived and attained.

With these thoughts in mind, many socially attuned architects still define their task as that of ordering and articulating the spaces of households, as physical and spatial backdrops for a life lived for common benefit; albeit many projects imply or serve an *oikos* of daunting complexity and scale – as, for example, schools commissioned and funded from the public purse. Clearly, to sustain a vision that maintains an appropriate, humane and nuanced articulation of the life of the *oikos* as a central architectural value in the face of everyday market, economic pressures – cost control, performance specification, branding, value engineering and the rest – takes constantly renewed efforts. Architects must negotiate their immediate economic markets, whilst imaginatively engaging with the wider horizons of life, where economy is not wholly grounded in production, consumption and exchange; where mutuality, altruism and non-purposive spontaneous enjoyment of the given world form a part of the 'goods' to which humanity aspires. An architecture that aligns itself only with the demands of markets, providing the architectural commodities that different consumer groups 'want' and ignoring deeper needs – ones that cannot be easily articulated to suit the balance sheet – is indeed a failing architecture.

This tension is familiar both to those who have graduated from architecture school with aspirations for making a better architecture in the wider world only to encounter resistances, and also to non-professional communities seeking to improve their *oikos*. To maintain this vision is to consider architecture not only in market economic terms, but in its situated humanistic settings; it is to foreground qualitative values in a scenario where the lingua franca of value engineering and building information modelling (BIM) increasingly ignores all value that escapes measurable performance criteria. Many of the contributions in this book seek the creative moment within what appears to be unpromising conditions. They focus not only on the familiar difficulties of obtrusive economic pressures, but present structures of a common ethos whose creative potential supports a richer understanding of our designed spaces.

This book engages with these issues around the following key questions: how do we define our economies? How are the values of architecture negotiated among the various actors involved? How do we manage the production of a good architecture within any particular system? How does political economy frame and influence architecture? Accordingly, the book is structured into the following four sections: 'Defining household'; 'Negotiating value'; 'Managing production'; and 'Politics and economy'.

'Defining household' concerns itself primarily with issues of identity, considering the ways in which the members of a household or community – or those who envision a household or community for others – articulate their idea of what it is to be a good citizen, or a good member of the household, and how this appears as a spatial vision or design ethos. The 'households' studied operate variously at the scale of a region, a city, a neighbourhood or an individual dwelling. Here the systematic approaches that we have introduced as a definition characteristic of modern economics appear in various guises and in dialogue with more traditional ideas of household. Although contemporary homes often still look more or less traditional, they are now, more than ever before, atomized and connected by invisible digital architectures never conceived in even the most fervent dreams of Reyner Banham or Superstudio. These are the economies of Italo Calvino's *Eudoxia* – spun from infrastructures, tracings and networks.[8]

To elaborate this idea, take a basic product like grain and its marketing. When this crop came in a labelled sack, its relationship with the homestead that produced it remained intact. But in the Great West of the USA as the grain came out of the sacks into huge steam-powered grain elevators – under the pressure of greater production – nothing could disguise the fact that now the grain *flowed*.[9] It had become an abstracted market good, with no discernible relationship either to the place or people of its production, a circumstance that could not be belied even by the monumental 'architecture' of the elevators of Chicago and Buffalo, so beloved by Modernism. Grain was no longer physical produce linked to the household that had grown it, but an item of Capital that could be speculated on in the newly-created Futures Markets. Using the power of their *Eudoxian* spinnings City Traders have gone on to turn every product of hand and mind into abstract currents transgressing any recognisable geographical or physical borders. Against such fluxes, architecture's attempts to lay down any markers of physical and tectonic resistance, or identity, can appear progressively desperate and futile. But there are moments of resistance. Some develop visions of the good economy as a *Hortus Conclusus* or enclosed garden – a manageable space for experiments in economy. Others develop visions of a common ethical life and a shared identity developed within the familiar banality of a commercialized landscape, in creative dialogue with systematic abstractions. Some of these investigations have been Edenic, aspiring to wider Utopias; others more instrumental, seeking for example an *existenzminimum* through the lingua franca of measurable performance.

The unstable economic terrains laid out in the first section prompt the questions addressed in the next part of the book – 'Negotiating value'. Here we ask how the various actors making the spaces of our economies negotiate the value of architecture – insofar as they even recognize a need for architecture, or indeed architects. These questions concern the worth of what architects themselves do, identifying their skillsets in the various overlapping economic arenas in which they operate – whether specifically social, commercial or cultural in orientation. Architectural values are negotiated in many settings: in the discourse between client and architect; in literatures – academic, policy-making, trade journals, narratives, etc.; in the human body and its encounters with the surfaces and spaces of architecture; and in the stories through which we establish and renew the bonds and values of our various households.

The third 'Managing production' section considers the question of how architects and non-architects navigate the turbulent currents of everyday economic pressures, managing both the production of 'good' architecture and their own survival in a market where a real or constructed scarcity creates increasingly difficult conditions. Within the presiding limits of the planetary ecology itself – limits that most would at least *claim* to recognize – globalization has weakened localized democratic functioning and produced increasingly uneven income distribution and privation. Nonetheless, throughout the world, the harshest odds have produced extraordinarily vital informal economies and 'architectures without architects' in contexts where access to even basic professional services is denied.[10] These are probably the most common economies of place-production, yet even in these extreme situations community-minded architects have managed to produce and facilitate worthwhile contributions. In the better funded realms in which architects operate they have often seized the opportunity to reflect the wider existential conditions of angst and scarcity in ethics and aesthetics of *Arte Povera*, Brutalism and the like.[11] Another longstanding competition is the 'sibling rivalry' between architect and engineer, characterized in one case as engineer Dankmar Adler at one end of the office, and art-architect Louis Sullivan at the other – 'the solidity of German technique seemingly balancing mercurial Celtic artistry'.[12] In times of cultural confusion and scarcity – whether real, perceived or politically motivated – the architect's contribution, if conceived as 'art-dressing', can look very dispensable. In defining their value, architects have swung between stressing the essential poetics and symbolic import of their *Bekleidung* – as in the various PostModernisms and calls for a return-to-ornament – to protesting the through-composed, integral structural integrity of their every design move.

Having defined and distinguished architecture and economy within the levels of *oikos*, in its scales of value and the organization of its production, the final part of the book specifically considers 'Politics and economy'. In the foregoing sections, architecture, as a culture and discipline, has often appeared highly challenged and marginalized. At the same time building and development continue to be powerful political instruments: as economic regulators, as ways of making money (if not always creating much enduring 'value'), in ordering societies and as iconic images in the arenas of identity politics. Too often object-cities result; territories of indeterminate value with their loosely aggregated and isolated lunges at form. In the better cases when architects and urban-designers are meaningfully involved early on, public realms of high quality can be made and mixed-uses fostered even in the most corporate of scenarios. Sometimes architects get caught up anyhow in the slipstream of 'development' waterfronts, malls or downtowns. Even if not initially in the forefront of the minds of the policy-makers or venture capitalists, the savvier find ways to display their worth, to announce the possibilities of architecture and to elbow themselves to the decision tables. Others work bottom-up with economically smaller or disadvantaged user groups – those off the radar of the power-brokers and the breaking wave of the development strategies. Their campaigns of resistance and micro-intervention often achieve economic impacts far beyond the actual euros or dollars paid in.

In the conversations in each of these parts of the book the majority of examples are taken from current or recent architectural practice. Historical examples in each section place the various situations in a more extended critical perspective.

In most current studies, economy and architecture are discussed in fragmented ways within the separate debates concerning: development finance; project management and professional education; sustainability and ecology; globalization; and leisure and the self-sustaining economies of architectural history and theory. Here the intention is to promote a more holistic treatment that dismisses neither the professional managerial concerns of practice, nor the poetic, social and ethical concerns implied in any *praxis*. Instead, common ground is found for a more inclusive and creative discussion. The intention is that in bringing these concerns together, unexpected and fresh insights may be brought into some of the persistent dilemmas of economy and architecture. In treating such a central cultural issue there must necessarily be focus and limits. This study is firmly situated within the architectural humanities, and the chapters – though diverse in the material that each addresses – take common standpoints in placing architectural practices or artefacts in their varied cultural contexts.

Notes

1. Neil MacGregor, *A History of the World in 100 Objects* (London: Penguin, 2011).
2. See Anthony F. Mangieri, 'Legendary Women and Greek Womanhood: The Heroines Pyxis in the British Museum', *American Journal of Archaeology*, vol. 114, no. 3 (July 2010), 429–45.
3. 'Introduction' in William James Booth, *Households: On the Moral Architecture of the Economy* (Ithaca, NY; London: Cornell University Press, 1993), p. 1.
4. The editors have all engaged in architectural practice over a significant period.
5. Karl Polanyi and Harry W. Pearson, *The Livelihood of Man* (New York; London: Academic Press, 1977).
6. Booth, *Households*, p. 1.
7. Pearson, 'Editor's Introduction' in Karl Polanyi and Harry W. Pearson, *The Livelihood of Man* (New York; London: Academic Press, 1977), pp. i–iv (p. xxxiii).
8. Italo Calvino, *Invisible Cities* (New York: Harcourt Brace Jovanovich, 1974).

9 William Cronon, *Nature's Metropolis: Chicago and the Great West* (New York; London: W. W. Norton, 1991), Chapter 3, 'Pricing the Future: Grain'.
10 The phrase is borrowed from Bernard Rudofsky's classical study of vernacular traditions in architecture, *Architecture without Architects: A Short Introduction to Non-Pedigreed Architecture* (New York: Doubleday, 1964).
11 Reyner Banham, *The New Brutalism: Ethic or Aesthetic?* (London: Architectural Press, 1966); Alexander Clement, *Brutalism: Post-War British Architecture* (Ramsbury: Crowood, 2011).
12 Andrew Saint, *Architect and Engineer: A Study in Sibling Rivalry* (New Haven, CT; London: Yale University Press, 2007), p. 197.

PART 1
Defining household

Writing in the 1970s, Colin Rowe argued that:

> For the architect, of course, the ethical content of the good society has, maybe, always been something which building was to make evident ... for, whatever other controlling fantasies have emerged – antiquity, tradition, technology – these have invariably been conceived of as aiding and abetting an in some way benign or decorous social order.[1]

Putting aside the characterisation of the architect as 'he' (then dubious and now wholly untenable) what remains of the statement still, probably, holds true. Consequently, the primary question that informs the chapters in this section is – if the aim of economy is to promote the 'good life', how is this 'good' conceived and played out in the shared spaces of the 'household'? The chapters presented here offer definitions of economy in relation to that version of the 'decorous social order' proposed by a variety of 'households'.

We include five studies at five different scales – the region, suburb and town, the estate and the dwelling unit. The chapters address the radical kinetic spaces of twentieth-century California; the *économie sociale* of the Parisian garden city; a contemporary suburban experimental 'gift economy' at Todmorden; the 'divine economy' of a seventeenth-century godly household; and the late twentieth-century 'space standardised' home itself. So who is it who imagines and defines the good *oikos* in these various situations? Government and its agencies are the defining bodies in one case; others present the vision of the *pater familias*; a grass-roots community group; and the diffuse, but nonetheless identifiable, design community of a region. Each *oikos* holds a different relationship to place, some existing only in a space of extreme abstraction; others rooted in the specifics of both site and community; yet others identifiable in the tension between place and systematic abstraction.

In the opening chapter, **Simon Sadler** offers a portrait of what he calls the 'equalitarian' design ethos of California. California has long been characterized as a 'placeless' territory (we remember Gertrude Stein famously writing of Oakland California, 'there is no there there'). Sadler presents California in a more positive light, locating the shared architectural good of the region in the idea of an accessible connectivity. He argues that Californian designers see their task as providing a communal tissue of connectivity that links humans with technology and with nature. This common good – the mutual participation in common structures of communication and production – is exemplified by Apple computers, infrastructure projects, the pages of the *Whole Earth Catalog* and the Bay Region Style architects.

In the early years of the twentieth century, Paris was encircled by a ring of new garden city suburbs. These were consciously planned as experiments in ideal living, defined in terms of *économie sociale*, or 'the totality of the moral and material conditions of a society', to give a contemporary definition.[2] **Diana Periton** presents this new urbanistic paradigm in terms of two opposing ideas of Eden – a paradise of social harmony, and a paradise of luxurious hedonism. She draws both on the designs for the International Exhibition of 1900, which included a didactic display on the *économie sociale*, and on contemporary literature on the topic, including the writings of André Gide, and his less famous nephew, Charles Gide. How, she asks, was good citizenry in this new suburban Eden to be understood? Was it through participation in an efficient economy of consumption, or was a fuller vision of engagement on offer?

Moving to Britain in the 1960s, **Gary A. Boyd** presents us with a study in government-authored space standards for the home, the Parker Morris report of 1961. He argues that report represents not only a response to the imperatives of the industrial production of housing – the efficiencies of volume building, prefabrication, modularization and so on – it also envisions the spaces of the home itself in terms of industrial production and consumption. Illustrated by Gordon Cullen, the Parker Morris domestic interior is as much planned around the accommodation of domestic consumer durables as it is around the 'tasks' of the modern consumer inhabitants. Cullen's apparently placeless and scale-less diagrams emblematize these relationships, as walls dissolve and space flows from inside to outside in a homogenized and ephemeral landscape whose limits are perhaps only the boundaries of the nation state and the circuits of capital. In this way the home is placed in seamless continuum with the spaces of Fordist production.

In contrast to the top-down vision of state-sponsored programmes represented by the previous two chapters, **Kim Trogal** presents us with a study of a contemporary local 'gift economy' – the Incredible Edible project of urban gardening in Todmorden, Yorkshire. This project attempts to engage the entire community in growing food within the territory of the town – their aim is to promote eventual food autonomy. Though money is involved at various levels in this economy, both the labour and the food produced by that labour is given freely. The project thus presents a challenge to the accumulative tendency of capitalist economics through its 'economy of generosity'. Care is so often given freely and privately, and often by women. Here it is brought into the public spotlight through the disruptive practice of giving away produce that is grown in publicly situated plots. The gift economy operates *with* and *in* space, disturbing the prevalent enacted boundaries of ownership and privacy.

As a radical contrast to the open 'Equalitarian' systematic connectivity described by Sadler, **Juliet Odgers** presents a seventeenth-century domestic economy – the 'villa' of John Evelyn at Deptford in the suburbs of London. The household is described through Evelyn's drawings and writing, and is presented primarily as a tightly circumscribed domain of ethical action – an Edenic microcosm predicated on central duties of love and labour, attitudes similar to the generosity and care that motivate the acts of giving amongst the citizens of Todmorden described by Trogal. Evelyn's household is, however, a hierarchical structure instituted through a legally understood set of relationships and an equally definite spatial enclosure. Nonetheless Evelyn aspires to transcend the limitations of these structures through the religiously predicated ethical orientation of the household.

Notes

1 Colin Rowe and Fred Koetter, *Collage City* (Cambridge, MA; London: MIT Press, 1984), p. 87.
2 Littré's dictionary (1872).

1
EQUALITARIANISM[1]

Simon Sadler

What is Bay Area design?

In his most recent book, Stewart Brand mentions his custom of 'see[ing] everything in terms of solvable design problems.'[2] Brand is here trying to summarize his vision as an ecologist, yet the phrase strikes me as peculiarly applicable to a certain holistic and pragmatist view of the world cultivated in the Bay Area of Northern California, whose intellectual life Brand has influenced for a half-century. The prominent Silicon Valley design practice IDEO, for instance, vigorously promotes so-called Design Thinking—a widely proliferating method in product design and business consultancy which, lacking a clear single formula, might be simply summed up as the habit of seeing everything in terms of solvable design problems.[3] In Design Thinking, no design problem is localized—every design is considered in terms of smaller and larger scales, as though part of a web of life and commerce. This presents the historian of Northern California design with the difficulty of describing an approach to design that seems persistently to abjure style, authorship and form in favor of anonymity, process and connectivity within grand economies.

Note, for instance, the Bay Region's diffidence about monumentality. It is striking in the work of that consummate Bay Region architect, Bernard Maybeck: the Maybeck who designed the grandiloquent Beaux-Arts Palace of Fine Arts for the 1915 Panama–Pacific Exposition is the same Maybeck who designed self-effacing Arts and Crafts cottages in the hills of Berkeley and Oakland. A fair division between public and private, perhaps, but what then to make of Maybeck's 1910 First Church of Christ Scientist in Berkeley (Figure 1.1), where he seemingly ends monumentality and the arrogance of a single architectural language when designing that most enduring typology of the western canon, the church?

FIGURE 1.1 Bernard Maybeck, First Church of Christ Scientist, Berkeley, California, 1910

The building feels more like an apparatus than a monument, composed out of sets of relations—between inside and outside, between classicism, the arts and crafts and industrial technology, between East and West, Beaux-Arts, Romanesque and Byzantine, all captured in a momentary, unlikely, Zen-like fusion. (The puzzled Detroit-based supplier of the industrial steel windows for the church was reluctant to send them West to California, fearing that Maybeck had specified them in error.)

Across from the church, in 1969 activists turned an empty lot awaiting development by the University of California into the infamous experiment in anarchic social ecology known as the People's Park. Looking from the church to the park, one starts to see the story of Bay Region design as one of inexorable, anarchic, ecological dematerialization—from 'the magnificent mad hand of Bernard Maybeck, the local culture hero,'[4] as architect Charles Moore referred to him, to an 'architecture' of ineffable social relations around Berkeley in the 1960s, and then forwards toward the spread of electronic networks from Silicon Valley at the end of the century. Alas, the story is not quite that neat; five minutes' walk away from the First Church of Christ Scientist and the People's Park, John Galen Howard (following plans afoot since the turn of the century) laid out the main campus of the University of California, Berkeley, in 1922, replete with campanile, in a grand international Beaux-Arts style localized only by ceramic-tile roofs evoking Mission architecture but which are nearly illegible from the ground. And four decades later, it would be sometimes hard to differentiate between work supposedly representative of the Bay Region and the international concrete monumentality of Brutalism (most obviously in Berkeley's own School of Architecture, somewhat incongruously named after Bay Region Style leader William Wurster).

Still, these monumental gestures are a little anomalous in the area, and historians have mostly struggled to account for the architecture of the Bay Region, as though they faced something recognizable, and yet mutational, and astylar. 'I was asked to ferret out some [monumental architecture] on the West Coast, especially in California,' Charles Moore reported from Berkeley to the Yale journal *Perspecta* for his celebrated essay 'You Have to Pay for the Public Life' in 1965. He goes on:

> *Perspecta*'s editors suspected, I presume, that I would discover that in California there is no contemporary monumental architecture … Their suspicions were well founded; any discussion from California … is bound to be less about what we have than about what we have instead.

What existed instead was the 'small scale,' 'carefully understated, spare, almost anonymous efficiency of a well-understood carpenters' constructional system' known as the Bay Region Style. Moore was able to list some features of the Bay Region Style—above all its simplicity and domestic scale, the use of redwood, stucco walls, aluminum windows, wooden shakes 'and casual, if not cavalier, attitudes toward form.'[5]

In his earlier and well-known bid to define a Bay Region style in the *New Yorker* magazine in 1947, the historian and philosopher Lewis Mumford defined the work of Maybeck, Howard and William Wurster more as an ethic than aesthetic. The Bay Region was, Mumford claimed, the home to 'that native and humane form of modernism' that might be compared to other 'anonymous,' 'empirical' styles of modern architecture at the time such as those of England and Sweden.[6] The Bay Region Style was therefore broadly aligned with those post-War tendencies that saw in modern design the projection of a framework for progressive social policy (Mumford's lover Catherine Bauer, who later married Wurster, similarly insisted on the role of public policy in modern architecture). Landscape architects of the Bay Region Style such as Garrett Eckbo, Thomas Church and Lawrence Halprin were meanwhile all influenced by the public spiritedness of the New Deal in the 1930s.[7] Bay Region Style was, in the eyes of Mumford, 'a free yet unobtrusive expression of the terrain, the climate, the way of life on the Coast,'[8] inferring a geographical foundation to the Style, a notion echoed a couple of decades later by Moore, who explained that it hailed from a time 'when California was rural, a golden never-never land with plenty of room, with open fields for the public realm.'[9]

This is not the same sort of geographical determinism that leads to an architecture that resembles fishing villages (say) on the basis that the Bay is a coastal region. It is more metaphorical, evocative, speaking of liberation, low-density construction, open space and temperate weather (and thus distinct from the East or Midwest). And so we find the Bay Region becoming associated with a wide-ranging ethos of openness that Moore described as 'equalitarian.'[10] This pleasantly indistinct ethos asserted a generally progressive, liberal image of a state that for much of its first century of statehood had manifested conservative, even reactionary dispositions. It also affirmed a trajectory for the modernization of California reacting against the interiority that characterized bourgeois cultures of Europe and the East Coast.

16 Simon Sadler

This was especially apparent when the Bay Region Style became a staple of the area's 10,000 Eichler houses, built from 1949 on, and at the Sea Ranch development initiated in 1964 on the Sonoma Coast (some 100 miles north of the Bay, but really an extension of Bay Region Style by dint of its provision of second homes to Bay Region clients by key Berkeley practitioners—Moore, working in partnership with Donlyn Lyndon, William Turnbull and Richard Whitaker from the practice MLTW, plus Halprin and Joseph Esherick) (Figure 1.2). The Sea Ranch was recognized as a pioneering effort at 'ecological design,' in which the buildings 'learn' from the landscape and weather. For instance, homes were shaped to lean into the wind and the hedgerows, and the condominiums were agglomerated into a distinctive mass to lend a restrained, impermanent presence alongside trees, rocks, ridges. Meadows were left as commons or, as Halprin put it, 'outdoor rooms.' According to this school of design—this imagining and projection of California—quality of life in the state, ideologically and architecturally, was to be pursued less through the enclosure of the commonwealth, more through its seeming distribution across space.

And so Bay Design preferred to *present* than *represent* phenomena, be it a sightline, some data, a destination, another culture. It became ever-more restrained and cool—showing us the world as yet more patterns, systems, connections, adjustments. It suggested a revised sensibility toward, and renewal of, the public realm. It was not the explicitly political sense of the public realm propounded by late eighteenth-century Europe, where it was staged through great art, streets, parliaments and media. It was a sensibility more based around the state's connecting

FIGURE 1.2 Joseph Esherick, Hedgerow House 1, the Sea Ranch, California, 1966–1967

tissue of communications through infrastructure, water, landscape architecture, information and education. California was imagined as the apotheosis of middle-class American existence as a 'smooth space' of opportunity and mobility.[11]

Like most grand modernizing projects in design history, it was not necessarily realized, unvarying or indefinite. Other histories are necessary, for instance, to acknowledge the ongoing separation of Californians along the lines established by race and class, accelerated recently by disorienting escalations in the region's real estate prices. No culture is universal; the civilization of the Bay, if that is what it is, will be but the work of a coterie ('a hundred men,' as Friedrich Nietzsche once remarked about the civilization of the Italian Renaissance),[12] and politically, then, the design ethos examined here is more or less the project of a hegemonic (white, male) elite. Even in respect to Moore's equalitarian aesthetic sensibility, one senses his perturbation as a Northern Californian looking at Southern Californian alienation in the very title of his essay 'You Have to Pay for the Public Life'—where he proposes, if needs be, the shoring up of spatial quality by landscaping freeways. 'If California should neglect or trash its public landscapes,' the historian of California Kevin Starr writes of the landscape architecture tradition that begins with Church, Eckbo and Halprin, and which might still be felt today in the work of a designer like Walter Hood, 'the private garden would become a flight from reality, a retreat into unearned privilege, a mode of self-deception.' And so, Starr implies, Bay Region landscape architecture tried to project its spatial ideology across all scales and places:

> Within each private California garden could be found California itself; hence the visual well-being of that larger California was crucial to the success of those arrangements of earth, rock, water, stone, trees, shrubbery, and flowers that mysteriously reordered the world for purposes of private recreation and renewal.[13]

I posit that Bay Area design from Maybeck forward imagined an endless set of avowedly 'equalitarian' relationships.

A Bay Area state of mind

A Zen-like transcendence seemed attainable amid the beauty of large swathes of the Bay Region—the Bay Region Style bore the clear imprint of Japanese Zen architecture, and Mumford described the Bay Region Style as 'a product of the meeting of the Occidental and Oriental architectural traditions.'[14] ('I have always found … Japanese Zen Buddhism … to be aesthetically sublime,' Bay Area computer impresario and Apple Computer co-founder Steve Jobs concurred six decades later; 'The most sublime thing I've ever seen are the gardens around Kyoto.'[15]) But it was precisely that *relation between* diverse modes of design that made the Bay Region Style, Mumford said, 'far more truly a universal style than the so-called international style.'[16] Mumford moreover explained in an essay defending the Bay Region

Style that 'the main problem of architecture today is to reconcile the universal and regional, the mechanical and the human, the cosmopolitan and the indigenous,'[17] so establishing the larger technocultural agenda for Bay design.

The Bay tacitly emerged for Mumford as an instance of his theory of cultural syncretism found in his book *Technics and Civilization* of 1934. Civilizations, the syncretist theory held, are composites of elements and achievements taken from preceding and accompanying cultures. Drawing upon his admiration for Patrick Geddes' theory of biotechnics—which held that technology was evolving into a benign force in culture—Mumford further contended that nature, culture and technology would increasingly be recognized as related parts of an organic whole. In the same way that scientists were relinquishing a compartmentalized, linear, mechanical view of the world in favor of a more relativistic view of a world 'described as systems of energy in more or less stable, more or less complex, states of equilibrium,' Mumford argued, then humanists and scientists alike would soon have to accept that 'the world has conceptually become a single system.' 'Form, pattern, configuration, organism, historical filiation, ecological relationship are concepts that work up and down the ladder of the sciences,' Mumford stated.[18]

Mumford's optimism would be tempered by the horror of the Second World War, so it is ironic that the more systematic and organic technologies deemed necessary for the war effort accelerated California's economic development and initiated the development of cybernetics, the general science of control and communication which found an enthusiastic and diverse reception in the post-war Bay Region.[19] Cybernetic theory underwrote both the industrial development of computing in Silicon Valley and the countercultural ideology that developed around the Bay Region's *Whole Earth Catalog*. The *Whole Earth Catalog* was published by Stewart Brand from 1968 as a sort of storefront for the counterculture. As its reader gamely imagined filling a shopping cart with the bits and pieces featured inside the *Whole Earth Catalog*—pickaxes, books, early electronic computers, sex guides and gardening manuals—the *Catalog* promoted design as an ethic, as an ecology, as a mind, as a patterning of the universal economy symbolized in the famous images of planet earth featured on its covers. The *Catalog*'s editors encouraged interest in Bay Region architects and in their champions such as Lewis Mumford. It argued that technology, nature and culture are partners, not adversaries, a sentiment echoed in the state at large: Kevin Starr argues that from the Gold Rush to the comprehensive State Water Projects, 'Virtually the entire cultural history of American California revolved around this nature–technology dialectic: this tension of opposites, so tenuously reconciled.'[20]

But we could go further, to say that one oddity of the Californian project was that it short-circuited the dialectic between nature and technology, such that technology was not even mediating between nature and culture, but merged with them into a single, designed assembly. This vision of California was briefly de facto governmental policy when Brand became an advisor to State Governor Jerry Brown during his first period in office from 1975–1983, and when Sim van der Ryn—a Berkeley faculty member who founded the Farallones Institute, sister enterprise to

Brand's *Whole Earth Catalog*, and who helped organize the People's Park—became State Architect. Van der Ryn named the principal state building constructed during his tenure—Sacramento's Bateson Building (1977–1981) (Figure 1.3), a stand-out early ecological design—for Brand's mentor, the anthropologist Gregory Bateson.[21]

A Californian of British extraction, Bateson advocated the possibility that human and non-human assemblies (like whole regions) could think as singular cybernetic minds. By the 1970s Brown, Brand and Van der Ryn seem to have thought of California itself as a whole system, with State Government helping coordinate and engineer flows of energy, material and information between the different elements composing the system. Take as an example the state's remarkable 1979 *California Water Atlas*, the dramatic diagrams of which represented California as a coherent, natural, technological and cultural assembly.[22] Conceived under Governor Brown with Brand as an advisor, the *California Water Atlas* was not presenting a traditional, top-down image of government responsibility, but a distributed model that hailed the public–private image of New Deal public works and tacitly looked forward to the somewhat libertarian image of California as the entrepreneurial mêlée adored by Brand and his circle.[23] In the *Atlas*, that is to say, human agency, natural resources and technological intervention are as one, evolving over long periods of time. 'What thinks,' Bateson said—in a comment about cybernetics that seems germane when viewing the *California Water Atlas*—'is the total system which engages in trial and error, which is man plus environment,' such that 'wisdom' is not arcane, but 'a knowledge of the larger interactive system.'[24]

FIGURE 1.3 Sim van der Ryn and the Office of Alternative Technology, Bateson Building, Sacramento, California, 1977

Evidence of the existence of a system, according to Bateson, is found in its generation of patterns. Whether or not one subscribes to the Batesonian cybernetic model, the Batesonian observation of patterning might prompt us to notice the way that the groups of Californian designers under scrutiny here, from the Bay Region Style architects, through the *Whole Earth Catalog* editors to the interfaces of Apple computers, greatly valued self-effacing patterns, and backgrounds, and relays. California is a state of pergolas, atria, terraces, outdoor rooms, transit systems, grilles, signs, views, that constantly defer attention and connect points across space. As William Wurster wrote about Bay Region Style in 1956, 'Architecture is not a goal. Architecture is for life and pleasure and work and for people. The picture frame, not the picture.'[25] Or as Steve Jobs enthused about Eichler houses: 'His houses were smart and cheap and good ... I love it when you can bring really great design and simple capability to something that doesn't cost too much ... It was the original vision for Apple.'[26] (Jobs claimed to have lived in an Eichler house as a child. He was in error about this, though Apple co-founder Steve Wozniak's childhood home was an Eichler, and Jobs claimed the *Whole Earth Catalog* as a determining presence in his life.[27])

Apple products were of course more than simply indigenous to California and Californian good intentions. By the early twenty-first century, in their most iconic, oblong, metal-and-glass period, they became nothing less than summary forms of international modernism and global industrial capitalism, explicitly recalling the German industrial design of the Dessau Bauhaus of the 1920s and of Braun's Dieter Rams in the 1960s, admiration for which Jobs developed when attending the Aspen Institute's conferences in the early 1980s.[28] To an art historian, the 2009 Manhattan Apple store's minimalism is immediately evocative of European Rationalism and neo-Platonism (Figure 1.4); to the cultural critic, it is a temple to the commodity fetish, a building composed of nothing but shop windows. This is not the Bay Region Style as Maybeck or Wurster would recognize it. And yet Apple distinctively recombines all these influences as Californian. The floor-to-ceiling windows (of computers and stores alike), their seeming friendliness and democratization, their attention to creature comforts, their promise of fresh, mind-expanding views on the world, their Zen aura—these are all, in some admittedly abstract sense, of a Californian mindset.

The zealotry of a figure such as Jobs belongs to a Bay tradition of attunement to the whole by attending to its patterns, systems, engineering and overlooked details. A recent book compiled at IDEO (which had an early collaborative relationship with Apple) by engineer Andrew Burroughs presents the reader with close-ups of loose wires and corrosion and flanges.[29] It is cryptic: the techno-environmental complex in which we live, the book implies, is evolutionary—or rather, it is an evolutionary branch open to human, and usually collective, intervention. What made D'Arcy Wentworth Thompson's classic and curious 1917 volume of natural history *On Growth and Form* relevant to 'artists, inventors, engineers, computer systems designers, [and] biologists' (so asserted the *Whole Earth Catalog*)[30] was its emphasis on the roles of physical laws and mechanics in the formation of species: rather than allow the

FIGURE 1.4 Apple Store, Fifth Avenue, Manhattan, 2009

Source: Bohlin Cywinski Jackson for Apple Corporation.

brutal principle of survival of the fittest to operate alone, nature was a great *engineer*. So it becomes the great instructor, showing us that the forward movement of history is less a race than a splendid attunement to environment.

The special appeal of Bateson's model was its insistence that nothing develops *sui generis*, and that instead all entities co-evolve. Diversity in nature can then be read as homologous to diversity in culture, as advocated by Californian liberalism and counterculture. But it has more depth than that. Bateson's work suggested the possibility of *intervening* in the patterns of the world around us so as to reduce the occurrence of pathologies and dysfunctions—a proactive role immediately recognizable to the designer, the engineer or the social activist seeking the betterment of the world without aspiring to change it root and branch. It also emphasized that change takes place 'three-dimensionally,' so to speak, across time and space: a change here has to be understood with a change there, and there and there; a change now has to be understood in relation to change in the past and in the future (a metapattern, according to Bateson, is ultimately a pattern through *time*).

Herein is a view of a world without end, modifiable, somewhat learnable and subject to speculation, the more minds compounded into a bigger mind, the more systems compiled into a bigger system, the better—but with the world never wholly knowable or predictable. The whole instead becomes something around which we convene: Brand's Seminars About Long-Term Thinking have met since

2003 in front of a general public in San Francisco. One of the few professional architects about which Brand finds much to admire is Christopher Alexander; Alexander sought, principally at UC Berkeley, a rudimentary (some would say autocratic) pattern language presenting *The Timeless Way of Building* (1979), a mission that reputedly migrated from architecture to software engineering. Alexander and Brand propound a taste for economical, adaptable spaces in which to co-evolve social systems: Brand's 1994 book *How Buildings Learn* implies that lay intelligence and low-tech structures are part of a single, learning, engineered assembly.[31]

How the West Coast became delirious

With sufficient investigation we would likely find the Bay Area design tradition—to reiterate, an avowed equalitarianism working incrementally toward the revelation and furtherance of life—re-emerging in Silicon Valley computing and biotech endeavors. My wager is based on what I take to be a sort of animism peculiar to Bay Region design, one that has proven at once mesmerizing and uncanny to modern onlookers for whom life has otherwise been threatened constantly at a global scale by World War, then by Cold War, and by famine, and now by climate change (the latter a challenge met with gusto by Brand and his circle as just one more design problem). It has cut against the dominant history of modernist and postmodernist aesthetics formed on the East Coast.

We should not overstate this tension, because the cultures of the two coasts are also conjoined. (Two quick cases in point: though Charles Moore 'started out thinking of myself as a "Bay Region architect",'[32] his move from Berkeley to Yale, where he became Dean in 1969, made him a pivotal figure back on the East Coast. And the architect of record for the New York Apple Store, the Bohlin Cywinski Jackson practice, was founded on the East Coast (in Pennsylvania in 1965) and has a nationwide presence—though notably the opening of an office in the Bay in 1999 was initially to handle the Pixar campus for Steve Jobs.) Still, the long tradition of East Coast culture looking toward the western frontier of the US with skepticism surfaces in the antagonism with which Mumford and the Bay Region Style were received at the New York Museum of Modern Art in the 1930s,[33] and resurfaces in the 1960s and 1970s when Peter Eisenman, a high-profile and consummately East Coast architect, insisted that architecture is an *autonomous* practice, one disconnected from larger systems and dependent on its *own* artful internal permutations, not the contingencies of an ecological totality at large—a critique that began when Eisenman wrote his PhD thesis in Cambridge, England, specifically to rival the thesis written there by Christopher Alexander, prior to his departure for Berkeley.[34]

Much as the so-called Chicago School challenged the East Coast at the end of the nineteenth century, California—the most ambitious ascendant American region toward the end of the twentieth century—offered regional inflections to modern American design. Critics and historians in fields other than design have seen something unusual in the development of Californian culture—some British and French commentators go so far as to note (somewhat antipathetically) a libertarian 'California Ideology' or 'California Optimism.'[35] After all, the size, geography, history and economy of the state of California lend it the quality of a nation within a nation—or if not a nationalism, at least a 'higher provincialism.'[36] It is as though the 'delirium' of American modernization passed, after the Jazz Age, to California. Much of what architect Rem Koolhaas said of the delirium of 'Manhattanism' in his classic 1978 book *Delirious New York* can be inverted to aptly describe the 'delirium' of California.[37] Like 'Manhattanism,' the design culture of California is 'so outrageous that in order for it to be realized it could never be openly declared.'[38] If New York's contribution to modernity was its 'culture of congestion,' one collected (Koolhaas observed) by grids and plotted with monuments like the Empire State Building, California's contribution to modernity (I contend) was its 'culture of equalitarianism,' collected by matrices, and plotted with remarkable communications structures such as the Golden Gate Bridge and computer networks.

With each East Coast expression of ennui in the capacity of design to change life, it seems the West Coast responds by becoming more cheerful about its capacity to build a better day. The hierarchical, compartmentalized corporatism of the East was met by the loudly entrepreneurial culture of California. To offer another well-worn stereotype, the loafer-shod market speculators of Wall Street were met by the flip-flop wearing venture capitalists of Silicon Valley. And so the unstated contest goes on, back and forth across the twentieth century: New York's importation from Europe of an International Style in the 1930s was met by the Bay's importation of style from Japan; the International Style was authoritative, disciplined, non-regional, Cartesian, rationalist; Bay Region Style was anti-authoritarian, pragmatic, regional, ecological, intuitive.

Ultimately, though, the dialectic of East Coast/West Coast is symptomatic of a larger altercation between opposing notions of what design is and—because design is a type of praxis—between divergent political models. In short, California tended to embrace design as an 'evolutionary' practice, positing incremental reform, usually through reference to vernacular forms (as in the case of Alexander). Some of the leading architectural schools of the East Coast, by contrast, embrace design as a 'revolutionary' practice, usually through reference to avant-garde forms (stemming, for instance, from Constructivism, as in the case of Eisenman), even though avant-garde styles were largely separated from revolutionary politics upon their adaption to the US: by propounding architecture's relative *autonomy* from larger political and technocultural assemblies, architecture would be afforded a certain critical distance from the world of which it is a part, authoritatively 'speaking' about the world through the language of form. Californian design, as I present it here, has happily transmitted information and facilitated social interaction; it was not too squeamish about instrumentalism; it preferred mechanism to art. Or rather, it promised pleasure not simply through aesthetic response to form, but through technics, invention, association, nature.

Needless to say, the quest through design for a holistic totality of relations and links and insertion points is ideologically a mixed bag. The Bay Region's reverence for feedback loops, incremental adjustments and long-term patterns is at once politically conservative in its aversion to sudden change, but also rather radical in the way that it implies that steady change is inevitable, natural and necessary—at once a hegemony and a vitiation of hegemony. The ambition it seems to have harbored since the counterculture for a libertarian abolition of political society, along with any other separation of cultural spheres, is again intensely conservative and radical simultaneously. And somewhat paradoxically, the quasi-whole systems ideology of neoliberalism has promoted disinvestment in the state ideal that once undergirded California. Liberalism in the Bay Area ultimately evolved beyond New Deal progressivism to host the bellicose liberalism of counterculture, the ecumenical outlook of environmentalism and then the informational infrastructure of neoliberalism. Delaminated—the public from the private, the real from the virtual—equalitarianism is ever more mythic (you do indeed have to pay for the public life). Which oddly and lamentably begins to explain, one wonders, the allure of California to a wider world where the atrophy of the public realm seen in California is repeated over and over again, and into which California has exported its latest 'patches,' its designs for making people, technology and nature more whole (fine houses, landscape architecture, drugs, media, recreational equipment, sentiments, computers). Because even when Californian design offers little more than an ersatz commonwealth through consumption, it arrives in the market accompanied by the hope of something more than another consumer fetish. Most recently the beautiful boxes shipping from Apple Computer bear this covenant, illusory and real: 'Designed by Apple in California.' California design promises its customers a better and more replete future.

Notes

1 This chapter is a modified and abridged version of an essay originally published as 'A Culture of Connection,' in *Boom: A Journal of California*, 2:1 (2012), pp. 1–16.
2 Stewart Brand, *Whole Earth Discipline: Why Dense Cities, Nuclear Power, Transgenic Crops, Restored Wildlands, and Geoengineering are Necessary* (New York: Penguin, 2010), p. 21.
3 See for instance Tim Brown, *Change by Design: How Design Thinking Transforms Organizations and Inspires Innovation* (New York: HarperBusiness, 2009).
4 Charles Moore, 'You Have to Pay for Public Life,' *Perspecta*, 9:10 (1965), pp. 57–106 (p. 85).
5 Moore, 'You Have to Pay for Public Life,' pp. 83–84.
6 See too Stanford Anderson, 'The New Empiricism–Bay Region Axis,' *Journal of Architectural Education*, 50:3 (February 1997), pp. 197–207.
7 Eckbo was especially concerned that design should meet the mandates of the New Deal, but we might argue that even Church, as something of a paternalist, wanted his clients' taste to set a public example.
8 Lewis Mumford, 'The Skyline: Bay Region Style,' *The New Yorker* (11 October 1947), pp. 106–109, reprinted in Joan Ockman and Edward Eigen, eds, *Architecture Culture 1943–1968: A Documentary Anthology* (New York: Rizzoli, 1993), pp. 107–109 (p. 108).
9 Moore, 'You Have to Pay for Public Life,' p. 86.
10 Moore, 'You Have to Pay for Public Life,' p. 62 *passim*.

11 On 'smooth space,' see Gilles Deleuze and Félix Guattari, *Mille Plateaux*, 1980, trans. Brian Massumi, *A Thousand Plateaus: Capitalism and Schizophrenia* (London: Continuum, 2002).
12 Friedrich Nietzsche, *On the Use and Abuse of History for Life* (Sioux Falls, SD: NuVision Publications, 2007), p. 19. Nietzsche was drawing upon Jacob Burckhardt's analysis of *Die Cultur der Renaissance in Italien: Ein Versuch* (Basel: Schweighauser, 1860).
13 Kevin Starr, *Golden Dreams: California in an Age of Abundance, 1950–1963* (Oxford; New York: Oxford University Press, 2009), p. 38.
14 Lewis Mumford, 'The Skyline: Bay Region Style,' p. 109. By the 1920s in San Francisco, Kevin Starr argues that the juxtaposition of Eastern and Western furniture was suggesting an Eastern–Western fusion 'at the aesthetic core of the Bay Area.' *Golden Dreams*, p. 38.
15 Walter Isaacson, *Steve Jobs* (New York: Simon & Schuster, 2011), p. 7; 'Jobs' Likeler No Eichler,' *Eichler Network*, www.eichlernetwork.com/article/jobs-likeler-no-eichler (accessed 9/25/14), p. 128.
16 Lewis Mumford, 'The Skyline: Bay Region Style,' p. 109.
17 Lewis Mumford writing in the catalog of the exhibition 'Domestic Architecture of the San Francisco Bay Region,' San Francisco Museum of Modern Art, 1949, quoted in Joan Ockman and Edward Eigen's introduction to Lewis Mumford, 'The Skyline: Bay Region Style,' p. 107.
18 Lewis Mumford, *Technics and Civilization* (New York: Harcourt, Brace and Company, 1934), pp. 369–371.
19 See for instance Norbert Wiener, *The Human Use of Human Beings: Cybernetics and Society* (London: Free Association, 1989, 1954) and Norbert Wiener, *Cybernetics: Or Control and Communication in the Animal and the Machines* (Cambridge, MA: MIT Press, 1961).
20 Kevin Starr, *Golden Dreams*, p. 31.
21 See for instance Stewart Brand, *II Cybernetic Frontiers* (New York: Random House, 1974).
22 See Governor Edmund G. (Jerry) Brown, Jr.; William L. Kahrl, Project Director and Editor; William A. Bowen, Cartography Team Director; Stewart Brand, Advisory Group Chairman; Marlyn L. Shelton, Research Team Director; David L. Fuller and Donald A. Ryan, Principal Cartographers et al., *The California Water Atlas* (Sacramento: State of California, 1979).
23 The best sources on this trajectory of the counterculture are Andrew G. Kirk, *Counterculture Green: The* Whole Earth Catalog *and American Environmentalism* (Lawrence: University Press of Kansas, 2007), and Fred Turner, *From Counterculture to Cyberculture: Stewart Brand, the Whole Earth Network, and the Rise of Digital Utopianism* (Chicago, IL: University of Chicago Press, 2006).
24 Gregory Bateson, *Steps to an Ecology of Mind* (New York: Ballantine, 1972), p. 483, quoted in Jay Mechling, 'Mind, Messages, and Madness', in *Prospects*, 8 (October 1983), pp. 11–30 (pp. 19–20), http://journals.cambridge.org/action/displayAbstract?fromPage=online&aid=5664984&fileId=S0361233300003689 (published online 7/30/09; accessed 7/29/11).
25 William Wurster, 'Competition for U.S. Chancery Building, London,' *Architectural Record*, 119 (April 1956), p. 222, quoted in Marc Treib, ed., *An Everyday Modernism: The Houses of William Wurster* (Berkeley: University of California Press, 1995), p. 74.
26 Walter Isaacson, *Steve Jobs*, p. 7.
27 See for instance Jobs' Commencement Speech at Stanford University, 2005.
28 Walter Isaacson, *Steve Jobs*, pp. 126–127.
29 Andrew Burroughs, *Everyday Engineering: How Engineers See* (San Francisco, CA: Chronicle, 2007).
30 Stewart Brand, 'On Growth and Form,' *The Last Whole Earth Catalog* (Harmondsworth: Penguin, 1971), p. 14.

31 Christopher Alexander, *The Timeless Way of Building* (New York: Oxford University Press, 1979); Stewart Brand, *How Buildings Learn: What Happens after They're Built* (New York; London: Viking, 1994).
32 Charles Moore, quoted in David Littlejohn, *Architect: The Life and Work of Charles W. Moore* (New York: Holt, Rinehart and Winston, 1984), p. 125, cited in Jorge Otero-Pailos, *Architecture's Historical Turn: Phenomenology and the Rise of the Postmodern* (Minneapolis: University of Minnesota Press, 2010), p. 123.
33 Lewis Mumford, 'The Skyline: Bay Region Style,' p. 108.
34 Alexander, *The Timeless Way of Building*.
35 See for instance Steve Best and Douglas Kellner, 'Kevin Kelly's Complexity Theory: The Politics and Ideology of Self-Organising Systems,' *Democracy & Nature*, 6:3 (2000), pp. 375–399; Richard Barbrook and Andy Cameron, 'The California Ideology,' *Mute*, 3 (1995), www.hrc.wmin.ac.uk/theory-californianideology-main.html (accessed 7/29/11); Adam Curtis, dir., *All Watched Over by Machines of Loving Grace*, screened on BBC2 television May–June 2011.
36 I borrow the phrase from Kevin Starr's chapter on the emergence of a distinctively American Californian civilization at the end of the nineteenth century and beginning of the twentieth century in *California: A History* (Modern Library) (New York: Random House, 2007).
37 Rem Koolhaas, *Delirious New York: A Retroactive Manifesto for Manhattan* (London: Thames & Hudson, 1978).
38 Original publisher's text for the cover of Koolhaas, *Delirious New York*, reproduced at the OMA website, www.oma.eu/publications/delirious-new-york (accessed 3/30/15).

2

THE EARTHLY PARADISE OF *ÉCONOMIE SOCIALE*

Diana Periton

Introduction: the *cité-jardin*

Shortly after the end of the First World War, work began on a ring of so-called 'garden cities', *cités-jardins*, in the suburbs surrounding Paris.[1] During the war, *Offices publics d'habitation à bon marché*, public offices for low-cost housing, had been established both for the City of Paris and for the wider Department of the Seine; each had powers to borrow money with which to acquire sites and to build. But while the municipal housing built within Paris was mostly just that – blocks of workers' housing, consisting of well-ventilated apartments stacked around stony courtyards – in the *cités-jardins*, the Department of the Seine interpreted its remit for low-cost housing much more broadly. The *cités-jardins* were planned as entire, almost self-sufficient communities of 5–10,000 people. One of the most elaborate examples is in the western suburb of Suresnes. In addition to its housing (for low-level managers and skilled workers as well as for manual labourers), Suresnes has schools, a communal laundry, a *salle des fêtes*, co-operative restaurants and shops, a health centre, a retirement home, sports grounds and playgrounds, all set in extensive community gardens (Figure 2.1).

The *cités-jardins* were an interpretation of Ebenezer Howard's English garden city, first described in his 1898 manifesto *To-morrow: a peaceful path to real reform*.[2] But unlike Letchworth (founded 1903) or the later Welwyn (1920), stand-alone towns intended to multiply and eventually to render the metropolis of London obsolete, the *cités-jardins* were conceived as integral parts of a 'greater Paris'.[3] Within this 'greater Paris', they were state-sponsored 'workshops of social reform', 'experimental laboratories of social life'.[4] The *cités-jardins* were controlled applications of the newly developing 'science of urbanism', the study of the physical and administrative re-organisation of the city for the sake of the well-being of its citizens. As such, they were built experiments in *économie sociale*, also a nascent

FIGURE 2.1 *Cité-jardin de Suresnes*

Source: photo Chris Schulte, 2011.

discipline, and increasingly specifically defined as a 'science of betterment' through the study of the 'totality of the moral and material conditions of society'.[5]

The journal of Paris' new *Ecole des hautes etudes urbaines*, its School of Advanced Urban Studies, founded in 1919, indicates how the *cités-jardins* were funded.[6] State grants paid for municipal buildings such as schools or health centres, but most of the funding was in the form of loans from the *Caisse des Dépôts*, France's public but autonomous financial vehicle for the investment and safekeeping of state pension and insurance funds.[7] These loans, with interest at 2–3 per cent, were to be re-paid over a period of 25 or 40 years using rent collected from housing; the repayments were guaranteed by the Department of the Seine, who benefited from an increased tax base and increased land value.[8] The cumulative laws involved in making this possible, to mention but a few, were the Loi Siegfried of 1894, the Loi Bonnevay of 1912 and the Loi Cornudet of 1919. The Loi Siegfried defined what constituted low-cost housing (the new term for workers' housing), and established the principle that companies providing officially sanctioned low-cost housing could borrow from the *Caisse des Dépôts* at low rates of interest, as well as receiving various tax breaks. The Loi Bonnevay extended these provisions to new public organisations, not just private companies; it was this law that allowed for the creation of the *Offices publics d'habitation à bon marché*, with their attendant borrowing powers. The

Loi Cornudet demanded that all towns with populations of over 10,000 people should draw up development plans. In the development plan for 'greater Paris', the *cités-jardins* formed a ring of carefully cultivated seeds, germs of well-being intended to propagate order into Paris' chaotic growth.

In 1904, lawyer and economist Charles Gide (uncle of the more famous novelist, André), writing in support of the campaign to introduce the garden city to France, described it as a Paradise regained, a place of flowers and fruits, fountains, mossy banks and birdsong. But, he warned, 'it is not evident that everybody has the aptitude to return to the Garden of Eden, even if the archangel who guards it opens its gates'. The garden citizen must acquire passions different from those of the crowd, of the life of the street and the café; 'the "order of pleasures" will have to be modified in the souls of the people – a new education will be required.'[9] Hence the prevalence, in the *cités-jardins*, of trade schools (equipped, in Suresnes, with gym and swimming pool), of schools for girls with classrooms for home economics, of health centres that instructed citizens in hygienic living and of apartments whose planning (with separate bedrooms for parents, girls and boys, and sometimes a separate dining room) encouraged industrious families to live *bourgeoisement*. In the *cité-jardin*, its advocates wrote, 'man is improved morally and physiologically'; there, he learns to live in harmony, in 'solidarité sociale'.[10]

This chapter is a brief and partial exploration of the genesis of *économie sociale* and its role in the creation of Paris' *cités-jardins*. It asks what kind of science, or knowledge, social economy was expected to be if it could be applied in this way. It begins also to ask what kind of knowledge, or knowing, the *cités-jardins* were intended to engender – what kind of understanding is expected of the garden citizen, if he or she is to live in *solidarité sociale*.

Paris 1900

Shortly before his involvement in the campaign to promote the garden city, Charles Gide had been the government-appointed reporter for the *économie sociale* section of Paris' Universal Exhibition of 1900. Both festive and didactic, the world exhibitions of the nineteenth and early twentieth centuries might in general be described as settings to show, and to show off, the 'moral and material conditions' of the participating nations, their emphasis on progress – whether industrial, artistic or societal – a particular version of 'betterment'.[11] The official guide to the 1900 exhibition described it as a series of 'marvellous *villes nouvelles* that have risen up as if by enchantment on the banks of the Seine'.[12] Together, these new cities constituted a microcosm of the conditions in which the *cités-jardins* would find their place.

The exhibition organisers, overseen by the French Ministry of Industry and Commerce, proposed a route through its different sections that emphasised a cycle of increasingly sophisticated production, ultimately the production of society and its culture, condensed into a loop through the centre of Paris. The journey began south of the river, at the foot of the Eiffel Tower (a relic from the 1889 exhibition), with halls dedicated to education – for it is with education, the 'source of all progress', that 'man enters life', they declared.[13] From exhibits demonstrating the teaching of letters, arts and sciences, the visitor moved through mechanical, chemical, electrical and agricultural products – the *ville industrielle* – before speeding by electric rail or travelator to the refinements of the crafted products of the decorative and fine arts – the *ville des arts*, which straddled the Seine. To the south were the pavilions of the department stores and craft manufacturers, across a bridge to the north (the Pont Alexandre III) the palaces of painting and sculpture. Then came the sometimes bawdy, sometimes bucolic entertainment of the *ville des plaisirs*, the city of pleasures, on the Champs-Elysées, which provided the backdrop for the *Palais d'économie sociale* (Figure 2.2). Beyond the *Palais*, on the hillside of the Trocadero – opposite the Eiffel tower – lay the *ville exotique* of colonialism. Alfred Picard, overall director of the exhibition, described both social economy and colonialism as *la résultante*, the natural outcome, of the industrial and commercial process.[14]

One class of the *économie sociale* section – class 106, *habitations ouvrières*, or workers houses – was built as an eclectic model village in the wooded parkland of the Bois de Vincennes, to the east of Paris. Here, as in every section, participating countries showed their products side by side, in the 'peaceful rivalry of competition that accelerates progress'. All of the exhibition's *villes nouvelles* were constructions where 'the peoples of the world have laboured together' to display the 'balance sheet' of the new economic order.[15] In his speech at the prize-giving ceremony for the exhibition, President of the French Republic Emile François Loubet declared that 'the exhibition of 1900 will have given solidarity its most brilliant expression

FIGURE 2.2 *Palais d'économie sociale*, Paris Exposition: Paris, France, 1900

Source: Brooklyn Museum Archives. Goodyear Archival Collection. Visual materials [6.1.014].

– that solidarity ... which allows us to see our ultimate goals more clearly ... the reduction of misery ... and the realisation of true fraternity'.[16]

Économie sociale

In the midst of the exhibition's elaborate splendour, the *Palais d'économie sociale* was intentionally simple and sober.

Charles Gide writes in his report that he suspects the claim (made by Minister of Commerce and Industry Alexandre Millerand) that millions visited the palace was probably exaggerated – though they could have been going to the endless congress meetings held on the upper floor. But he acknowledges that 'perhaps its name, inscribed above the entrance to the building, did exert a certain fascination. Perhaps [its visitors] ... hoped they would find the secret of happiness there', amongst the maps, graphs and lists of figures, sometimes hidden in books untouchable in glass cases, filed differently by each country, that he goes on painstakingly to describe.[17]

Gide starts his report by making a distinction between political and social economy, a distinction he tells us is too often blurred. Where political economy has been called a 'science of wealth', social economy is the 'science of well-being' through the 'ordered distribution of wealth'. It has 'the labouring classes more especially in view', because it is they who suffer a deficit in the economic conditions for happiness.[18] We might now use different definitions or labels, but Gide's distinction is reiterated in sociologist Giovanna Procacci's 1978 essay 'Social economy and the government of poverty', which traces the emergence of social economy from classical political economy. The economic writings of the late eighteenth and early nineteenth centuries were without a specific discourse on poverty. Poverty was simply the limit at which political economy no longer held sway; it was the ever-present, necessary but opaque background to wealth from which the force of labour was drawn. Procacci suggests that it was Malthus, in his *Principles of Political Economy* of 1820, who was one of the first economic thinkers to recognise the pauper as a specific problem, as someone 'stubbornly indifferent to the lures of well-being, indolent in regard to that fundamental activity for the economic system, the perpetual expansion of "needs"'.[19]

For Frédéric Le Play, founder in 1856 of France's *Société d'économie sociale*, it was classical economists' insistence that labour should be understood as a variably-priced commodity, leading inevitably to periods of unemployment or wages below subsistence level, that itself created the mass phenomenon of pauperism.[20] Pauperism's recruits, wrote a French commentator on the need for social economy, were to be found amongst 'this floating population of great cities ... which industry attracts, but is unable regularly to employ'.[21] With pauperism, the labouring classes became synonymous with the dangerous classes. They were a threat not only to the economic order, but also to the social order – a threat to Le Play's ideal of *la paix sociale*, social peace.[22]

Social economy, then, emerged as a necessary pendant to political economy. It was the making-safe of labour through the government of poverty. Le Play and his *Société d'économie sociale* saw its study as a science of observation, from which society's natural laws of prosperity and harmony can be deduced. The object observed was *la famille ouvrière*, the worker's family. Le Play and his colleagues studied its habits and beliefs and, in particular, its patterns of income and expenditure – its family budgets. For Le Play, the family was the fundamental unit of society, the *véritable unité sociale*.[23] His comparative research, which consisted of a huge number of 'monographs' of family types from across Europe, concluded that the most prosperous family type, least susceptible to pauperism, is the *famille-souche*, the stem or root family, its paternal authority grounded in place and in property – in the home. It is the home from which the *famille-souche* derives its stability, and can send out its shoots. Le Play argued that the most stable conditions for the worker's family, and thus for prosperous industries and a harmonious nation in general, is a situation in which the employer echoes the paternal role, and enables the worker to become rooted in his home.[24]

Le Play was also the overall organiser of Paris' 1867 Universal Exhibition, the first to include *économie sociale* amongst its different classes. There was no physical space allocated for the display of the study or application of social economy, but prizes were awarded to manufacturing businesses where 'well-being, stability and harmony' were seen to reign. Le Play hoped not just to show the marvels of industry, but also to draw attention to the 'material and moral conditions' of the people who produced them.[25] Gide's report is full of praise for Le Play's introduction of *économie sociale* as one of the categories of French universal exhibitions, but he identifies the 1889 exhibition as the one in which its possibilities were fully established. There, an entire *cité sociale*, including a working men's club and a 'hygiene pavilion', was built on the Esplanade des Invalides.[26] The first congress on *habitations à bon marché* was held under the 1889 exhibition's auspices; its discussions (led by Jules Siegfried) laid the groundwork for the Loi Siegfried of 1894, which gave state-backed financial encouragement to those supplying government-vetted, low-cost housing.

Charles Gide was respectful of Le Play (Gide was a member of the *Société d'économie sociale*, by this time over 40 years old), as well as of the organisers of the 1889 and 1900 exhibition sections on social economy, but he was also critical. For Gide, while political economy *is* a science of observation, from which apparently natural laws of behaviour can be deduced, social economy – and here he disagreed directly with Le Play – is not. Social economy, he wrote, studies not spontaneous, but 'purely voluntary relations that men create amongst themselves, with a view to improving them'; political economy, by contrast, makes no moral pronouncements.[27] Social economy, he said, has 'no trust in the free play of natural laws to assure men's happiness, nor in the inspirations of a vague philanthropy. It believes in the necessity, and the effectiveness, of willed, reflective, rational organisation.'[28]

Gide's report makes clear that he was disappointed by the exhibition in the *Palais d'économie sociale* that he reviewed. The 12 different categories of material defined by the organisers seemed to him to be without a coherent system of classification. Some classes were huge, based on a loosely identified aim (such as class 111, 'hygiene'); some highlighted the provenance of institutions for betterment (class 110, 'public or private initiatives for the well-being of citizens'); some were grouped around an institutional type (such as syndicates and co-operative societies for the improvement of labour conditions).[29] Participating countries mostly sent material on individual organisations and their good works, without suggesting how those organisations might work together, or how they might adapt to address newly identified problems – the material showed only existing situations, and avoided any theoretical speculation on what ought to be. And although Gide acknowledged it was difficult to convey ideas, much easier simply to show concrete things (a full-size model of part of a temperance steam-boat for Sunday trips on the Neva, and the model dwellings in their separate setting in the Bois de Vincennes were amongst the most compelling pieces on display), too many of the exhibits were just dry lists of figures or graphs that were indecipherable to a general audience.[30] Overall, social economy's possibilities as a rational science of betterment were not exploited, whether by the participants in the exhibition or its organisers.

In response, Gide sketched out an alternative plan for the didactic display of *économie sociale* that would be, not a palace to be wandered through, but a cathedral, in which aisles and bays would provide the built version of a carefully ordered comparative table.[31] The aisles of Gide's cathedral are dedicated to the provenance of institutions for social reform, the main aisle to well-being through co-operative association, one side aisle to state intervention, the other to patronage or philanthropy. Each of the bays represents a specific 'social goal', starting with those concerned with working conditions and salary, moving through those of long-term comfort and stability (including housing and education), culminating in possibilities of self-sufficiency through credit schemes and co-ownership.[32] What is being compared is the effect of different sources of intervention on the goals of betterment.

Gide mentions as a precedent Le Play's layout for the 1867 international exhibition as a whole. There, in a vast building made up from a series of concentric oval-shaped rings, each ring housed a particular kind of product, and each nation was allotted a wedge, or a slice. A visitor could compare different countries' goods of the same kind by walking round one of the rings, or focus on the goods of one country by walking inwards through the various orbits, from the products of industry to the works of art. The centre of the building was left empty of man-made objects, given over to a garden. In Gide's proposed cathedral, the division by nation states is abandoned ('we are no longer in the kingdom of competition, but in that of fraternal cooperation').[33] What is collated instead is a series of different ways in which well-being might be procured and distributed. As the visitor progresses from one end of the building to the other, stopping to study each of the side chapels as well as the display in the main aisle, he or she moves inexorably towards the ultimate objective, 'the emancipation of the working class'. The raw and terrifying neediness that is pauperism has been overcome, and lies buried in the crypt below.[34]

It is in order to free the working classes from the oppression of their labour that Gide argues for the reasoned and ordered application of the findings of *économie sociale*. The *cité-jardin* that he advocates (Le Play's central garden becomes also city) is a means to the same end, a means to a highly structured version of freedom. When he calls it Paradise regained, it is not a transcendent Paradise to which we return — and it is not, as Le Play might have imagined, a place in which, once rooted, we follow natural laws of a social harmony. Instead, it is a 'willed, reflective, rational organisation' of salvation, a consciously made and purely immanent Garden of Eden, where, to quote another of its advocates, people 'die less, and procreate more, where the spirit of association and solidarity grows'.[35]

Les Nourritures Terrestres

When Charles Gide was formulating his earthly paradise of social economy, his nephew André was writing *Les Nourritures Terrestres*, 'The Fruits of the Earth', his quasi-evangelical call for a return to sensual pleasures. André Gide's work is a hymn to nature, in which air 'shines with an effusion of light, as if the blueness of the sky has turned liquid', 'golden spray is left on the tips of the branches' and all such liquid is there to be drunk.[36] In André Gide's earthly paradise, 'every fecundation is accompanied by pleasure — all urge to life is enveloped with enjoyment'.[37] He insists that well-being — that key word of the proponents of *économie sociale* — should be synonymous with pleasure, then that pleasure and well-being should be synonymous simply with being.

In *The Human Condition*, philosopher Hannah Arendt argues that both the pain of labouring and the sensual pleasure of hedonism are equally private experiences, unshareable, a-political and unfit to be the basis for solidarity. They leave nothing between necessity and freedom; both are experienced only in the infinite present of sensation.[38] Seen in this light, the approaches of the two Gides represent two sides of the same coin. Charles Gide aims to liberate the labourer from his state of painful toil into a realm of relative comfort, where he is able to make rational choices. But in the garden city, living in carefully, didactically designed dwellings, attending specifically worker-oriented schools, labourers labour still, learning the techniques and skills to turn out a new product, the good garden citizen (Figure 2.3). They are both object and vehicle of a benign economic order, in which economy, whether social or political, is the production of society as a system, from its vegetable plots tended at weekends to its culture as a whole, displayed in international exhibitions. Solidarity, here, is simply the smooth functioning of this system.

Unlike his uncle's mode of knowing, predicated on rationally deduced truths of cause and effect, André Gide's is instead a passion for that which will always remain inappropriable, but can only be discovered through sensual involvement. Perhaps — and only perhaps — beyond sensual pleasure, there is in his version of being an open-ness to the world that might provide the basis for a different kind

FIGURE 2.3 *Cité-jardin de Suresnes*, avenue Edouard Vaillant

Source: photo Chris Schulte, 2011.

of solidarity. Perhaps there is the possibility of a solidarity that comes, not from learning pre-ordained techniques of harmonious citizenship, but from reaching understanding, common ground, through mishap and misunderstanding – from taking the risk of becoming involved.[39]

Notes

1 Ginette Baty-Tornikian, *Architecture et social démocratie, un projet urbain idéal typique: l'agglomération parisienne 1919–1939*, Paris: Institut d'études et de recherches architecturales et urbaines, 1978, lists nine principle *cités-jardins* in the Paris suburbs – Suresnes, Stains, Drancy, Champigny, Plessis–Robinson, Châtenay–Malabry, Gennevilliers, Pré-Saint-Gervais and Arcueil–Cachan.
2 Ebenezer Howard, *To-morrow: A Peaceful Path to Real Reform*, London: Swann Sonnenschein, 1898, republished 1902 under the title *Garden Cities of To-morrow*.
3 Hampstead Garden Suburb, founded 1906, was studied closely by French proponents of the *cité-jardin*.
4 Jacques Parisot, preface to Louis Boulonnois, *L'Oeuvre municipale de M. Henri Sellier à Suresnes*, Paris: Berger Levrault, 1938, p. vi; Paul Grunebaum-Ballin, president of the Office public d'habitation à bon marché du Département de la Seine from 1926, quoted in Ginette Baty-Tornikian, op. cit., n.p.
5 Littré, *Dictionnaire de la langue française*, definition of *économie sociale*, 1872 edition.

6. See e.g. Paul Strauss, *La vie urbaine*, no. 11, 1921 (*La vie urbaine* was the journal of the Ecole des hautes etudes urbaines).
7. See www.caissedesdepots.fr and http://fr.wikipedia.org/wiki/Caisse_des_dépôts_et_consignations (accessed 30.06.11).
8. This somewhat approximate summary of the funding mechanism for the *cités-jardins* is also gleaned from Louis Boulonnois, op. cit., pp. 81–85.
9. Charles Gide, introduction to Georges Benoît-Lévy, *La cité-jardin*, Paris: Jouve, 1904, pp. iv–v.
10. Léon Jaussely, *La vie urbaine*, 1919, p. 136; Henri Sellier, quoted in Baty-Tornikian, op. cit., n.p.
11. See Littré's definition of *économie sociale* as a science of betterment through the study of the moral and material conditions of society, note 5, above.
12. *Paris Exposition 1900*, Paris: Hachette, 1900, p. 171.
13. Ibid., p. 178.
14. Alfred Picard, quoted in ibid., p. 178.
15. *Paris Exposition 1900*, p. 171.
16. Emile-François Loubet, French president 1899–1906, quoted by Charles Gide in *Exposition Universelle de 1900, rapports du jury international, sixième section: Économie sociale*, Paris: Imprimerie Nationale, 1902, p. 55.
17. Charles Gide, *Exposition Universelle de 1900 ... Économie sociale*, op. cit., p. 1.
18. Charles Gide, *Political Economy*, trans. Constance Archibald, London: George G. Harrap, 1914 [*Cour d'économie politique*, 3ème édition, Paris: Imprimerie Nationale, 1902], p. 3; Charles Gide, *Exposition Universelle de 1900 ... Économie sociale*, op. cit., p. 3.
19. Giovanna Procacci, 'Social economy and the government of poverty', in *The Foucault Effect*, eds Graham Burchell, Colin Gordon and Peter Miller, Chicago, IL: University of Chicago Press, 1991, p. 155. Procacci is quoting from Thomas Malthus, *Principles of Political Economy, Considered with a View to their Practical Application*, London: John Murray, 1820, vol. IV.
20. Fernand Auburtin, preface to Frédéric Le Play, *Economie sociale*, Paris: Guillaumin, n.d., p. xlix.
21. Buret, *De la misère des classes laborieuses*, Paris, 1840, quoted in Procacci, op. cit., p. 158.
22. Fernand Auburtin, preface to Le Play, op. cit., p. xvi.
23. Ibid., p. xxi.
24. See Frédéric Le Play, *Les ouvriers européens*, 6 vols, Tours: Alfred Mame et Fils, 2nd edn 1877–1879 (the first volume of the first edition was published in 1855); Le Play, *Instruction sur la méthode d'observation dite des monographies des familles*, Paris: Société d'économie sociale, 1862.
25. Auburtin, preface to Le Play, op. cit., p. xii. See also Littré, notes 5 and 11, above.
26. Charles Gide, *Exposition Universelle de 1900 ... Économie sociale*, op. cit., p. 11.
27. Charles Gide, *Political Economy*, op. cit., pp. 3, 8–9.
28. Charles Gide, *Exposition Universelle de 1900 ... Économie sociale*, op. cit., p. 3.
29. Ibid., pp. 27–29.
30. Ibid., see for example pp. 3, 8, 19, 20.
31. Ibid., p. 3 – see note 28, above.
32. Ibid., pp. 31–34.
33. Ibid., p. 11.
34. Ibid.
35. Ibid., p. 3 (see note 27, above); Léon Jaussely, *La vie urbaine*, nos 1–2, 1919, p. 136; Henri Sellier, quoted in Baty-Tornikian, op. cit., n.p. Charles Gide argued in favour of 'association' rather than state intervention in the building of housing. He saw the state as an external, paternalistic authority, separate from the people. For those such as Jaussely who helped make the *cités-jardins* a reality after World War I, state intervention was not merely a necessity, the state itself should be understood as a democratic manifestation of the people.

36 Paraphrased from André Gide, *Fruits of the Earth*, London: Vintage, 2002, p. 30 [*Les Nourritures Terrestres*, Paris: Gallimard, 1917 (1898)].
37 Ibid., p. 81. André Gide is talking here about spitting out apple pips.
38 Hannah Arendt, *The Human Condition*, Chicago, IL: University of Chicago Press, 1958, pp. 112–115.
39 On solidarity as involvement in and interpretation of situations held in common, see Hans-Georg Gadamer, 'What is Practice? The Conditions of Social Reason' and 'Hermeneutics as a Theoretical and Practical Task' in *Reason in the Age of Science*, trans. Frederick G. Lawrence, Cambridge, MA; London: MIT Press, 1981.

3
PARKER MORRIS AND THE ECONOMIES OF THE FORDIST HOUSE

Gary A. Boyd

Introduction

In 1980, Margaret Thatcher abolished the housing standards set out by the Parker Morris report in 1961. This provoked decades of muted elegies before a resurrection of interest in the analytical measuring of domestic space and its uses in the mayoralty of Boris Johnson's London.[1] This chapter re-examines the scope and iconography of the original Parker Morris report arguing that – despite its recent exhumation in twenty-first century London – it expresses a particularly modernist approach to space, one that presupposed equally specific modernist economic conditions and geographies.

The Fordist house

'The war is sixteen years and three and half million houses away.'[2] Thus, the conclusion to the Parker Morris report began with a description of time measured not only in conventional units but also in terms of space, *houses*. The purpose of this was perhaps threefold: to draw attention to the enormous quantity of housing produced in this period; to ascribe housing issues with a heightened sense of social significance; and to suggest new means in which this emerging space could be measured, organised and ultimately used.

Notions of time and space conflate regularly in the report not least in its official title, *Homes for Today and Tomorrow*, where the idea of domestic space is projected to the future. In the search for new housing standards, Parker Morris represented both a continuation of and reaction to a tradition of scientific enquiry. The origins of this lay not in the home but rather in the early twentieth-century factory where time was prioritised over space. Frederick Winslow Taylor's seminal text of 1911, *Principles of Scientific Management*, for example, sought to increase the efficiency of the production of goods by fragmenting work routines and re-calibrating them according to principles of time and motion.[3] When his theories were adopted by Henry Ford to create the conditions for mass production, the result was an assembly line system where stationary workers connected with moving conveyor belts bringing components to them. Productive space in the Ford factory, therefore, was reduced to a diagram of linear movements articulated by the intersection of points and lines.

Perhaps as a corrective to its absence in European industry in the 1920s and 1930s, the idea of the Fordist paradigm as a technological salve to social ills occupied a central place in the imagination of progressive European thinkers. Conspicuous among these was the architectural avant-garde. As early as 1910, for example, Walter Gropius explored the possibilities of extending techniques of mass production to domestic architecture in his essay, 'Program for the Founding of a General Housing-Construction Company Following Artistically Uniform Principles'.[4] Perhaps significantly, in his descriptions of the desirability of mass-produced elements (doors, staircases, walls etc.) – and his calls for their realisation in standard sizes and a pre-emptive celebration of the expected aesthetic harmony – he singularly failed to mention the space in between these components or the activities likely to take place there. Perhaps also significantly, this omission was to an extent corrected by a woman, Christine Frederick, who published *The New Housekeeping: Efficiency Studies in Home Management* three years later in 1913.[5]

As Paul Emmons pointed out, the latter publication was important for two reasons. First, it extended the principles of Taylorism to the interior of the home for the first time. And, second, it did so through a series of diagrams that concurrently began to assume the irrefutable qualities and authority of scientific measurement. Indeed, Emmons asserts that by the time Alexander Klein was configuring his famous 'Functional House for Frictionless Living' in 1934, he considered conventional house plans to be fit only for 'subjective evaluation'. His own diagrams, meanwhile, provided 'direct access to the facts [acting as X-rays to reveal … underlying skeletal conditions'.[6] But the limitations are obvious. If Gropius's notion of mass-production neglected the space in between, then the diagrams of Frederick and Klein seem to propose an absolute interior. Here, there is no mediation between inside and outside space and instead the envelope of the building is of no apparent consequence. Its physicality un-described, it is effectively dematerialised.

Furthermore, this application of scientific enquiry took place in an uneven and limited pattern across the geography of the house. Frederick's deliberations in the kitchen, for instance, began a series of preoccupations with this space that would be emblematised by the *Frankfurter Küche* designed by Grete Schütte-Lihotzky in 1926. The development of the lesser-known Frankfurt bathroom suggests that this area too was the site of much observation and speculation.[7] That such detail was not necessarily afforded other spaces provides insights on the premises under which the scientific study of the home was being conducted. Sharing a seductive mixture of new, ready-made, mass-produced equipment and fittings, the kitchen and bathroom were areas closely connected with production and technology. This is self-evident in the case of the kitchen, while the bathroom's intimate association with hygiene – and, by extension, to bodily fitness, etc. – also made it a key site in the creation of healthy workers. Bruno Taut famously took this one step further suggesting that a close relationship between function and space would invoke a psychological reaction, producing 'a new mental attitude, more flexible, simpler and more joyful'.[8]

The house, conceived as both product and site of mass production, is central to the notion of *existenzminimum* that so exercised practitioners such as Taut throughout the 1920s. This concept presupposed a standard of living that would effectively preclude certain activities and choices from taking place in the home. Instead, a symbolic proximity emerges between the factory and the house. For Robin Evans, this was encapsulated in Klein's ideal of a frictionless home, a well-oiled machine dedicated to the pursuit of clear pre-meditated tasks conducted without diversion.[9] That such a level of subsistence and single-minded living was to be actively pursued as a positive feature is not only revealing of the puritanical characters of some proponents but also of their economic naivety. As Henry Ford had long since recognised, to pursue a total system of mass production, it is necessary for workers to mass consume as well as produce. The home would increasingly become the site for both.

New patterns of living

The first section of *Homes for Today and Tomorrow* stresses that the world of the 1930s is no more. Emphatically entitled 'New Patterns of Living' here the report presents itself as a necessary update to its predecessor, the Dudley report of 1944.[10] The latter, it claims, was conceived against the austerity of the depression, a period of 'vastly different problems, outlook and trends'. Since then, 'the country has undergone a social and economic revolution'. This had manifested itself not only in 'full employment, a national health service [and] retirement pensions' but also in material terms: 'People are better off than ever before; the average pay-packet buys a good deal more than it did in 1939.'[11] Much of this increased spending power, the report suggests, registered itself in the home where the temporal freedoms offered by new, labour-saving devices promoted the acquisition of other commodities dedicated purely to leisure. It is the search for the spatial accommodation of these new freedoms that begins to underpin Parker Morris's key recommendations: larger houses and better heating. This begins to explain the appearance and form of the famous and very curious diagrams by Gordon Cullen (Figure 3.1) which accompanied the report and perhaps most potently conveyed its spirit. Once again, comparison with Parker Morris's predecessors illustrates this more clearly.

In the Dudley report, the accompanying diagrams illustrate what feel like a series of tight, partitioned spaces conspicuously constrained by the material that makes and surrounds them: walls. Furthermore, and similar to the functionally orientated houses of the 1930s, the productive space of the kitchen is given a prominent

FIGURE 3.1 Diagram by Gordon Cullen, from *Homes for Today and Tomorrow*

Note the floating baby.

role. This is reiterated in another, more recent publication which appears to have been very influential on the Parker Morris report, providing not only some key data but also techniques of information retrieval and even prototypes for Cullen's images. *Meals in Modern Homes* was produced in 1956 by the Council of Scientific Management in the Home, an exclusively female research committee. Its stated premise was to investigate how the kitchen – evocatively described as the 'housewife's machine in which she is both worker and manager' – could be reconfigured spatially to become more productive and efficient.[12] Gleaning information on a national scale from questionnaires disseminated across Great Britain, this report classified a whole series of cooking activities and kitchen arrangements – often using scientific sounding acronyms like ws/c/ws/s/ws (work surface/cooker/work surface/sink/work surface) – before finally making generic recommendations.[13] *Meals in Modern Homes* was generously illustrated – somewhat spuriously with photographs of mealtime activities that manage somehow to remove men completely from the kitchen – but more intriguingly with a series of diagrams representing the sequencing of kitchen equipment, arrangements of kitchen doors and, most significantly, movement across space. The latter, in a diagrammatic plan describing meal service arrangements (Figure 3.2), is conveyed through a large darkly toned arrow that delineates a female figure's route from kitchen to dining room.

Whereas this arrow has to constrict and deform to negotiate spaces that – like those in the Dudley report – are constrained by material, when Cullen adopts a similar convention in Parker Morris, it is subverted and critiqued in a number of ways. Cullen's arrow enjoys a space that is emphatically free. No longer confined to a plan, it roams about in three-dimensions, flexing and twisting according to a logic of flow and connection. Moreover, it ceases to describe a linear route, instead splitting up to arrive simultaneously at a series of points. Just as it presupposes the

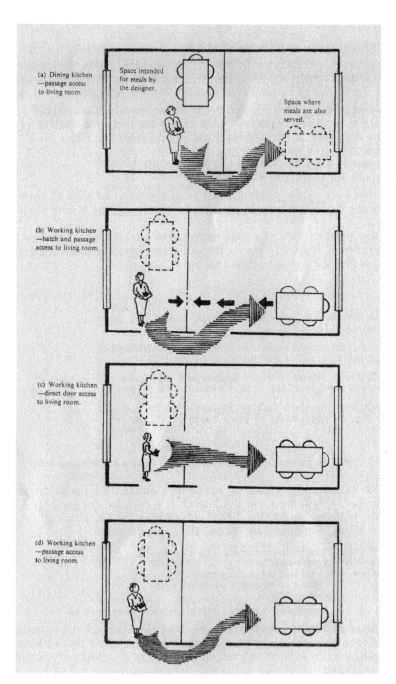

FIGURE 3.2 'Examples of Meal Services Arrangements' from *Meals in Modern Homes*

dematerialising of walls and floors, it suggests the disembodiment of the individual into a ghost or perhaps even a puff of hot air (Figure 3.3).

Elsewhere, the report suggests that better heating will promote both spatial *and* social emancipation by allowing the occupants 'to move away from the fireside to somewhere else in the home'.[14]

This point was reiterated in the contemporary architectural press where the opportunities offered by advances in heating and other technologies were being actively celebrated. Cullen's diagrams of transparent spaces populated with figures pressed close to vague, dematerialising walls found an equivalence in a whole series of advertisements for building technologies, products, components and appliances. These seem to suggest new ways of experiencing and using space; new relationships between outside and inside; and other new spatial freedoms. Thus, Cullen's eerie floating baby, free from the vicissitudes of gravity, can be viewed as another example in a contemporary spirit of utopian thinking that seemed to equate technology and transparency respectively as the means and essence of modern ways of living.

So while the negated walls of Christine Frederick's diagrams appeared to represent an indifference to their quality, by the time Parker Morris is published, this apparently negative example of expediency is being actively pursued as a positive design ideal. This was nothing new, the dematerialised wall lay at the heart of the pre– and post-war theories of Frank Lloyd Wright, Mies van der Rohe and countless others. Meanwhile, in Britain in 1939, in a publication called *The Social Function of Science*, the famous scientist J. D. Bernal was contemplating the

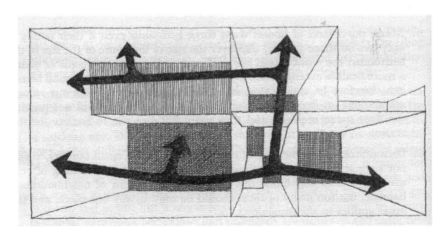

FIGURE 3.3 The promiscuous arrow, from *Homes for Today and Tomorrow*

Source: diagram by Gordon Cullen.

scientifically designed window wall to be 'guarded either by the wind itself or by jets of air forming part of the general ventilation system'.[15] What was different was that by 1961, not only had such ideas seeped into mainstream thinking but they were also being considered as achievable in everyday dwellings. Paradoxically, given Parker Morris's acceptance and expressions of the benefits of technology, the report actually owed its existence to a concern surrounding a perceived lack of freedom resulting from technological systems.

Systems building

By the time the Parker Morris report was commissioned in 1959, Walter Gropius's dream of the mass-produced house had, to some extent, been realised in Britain. A significant proportion of the three million houses built since the war had been created through factory-made prefabricated components. Central to this huge undertaking was the role of a government dedicated to creating a Welfare State articulated by some of the economic principles of John Maynard Keynes. This ideology had underpinned the deployment of a series of hitherto unconnected forces – various ministries, local authorities, large building firms, scientists, engineers and architects – to the provision of industrialised housing. The latter was deemed to be the only form capable of solving the 'housing crisis'. And while government sponsored research had taken place before the war, it was really only in the 1950s that the idea of systems building began to be investigated in any great detail. Much of this concerned itself with so-called modular coordination, the development of a series of standard measurements for components and, just as critically, how they connect. The manufacturers of the building parts themselves contributed a significant amount of this research, which often involved ways of producing the components more cheaply.[16]

Parker Morris was set up by the Ministry of Local Government and Housing as a spatial corrective to these material investigations, one that purported to give centrality to the inhabitant and their activities and advocated a notion of flexibility. It is this last quality that situates the report within a particular and ongoing discussion surrounding the nature of systems building. This was conceived under two terms: open and closed systems. Closed was basically a complete package delivered by a building company to which, rather like in classical architecture, nothing could be added or taken away without adversely affecting the whole. Unsurprisingly, given the lower costs involved, these were favoured by manufacturers. Open systems, on the other hand, represented a more complex creation of a series of components that could be assembled and conjoined in a number of different configurations. The Modular Society, founded in 1953, favoured the flexibility inherent in this approach, as did the Royal Institute of British Architects because it allowed continuing creative control.[17]

By favouring flexibility and proposing the quite radical idea that a home should be adaptable over time, Parker Morris implicitly endorsed open building systems. This is reinforced in a number of ways. For example, the report recommends unequivocally that an architect should be used. It also eschews minimum standards for individual rooms and instead recommends overall areas for entire houses. How these houses are configured internally is left for others to decide but in any case should respond to use and other conditions such as sunlight and view. Thus, the intimate connection between wall and space proposed by closed systems is disrupted: walls are now subjected to spatial imperatives and not the other way around.

Again, this new relationship is expressed eloquently in Cullen's diagrams where roaming arrows seem to be prodding now dematerialised walls into some sort of reaction. Yet paradoxically, the increase in space recommended by Parker Morris would have the effect of actually accelerating the deployment of closed systems. More space meant higher costs, which inevitably were counteracted with cheaper, less flexible components. Indeed, the relationship between economics and space is always the key to understanding *Homes for Today and Tomorrow* and its limitations.

Commodities and flexible living

In their book, *Flexible Housing*, Tatjana Schneider and Jeremy Till commend Parker Morris for seeking to promote issues of flexibility and for giving increased importance to the user and their activities.[18] For Adrian Forty, however, the term 'user' – which is implied but never actually used within Parker Morris – was, in the 1950s and 1960s, essentially a fiction, an abstraction that allowed architects to believe they were placing the occupant at the centre of their designs while in fact they were producing primarily for the State.[19] This view is perhaps endorsed by the means used by the Parker Morris committee to retrieve its information. Borrowing methods from *Meals in Modern Homes* they sought to achieve a nationwide consensus, receiving and classifying data from across Great Britain. Within such abstract ideas of placelessness and 'the user', other registers emerge to address social ties, individual needs and the spaces to accommodate them.

This is best illustrated by the design manual, *Space in the Home*, which was produced by the Ministry of Housing and Local Government in 1963 to facilitate the application of the Parker Morris standards. Here, the visionary qualities and promises of freedom conveyed by Cullen's drawings are transposed into schedules listing the sizes and shapes of mass-produced objects and diagrams of social situations organised around these new commodities. Meanwhile, other diagrams describe diurnal rhythms shaped by factory and office times, lifetimes organised in nuclear families and both articulated by gender-orientated divisions of labour. Whereas, 1930s examples such as Klein's functional house had tended to limit themselves to the creation of the productive individual, Parker Morris is more pervasive and, in its assumptions, perhaps even less flexible especially with regards to time. Both site and product of the Welfare State, *Homes for Today and Tomorrow* and *Space in the Home* represent the completion of the Fordist house project. Their diagrams are icons of a dream of a planned economy where domestic technologies and living space would be deployed by the State as a means of achieving a balance between production and consumption at the level of the nation.

While we know this dream was complicated by the social events of the 1960s, problematised by the 1973 oil crisis and ultimately dismantled by Thatcher, it is worthwhile remembering the consensus in the 1950s and 1960s that surrounded, not only the desirability of a Welfare State, but also the role of building technologies and services as neutral, value-free means towards a better tomorrow. As well as being central to the assumptions of the State-sponsored Parker Morris report, reiterated by scientists and emphasised in contemporary advertisements, this conception also seems to have exercised some of the more progressive and radical thinkers of the architectural profession. The apparent intersections between Gordon Cullen's drawings and the icons of an avant-garde dreaming of technological freedoms is striking. Cullen's arrows seem to equate to the Smithsons' ideal of 'an endless architectural equivalent to the present cosmology of endless continual space'.[20] And his wall-less electrical services diagram corresponds to a non-architecture of services dreamt of by Cedric Price (1964) in Fun Palace (Figure 3.4); extended into a continual landscape by Superstudio (1972); and reconceived at the level of the dwelling by Reyner Banham and François Dallegret in 'Un-house: Transportable Standard of Living Package, and A Home is not a House' (1965).[21]

Conceived in the context of a Fordist/Keynesian economic system underpinned by State-sponsored regulation, it is easy to see why Parker Morris was unpalatable to the free-market ideologies of Thatcher. And yet, within the assumptions of *Homes for Today and Tomorrow*, agendas can be discerned that are not inconsistent with aspects of post-Fordism or neo-liberalism: an accelerating acquisition of commodities, the evocation of individual freedoms,[22] and the notion of possessive individualism as an increasingly critical facet of a family's social contract. It is, then,

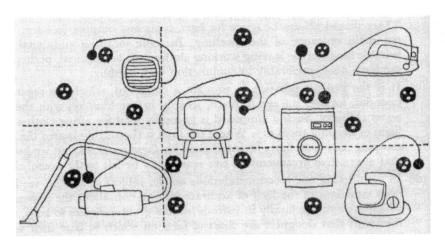

FIGURE 3.4 Wall-less electrical services, from *Homes for Today and Tomorrow*

Source: diagram by Gordon Cullen.

significant that Parker Morris concerns itself almost entirely with private spaces within the domestic unit and that shared or communal areas are mostly conspicuously absent. The home, a framework for the accumulation of commodities, is poised to increasingly become a commodity itself. It is, then, perhaps both fitting and paradoxical that the Housing Act of 1980, which authorised the selling of council houses, was the same act that dissolved the Parker Morris standards.

Notes

1 The *London Housing Design Guide* (Interim Edition) which makes a series of recommendations for domestic space standards was published in 2010.
2 Parker Morris Committee, *Homes for Today and Tomorrow* (London: Her Majesty's Stationery Office, 1961), p. 47.
3 Frederick Winslow Taylor, *Principles of Scientific Management* (New York: Dover Editions, 1998).
4 Walter Gropius, 'Program for the Founding of a General Housing-Construction Company Following Artistically Uniform Principles' (1910) in Barbara Miller Lane, ed. *Housing and Dwelling: Perspective on Modern Domestic Architecture* (London: Routledge, 2007), pp. 237–240.
5 Christine Frederick, *The New Housekeeping: Efficiency Studies in Home Management* (Garden City, NY: Doubleday Page & Company, 1913).
6 Paul Emmons, 'Intimate Circulations: Representing Flow in House and City', *AA Files*, 51 (2005), p. 52.
7 Alexander Kira's seminal *The Bathroom* (Harmondsworth: Penguin, 1976) deepened scientific enquiry into this domestic space.
8 Bruno Taut quoted in Peter Rowe, *Modernity and Housing* (Cambridge, MA: MIT Press, 1995), p. 131.
9 Robin Evans, *Translations from Drawing to Building and Other Essays* (London: Architectural Association, 2003), p. 85.
10 The Dudley report (London: Housing Advisory Committee, 1944).
11 Parker Morris Committee, p. 1.
12 Council of Scientific Management in the Home (A Specialist Committee of the Women's Group on Public Welfare), *Meals in Modern Homes* (London: Council of Scientific Management in the Home, 1955), p. 41.
13 Council of Scientific Management in the Home, pp. 14–15.
14 Parker Morris Committee, p. 2.
15 Quoted in Brian Finnimore, *Houses from the Factory: System Building and the Welfare State 1942–74* (London: Rivers Oram Press, 1989), p. 30.
16 See Finnimore; also Miles Glendinning and Stefan Muthesius, *Tower Block: Modern Public Housing in England, Scotland, Wales and Northern Ireland* (New Haven, CT; London: Yale University Press, 1994); Emmett Scanlon, 'The System and the Art of Relationship: The Ordinary as Method in Post-War Britain' (Dublin: unpublished Masters thesis, University College Dublin, 2000).
17 Christine Wall, *An Architecture of Parts: Architects, Buildings and Industrialisation in Britain 1940–1970* (London: Routledge, 2013), p. 2. Wall discusses the Modular Society in great detail in Part II of the book.
18 Tatjana Schneider and Jeremy Till, *Flexible Housing* (London: Architectural Press, 2007), pp. 38, 146.
19 Adrian Forty, *Words and Buildings: A Vocabulary of Modern Architecture* (London: Thames & Hudson, 2000), p. 314.
20 Charles Jencks, *Modern Movements in Architecture* (London: Penguin, 1985), p. 256.

21 Cedric Price, *The Square Book* (London: Wiley Academy, 2003).
22 Katherine Shonfield memorably equated Cullen's arrow with the visceral figure of Michael Caine's fictional character *Alfie* enjoying new spatial freedoms and using transparency as a means to sexual conquest in the emerging permissive society of 1960s' London. Katherine Shonfield, *Walls Have Feelings: Architecture, Film and the City* (London: Routledge, 2000), p. 86.

4

CARE OF COMMONS

Exploring questions of care, gifts and reciprocity in making new commons

Kim Trogal

This chapter explores some of the economies and ethics involved in the creation of new commons.

Commons is a term we hear with increasing frequency. It often refers to 'common-pool resources', such as fisheries, rivers or forests, usually involving a cooperative or mutual form of management.[1] Commons include the material resources of the earth as well immaterial ones, like knowledge, languages or culture.[2] New kinds of commons are being made and claimed all the time, for example, 'creative commons', digital commons, as well as commons forming in ecological movements and in anti-capitalist movements.[3] Whatever kind of commons we are speaking about, as Mies and Bennholdt-Thomsen say, 'commons presupposes a community', no commons can exist as such without a group to care for it.[4]

Commons bring questions of management and governance but, importantly, as a collective practice they bring different economies and ethical relations. Commons are the spaces of reciprocity and of care, they involve labour (taking care of something) and responsibility; they involve ethical–economic relations with others. This chapter focuses specifically on this latter aspect, and aims to question the ethical economies of 'giving and taking' in an emerging commons in a study of local food project, Incredible Edible, Todmorden UK, in 2011.[5] I look particularly at aspects of gifts and gift economies involved in theses commons. Drawing on Derrida, I discuss some of the paradoxes involved, when considering commons and gifts, not only the questions of responsibility in reciprocity, but the problem of the (in)visibilty of care labour involved in sustaining a commons. I end with a short discussion of the relation of commons (and gifts) to neoliberal economies, and draw on Gibson-Graham's notion of economic diversity to situate commons, within wider economic practices.

Commons and local food production: Incredible Edible

In recent years feminists such as Silvia Federici, Maria Mies and others have pointed to urban gardening practices and urban agriculture as possible locations for new commons. Whilst urban agriculture is not a new phenomenon, it has become increasingly prevalent in the North within environmental movements concerned with peak-oil, or community movements that are attempting to counter the effects of deindustrialisation. The sites of ecological food production, focusing on the local, organic and seasonal, may not only provide a contribution to subsistence and build local economies, but may also become potential locations for more reciprocal economies, new forms of sociality and cooperation. The example I take to explore this potential is Incredible Edible.

Incredible Edible is a grassroots initiative in Todmorden, Calderdale, whose overall, long-term ambition is for the town to be self-sufficient in producing their own food (Figure 4.1). The project has many layers of activity, including fruit and vegetable growing, beekeeping, orchard planting, medicinal herbs, aquaponics and chicken farming. They work with groups and schools, holding events and classes on: how to prune trees; how to sell eggs; grow mushrooms; how to build raised beds; pick wild plants and so on. Other areas of activity include developing future

FIGURE 4.1 Gifted produce: outside the college, Todmorden, March 2011

livelihoods and businesses; creating an edible 'green route' through the town; a study and learning centre, and business incubator in Walsden; a fish farm and food hub at the secondary school; working with all the schools to create a town wide orchard; and a hilltop farm in Gorpley.

In Incredible Edible, a small common resource is established through the appropriation of private and public (state) land. Through agreements or guerrilla gardening, the group have set up forty plots, which are now adopted by individuals or groups.[6] Some of the growing sites are located in school grounds or private gardens, others sites are publicly accessible. In the public sites, food is grown by volunteers in raised beds, on street corners, outside the police station, in diverse locations from graveyards to train station platforms. The group calls these 'propaganda gardens' and their aim is to engage people with the idea of growing food, showing what it looks like, and suggesting the idea that this might be something to participate in.

The propaganda gardens are named by the group as 'food to share', everything grown in these publicly accessible plots is free to anyone who wants to take it. The group, with volunteers, had planted over 700 fruit trees by 2011, mostly in public spaces. For some involved, the town based growing is not their focus and their concerns are directed towards the surrounding rural areas. Here they work with local farmers, as well as cultivating their own farm land. Although I focus on the town based growing in this text, it should not be understood as their main activity.

Incredible Edible do not claim to be making a gift economy or a commons, these themes come from my research interests and provide the lens through which I look at their activities. What interests me especially about their project as a potential commons, is their emphasis on generosity and sharing in the public realm; in particular, their use of gifts to make connections between themselves and others, 'the public', outside the group. Historically, the commons in England and Wales were cared for by a group of commoners. In some ways an exclusive group (not everyone had commoners rights), but significantly they were a group defined by territory. It was a community of necessity: a community of people formed because they lived in the same locality and had to live together. But today, with the construction of new forms of commons we need to ask what kinds of sharing and relations could we have, that are not necessarily defined by territory? What do the edges of a group or community look like? In what sense do these gifts in public space open up new economic and ethical possibilities, without undermining their own sustainability?

Commons and the gift economy: care in giving and taking in Todmorden

In some ways, the community of a commons can be compared to a gift community in that both agree to impose strict rules on their individual members in order to ensure long-term welfare and sustainability. In the historic commons of England and Wales a commoner's right to, for instance, collect bracken, harvest fruit, to forage, to fish in a river or use common pastures were all highly regulated activities, mutually agreed by the commoners themselves.[7] Whilst there was high level of restriction on individual activity, taking from the commons also meant taking responsibility. Rules were agreed upon to protect the commons from degradation and therefore to support its capacity to support human life in the future.

Commons were never open access nor 'free gifts', neither are commons a 'gift economy' as such. What is notable however, is that gifts do bring a particular 'affective economy', creating connections in ways that monetary transactions do not.[8] The commons, and gifts, bring certain responsibilities and 'contracts' in the dynamics of giving and receiving. This is most famously elaborated in theories of the gift and counter-gift, by Mauss and later critiqued by Derrida, I return to this below.

So what are the relations of reciprocity in new commons? What are the gifts and how do they relate to care labour? What kinds of affective bonds are brought through this kind of economy?

Incredible Edible was initiated and is now run by volunteers. This signals the beginning of a gift economy, in which the primary gift is one of time. At the time of my conversations with the members of Incredible Edible, they employed two part-time community engagement workers and a part-time worker on the site in Walsden, to help build the facility, but most of the work is done on a volunteering basis. Other donations include monetary contributions, often small and from private enterprise rather than the state, as well as material contributions, gifts of produce, skills, materials, compost, seeds, tools, time, as well as instances of reciprocity.

The question of gifts is not a simple one, in terms of the economy they bring. One of the organisers, Nick Green, co-founder of Incredible Edible, spoke of the subjective shift required both to give and to receive:

> It's taken me a bit of getting used to giving. I used to be going past the beans that I planted in the town centre and think, 'shit! there's someone picking my beans!' Then a couple of hundred yards down the road I'm thinking 'oh! I just remembered, that's why I planted them. Getting passed that, thinking that they're my baby and I should get some, it's taken a while to appreciate what I am getting from all that, and that is, I have a sense that the public perception of me is quite different from what it was three or four years ago. Everyone knows who I am, for one thing, but very positive about who I am, what I'm doing, what Incredible Edible is, it's all very positive. So I get something from it other than eating the beans.[9]

This reminds me that reciprocity is not 'equal', we do not receive the same thing we give, but that it feels in some way approximate or commensurate.[10] It is an exchange of non-equivalents, in which the 'thing' received can often have strong meaning, value or feeling attached to it. The affective power of giving a gift can have profound effects. One of the participants, Kerry Morrison, told me an anecdote. She was standing at a bus stop as a young lad who had had a drink approached.

She asked him what he thought of the project and whether he ever took any of the food growing in the street. He replied that he felt it was a great project and yes, he took some of the produce. But, he remarked, he did not take too much because 'it is for everybody'. He knew it was a gift and treated it as such.[11]

Just as Nick noted that at first we might not be used to giving, many of us are not used to taking, either. Kerry also explained to me that from her perspective, sometimes the gifts are not gifts. One of the problems can be that people do not take what is there, even though it is marked as free. She told me that the group had, in some locations, put up signs to explain what the plants were and when they could be harvested. It was thought that people did not take, as they did not know what or when things could be taken. This was the reason a taxi driver gave me, for example, for why he never took anything himself. But despite the group providing this information, she thought that things mostly were not getting harvested. Others have more recently, in certain locations, reported the opposite response of 'overzealous' harvesting. Each of these responses gives interesting insights into commons, so I will take each in turn.

One obvious reason for the first response, of not taking, might be that what is produced here is somehow an excess. Whilst we all need food to survive, many in the UK are buffered from food insecurity, for now, and live in ignorance of it. However, borrowing from theories of the gift and gift economies there are other readings that can be made of Kerry's observations. When read as part of a gift economy they also tell us something about a commons without rules that contradicts the idea that a commons is 'tragedy' doomed to degrade under individual desire for gain.

We know from Mauss that there is no such thing as a free gift, the idea that something can be given freely, without expectation of a return.[12] Mauss argued that there must always be a counter-gift and the giving of gifts for Mauss was part of a gift exchange. This kind of gift economy could perhaps be called a reciprocal economy, where giving and taking are part of the same dynamic.

Pam Warhurst, one of the co-founders of the project, told me her favourite anecdote from the beginning of the project. She explained, eighteen months after Mary had turned her front garden over to the public and offered the produce there for free, people finally began to take a few things (Figure 4.2). A woman and her two children, strangers, asked her if it was okay to take things, and, assured that it was, they did. They returned cabbage leaves for composting in Mary's garden and the next day left a bowl of soup on Mary's doorstep, made from the vegetables.[13]

We do not necessarily need theories of gifts and counter-gifts to know that these are the gestures people make when the opportunity arises and when they know who to thank. This particular anecdote also raises an important question concerning the theory – why is the counter-gift, or reciprocity, so often seen as a negative aspect as a kind of bondage, rather than a connection or act of kindness?

With these gifts in the public domain, the propaganda gardening and town wide orchard, Incredible Edible could be said to be producing a common resource that is markedly different to the historic commons, for in the commons, one would

FIGURE 4.2 Gifted produce: Propaganda Garden, Todmorden, March 2011

have gathered wood or foraged, but would not have taken produce farmed by another. Traditional strip farming still has a remnant in today's cities in the form of allotment gardening. Whilst gift relations can be said to take place in allotments too, the sharing is reciprocal between producers. As passers-by of Incredible Edible sites are not always giving and are not contributing, there is no reciprocity and this may perhaps be a reason why they may not take what is given. There is then a question, how can reciprocity and production be further supported in order to allow a gift economy to evolve? Or, alternatively, how is it possible to move beyond reciprocity and the need for counter-gifts?

Derrida famously provides some answers to the second question. For Derrida, a real gift is not located within this kind of economy; if it is a real gift there will be no demand, or expectation of a return. For him, to speak of 'gift exchange' is a contradiction. In order to achieve radical giving, giving as a moral act has to be avoided and thus the paradox is that to truly give a gift, one cannot know one is doing so. It must be done without knowledge on the part of both the giver and receiver.[14] Whilst those participating in Incredible Edible do not actively seek counter-gifts by any means, the produce is offered freely and without expectation, as a recipient we will sometimes want to give back, or feel that we should.

Care labour here also has the potential to function in a way that accords with private property, rather than commons. The care that went into appropriating the space, planting, watering, weeding, protecting and growing the vegetables unwittingly functions as a sign of ownership and thus negates the gift by marking it. It is likely that people have respect for the effort that went into growing the produce. I certainly did not take anything on any of my visits. This respect might be increased by the marking of the beds; when a bed is adopted, it is sometimes marked showing who has responsibility and therefore who has made the gift. I am unlikely to take broccoli that a disabled child grew for example, however freely it is offered. Care can be present then, in both sides of giving and taking.

As well as their propaganda gardens, Incredible Edible have been planting trees around the town and planting edible plants, like raspberries, blackberries and blackcurrants in border spaces, such as the borders of the health centre car park (Figure 4.3). In these cases, unlike other crops, once the produce is taken, it will grow back next year; its supply is not exhausted. This kind of taking, and the

FIGURE 4.3 Invisible labour: fifty new fruit trees on the right-hand side of the image, March 2011

approach of the young man at the bus stop, is more in the spirit of commons and in the spirit in which it is offered by the group.

In these instances the gifts appear more 'natural', and in many cases the plants do not stand out. If you had no knowledge of the project you might not notice them, they seem to 'just be there'. But if we make care and labour the centre of attention, bringing Derrida's theory of the gift highlights a paradox. These plants and trees still need to be cared for, but the care is less visible and appears 'natural'. I take a feminist perspective, believing that care work needs to be valued and recognised, and so I cannot at the same time argue that in order for a gift economy and commons to succeed it needs to become hidden and unknown. This would situate reproduction in the 'natural' realm, and consequently it would remain unrecognised. The hidden care labour of commons is a frequent problem and one that emerges when we view commons only as resources and not as communities or practices. As historian Peter Linebaugh explains through the example of forests, these are not gifts of nature, rather they are often products of indigenous cultures and practices.[15] Thinking of commons only in terms of gifts can conceal the care involved in their maintenance.

Here there is respect and care in both giving and taking. According to others involved in similar projects, a common problem of a gift economy is that people will always put in more than they take. Some approach the gardens, seeing care as ownership, showing a respect for others' work, whilst others may approach them only as a resource from which to take. In either case, these opposite responses are illustrative of the difficulties in engendering the subjective shifts required to build common worlds.

Incredible Edible: commons and gifts within an economic diversity

As political economist Massimo De Angelis says, there are always necessary commons for capitalism to continue, but at the same time capitalism demands enclosures.[16] Similarly Caffentzis argues that the commons is not opposed to market capital *per se* and is in fact quite compatible with it.[17] In the context of neoliberal economies, and a 'Big Society' with its emphasis on volunteering and giving, what is the status of commons and gifts, especially the gift of time? Are they a means to legitimate the reduction of the state? Do they assist a form of value extraction based on the giving, from those with the least, materially speaking, to give? The question of how a commons, gift economies or other alternative economies intersect with markets, locally and globally then, needs to be much better understood. We need an awareness, as De Angelis says, of the power relations in a specific historic context. This is something that cannot be generalised but is specific to circumstances.

Incredible Edible emphasise providing opportunities for businesses and social enterprise. At first, I wondered whether, given this emphasis, we can still see the project in terms of commons, or whether the ethic of sharing, generosity and the possibility for an alternative economy was undermined. But this search for economic purity, or purity of ideas is my problem rather than theirs. Following the pioneering work of J. K. Gibson-Graham it is possible to escape the dichotomous logic of capital/alternative economy and instead recognise a heterogeneous picture of diverse economies.[18] With Gibson Graham, and their colleagues in the Community Economies Collective,[19] one can find in Incredible Edible an economic diversity of which commons is one part. It is not a pure gift economy, nor local economy and whilst there are commercial aspects, as well as donations from companies, government and lottery bids these do not appear to be dominant either. Incredible Edible is not pure but an iterative set of connections of different desires, interests and activities. Commons are present here, but they are one part of a diversity of relations. The extent to which commons may develop here is a question for the future.

Notes

1 'Common-Pool Resource' is a term developed by Nobel prize winner, Elinor Ostrom, see Elinor Ostrom, *Governing the Commons: The Evolution of Institutions for Collective Action* (Cambridge: Cambridge University Press, 1990).
2 Michael Hardt and Antonio Negri, *Commonwealth* (Cambridge, MA: Belknap Press of Harvard University Press, 2009).
3 See for example, Maria Mies and Veronika Bennholdt-Thomsen. *The Subsistence Perspective: Beyond the Globalised Economy*, translated by Patrick Camiller (London: Zed, 1999). Vandana Shiva, Afsar Jafri, Gitanjali Bedi and Radha Holla-Bhar, *The Enclosure and Recovery of the Commons: Biodiversity, Indigenous Knowledge, and Intellectual Property Rights* (New Delhi: Research Foundation for Science, Technology, and Ecology, 1997). The Commoner: a web journal for other values. www.commoner.org.uk.
4 Mies and Bennholdt-Thomsen, p.163.
5 This text is based on research and interviews with Incredible Edible in 2011.
6 This was the case in the summer of 2011, the time of research.
7 The rights of common came with responsibilities and strict rules regarding the care and maintenance of the environment. These rules were democratically agreed in annual, or bi-annual, meetings held either in a Manorial Court or at a village meeting. Rules were often highly place and time specific, for example:

> [At Cartmel] villagers were not permitted to cut rushes on Windermoor before 26th September; those with a meadow on common were ordered to mow the same on 1st or 2nd July; and no-one was allowed to gather nuts before Nutday, 1st September, or shear his bracken for thatching, bedding or burning before Brackenday, 2nd October.

Alan Everitt, 'Farm Labourers', in *The Agrarian History of England and Wales*, vol. IV 1500–1640, ed. Joan Thirsk (Cambridge: Cambridge University Press, 1967), pp. 396-465. See also: J. M Neeson, *Commoners: Common Right, Enclosure and Social Change in England, 1700–1820* (Cambridge: Cambridge University Press, 1993), pp. 110-133.
8 This is Sara Ahmed's term. See Sara Ahmed, *The Cultural Politics of Emotion* (Edinburgh: Edinburgh University Press, 2004), pp. 44–49.
9 Conversation with Nick Green, Incredible Edible co-founder and activist June 16, 2011.
10 See for instance David Graeber, *Debt: The Last 5,000 Years* (London: Melville House, 2011), pp. 104–105.
11 Conversation with Kerry Morrison, March 2011.

12 Marcel Mauss, *The Gift: The Form and Reason for Exchange in Archaic Societies* (London: Routledge Classics, 2002).
13 Conversation with Pam Warhurst, June 2011.
14 Jacques Derrida, *Given Time 1: Counterfeit Money* (London: University of Chicago Press, 1992), pp. 122–123.
15 Peter Linebaugh, *The Magna Carta Manifesto: Liberties and Commons for All* (Berkeley: University of California Press, 2008), p. 243.
16 Massimo de Angelis 'On the Commons: A Public Interview with Massimo De Angelis and Stavros Stavrides', *E-flux*, vol. 17 (August 2010), www.e-flux.com/journal/view/150 (accessed 10.02.2011).
17 George C. Caffentzis, 'The Future of "The Commons": Neoliberalism's "Plan B" or The Original Disaccumulation of Capital?', *New Formations*, no. 69 (n.d.), 23–41.
18 J. K. Gibson-Graham, *A Postcapitalist Politics* (Minneapolis; London: University of Minnesota Press, 2006).
19 Please see: www.communityeconomies.org (accessed 20.05.2011).

5

JOHN EVELYN'S VILLA AT SAYES COURT

A microcosm of labour and love

Juliet Odgers

In this chapter, I present an 'Œconomie' from the seventeenth century, the household established by John and Mary Evelyn at Sayes Court in Deptford in 1653, some few years after their marriage. I bring two documents to my discussion, a plan drawn by John Evelyn as a record of the intended improvements to both house and garden which he set in motion in the early 1650s (Figure 5.1); and a small volume of 'Instructions Œconomique', prepared by Evelyn as a present for his bride shortly after their wedding.[1]

Although both documents are well known, no one has yet thought to interpret the one in terms of the other.[2] My presentation proceeds along three thematic paths derived from the 'Instructions' – Microcosm, Love and Labour. Together these documents demonstrate the earnest efforts which John Evelyn made to establish his home as an ideal household. Although I do not wish to not deny Mary Evelyn any part in the plan, at the time of her marriage Mary was only fourteen years old; she lived in Paris with her parents (her father was the King's English Resident there); she had never seen Sayes Court and was scarcely in a position to exert a profound influence on its conception. For all that women were given a considerable responsibility in running domestic economics during this period, it is the perspective of the husband which is presented both in the documents and in my discussion.[3]

John Evelyn is perhaps best known to architects as the author of *Fumifugium*, a proposal for the improvement of air quality in London; and as translator of Fréart de Chambray's *Parallel of Ancient and Modern Architecture*.[4] To his peers he was known for his books on gardening and sylviculture, particularly *Sylva, or a Discourse of Forest-Trees*, the first book to be produced by the Royal Society, of which he was a founder member and lifelong supporter.[5] At the time when Evelyn composed the 'Instructions Œconomique', he was living in self-imposed exile in Paris, where he met and married Mary. By moving abroad he had escaped the civil war and

FIGURE 5.1 The plan of Sayes Court house and garden

Source: drawing John Evelyn, calligraphy Richard Hoare, c. 1652.

could observe the progress of events from across the channel, as rebellion climaxed in the beheading of Charles I in 1648, the year in which Evelyn composed his 'Instructions'. Once peace was restored, the young couple returned to settle in Sayes Court. Arriving in England in 1652, Evelyn was debarred from taking up any public employment due to his Royalist political affiliations and so settled down instead to plant his garden, manage his estate, to read, write and translate. This then is the strife-ridden background against which Evelyn develops his vision of a household of industrious and loving harmony.

Godly household

The 'Godly' household of the seventeenth century is a topic that has received considerable attention as it relates to 'Puritan' communities of England and New England. Less has been said on the topic in relation to Anglican and Royalist households, such as Evelyn's. As Margo Todd points out, however, the ideal of a household conceived in terms of divine order, transcends the much contested boundaries commonly drawn between 'Puritan' and 'Anglican'. Ultimately the idea, common to both camps, depended on a common foundation of Renaissance Humanism.[6] The ideal household is, of course, structured around the idea of divinely sanctioned marriage. In the early modern period, marriage started to emerge from its traditional function as a political and familial economic imperative to take on something of the role of an ideal state of intellectual and spiritual companionship. This is an idea that we see reflected in Evelyn's 'Instructions Œconomique'. He underpins the idea of the companionable and loving marriage by recourse to both biblical and natural ideals – comparing marriage to Adam and Eve in their 'innocency', and evoking the natural examples of the stork, swan, pelican and dove – birds that all mate for life.[7] As for the family at large, the community of parents, children and various employees, the primary metaphor that holds together both the operational social order described in the 'Instructions' and the spatial order described in Evelyn's plan, is that of the household as a little world – a microcosm that reflects the divine order of the Creation.

Microcosm

Evelyn's 'Instructions Œconomique' is quite sparse on practical considerations. It consists instead mainly of reflections on the duties of members of the household to one another, duties that Evelyn grounds in his religious and political beliefs. In describing these he returns time and again to the primary metaphor of microcosm to support the structures he seeks to uphold, writing to his beloved Mary:

> A *Family* may truly be called that Inferior Celestiall Spheare, wherein the *Master* and *Mistress* resemble the *Primum Mobile*, their Children the *Fixed Starres* where Gravity, Prudence, Fortitude, Religion, Humanity, Industry and Plenty make up the seven planets whose benigne Influence complicate that ravishing Conscent and Harmony of the whole family which consists under these as an immovable and indissoluble centre.[8]

Elsewhere, writing in his manuscript 'History of Religion', Evelyn inverts this metaphor, telling us that God 'looks on all the world but as one house', and therein, he continues, lies its beauty – beauty that 'consists not in its separate parts (which seem imperfect) but united, its order, economy, & concurrence to the end'.[9] The house is the world, the world is a house. In the 'Instructions' Evelyn extends the metaphor likening the household to a state, saying the family is 'an Image and prototype of a more considerable society, even of a Citty and Republique'. Within this 'Republique' the patriarch commands and must consequently 'be personally present in all places'. His duty is to 'dispose things and Affaires in due order and method', a thought that leads immediately into a lengthy description of the prayers that he must lead at the beginning and end of each day (not optional). Along with this religious leadership he must undertake the 'prudent disposition of revennue, the management of what is in the field'.[10] He is ruler, curate and manager of the garden and farm, whilst the domain of the wife is the house itself.[11]

Looking at the broader cultural picture, the locus of the metaphor of microcosm was primarily the individual human being, an idea familiar to architects through the image of Vitruvian Man. We find this neatly expressed in one of Evelyn's favourite authors from the early 1650s,[12] Jean d'Espagnet, who writes:

> Man, the Prince of all creature, and of the lower World, is accounted the Summary of Universal Nature: For his Soul is an immortal ray of the Divine Light, his Body is a beautified Composure of the Elements.
>
> ... Therefore was man deservedly called a Microcosm, and the accomplisht Draught of the Universe.[13]

This primary image of man as microcosm often becomes tacit as analogies proliferate in a chain of associations, for the metaphor of microcosm has vast applicability – once established, any bounded whole may be likened to any other as a world entire. Thus building becomes body, body becomes column, or here the household becomes the body, but before all of these body is cosmos. Thus when Evelyn writes:

> materially and formally ... this Domestique Society resemleth the Bodie: whose soule is Veritie; whose head the Husband: whose heart the Wife and Children; whose hands and feet are the Servants and whose possessions are the food and raiment that nourish and maintain it.[14]

... the image of the microcosm lies beneath the surface. I have explained elsewhere how, through the mediating structures of geometry, the formal figures that we see in the garden of the Sayes Court plan – the oval parterre and the grove with its criss-cross pathways – were intended by Evelyn as images of cosmos. My arguments there were based around Evelyn's understanding of the relationship of the heavens and earth, particularly in the arena of plant growth, a concern that he articulated along astrological lines.[15] Here I expand these themes not through an analysis of the figural construction of the garden, but through the idea of the collection of parts as it figures in the plan as a reflection of the human community that forms the household.

Labour

> Labour is intended that by which what is lawfully gotten is maintained and preserved: wherefore it ought to be pious, moderate and ordinate.[16]

Evelyn's idea of a harmonious household, for all of its universal aspiration, depended on a strictly enforced boundary. This appears in his plan of Sayes Court in the clear demarcation of the walls and fences that separate the heart of the estate from the surrounding land. The boundary establishes the house, garden and service courts as a whole simply by defining the outlying fields and the world beyond as 'not included'.

One way in which the ordering of that whole appears in the plan is as a collection of the parts, itemised in the key, the first item of which introduces the theme of collections: '1. Porch, susteind with two Dorick Collumnes, paved underneath, over it my wives Closset of Collections'. Evelyn was something of an expert in collections. The gathering, selecting, ordering, cataloguing of books, plants, 'rarities', prints was an important part of his attempts to map and understand the world. Over the course of the years, his enterprises in this direction included translating a book on librarianship, and helping to catalogue various collections (for the Royal Society, for the court); in gardening he applied himself to devising a system for a register of plants and collected a wide range of species in his own garden at Sayes Court.[17] Inventory-like, the key to his Sayes Court plan proceeds, listing every room, yard and improved facility, item by item: – '16. The kitchen Chiminey'; '57: My Elaboratorie'; '68: The new house of office over the dunghill', ending with '126. Divers Elmes growing irregularly'.[18]

A preoccupation with listing also informs his 'Instructions Œconomique', but here it is accompanied by explicit attempts at classification, which Evelyn refers to as 'distinction … of Substance'. He opens the discussion, saying: 'wee are to treat of domestique possessions, and those may be dissected into two parts the movable and immovable whereof the one is naturall and the other Artificiall.'

He continues, 'those I terme naturall possessions … consist in Lands, Rivers, fountains, lakes and the like, the artificiall are onely such as belong in the house'.[19] Shockingly, servants are classified with animals under 'moveable' and 'natural possessions', though Evelyn draws the line at slavery. His servants are 'free', that is to say parties to a voluntary contract, as indeed are the husband and wife.[20] In each relationship the legal, contractual nature of the mutual bond is completely explicit, He dwells on the issue at some length. With the master as the head, the wife and children the heart, the servants the hands and feet, it is clear who does the heavy lifting, carrying, scrubbing and digging. All are established in a hierarchical, 'natural' and 'divine' ordering, which runs through the legally defined mutual duties of the members of the household. It also informs the spatial order of the plan.

Examining the Sayes Court plan in more detail, it comes as no surprise to find that the master of the house gets the largest number of dedicated spaces – 'My Chamber', 'My Studie', 'My Private Garden' leading to 'My Elaboratorie'; the Mistress gets only one – the 'Closset' over the front door. The rooms belonging to the master and mistress overlook the front court and the gardens. The servants have a 'servants chamber' and 'garret lodgings' overlooking the less than elegant 'Kitching Backe yard'. In general the servant spaces are squeezed into the strip of land that passes between the house and the inconveniently close wall to the adjoining dockyard, to the east (south is at the top of the drawing). This extends further to the north of the house where the 'Stable, Kitching garden, privy and hog-pen' are placed in convenient and fertile arrangement with respect to one another. The doors passing from private to public areas are named. This mapping of territories also serves as a register of the various labours of the household members. The sites of the 'mean' labour of the servants – the saw pitt, garden and kitchens – are matched by the sites of the 'ingenious' labours of the Master – the study, flower garden and chemical 'elaboratory', though as we have seen it is the duty of the husband to 'be personally present in all places'. All are expected to labour, the master included, and Evelyn was certainly indefatigable in his diligent application to all his projects and duties. But in Evelyn's disquisition 'labour' is by no means presented as the primary force in the economy, for he writes, 'the conservation ... of a Familie Consists in these mutuall offices towards one another of *Love* and *Labour*.'[21] Love comes first.

Love

> *Love is the Base of the Universe, the Cube of Nature, and the fastening bond of things above and below.*[22]

The image of cosmos that Evelyn engages when first establishing the metaphor of the family as a little world follows the traditional Aristotelian geocentric scheme, which despite Galileo and Copernicus, still had considerable cultural currency in the mid-seventeenth century.[23] Evelyn places the master and mistress at the outer reaches of cosmos in the place of 'the *Primum Mobile*'; then, moving inwards, their Children are 'the *Fixed Starres*'; the virtues of 'Gravity, Prudence, Fortitude, Religion, Humanity, Industry and Plenty' are the seven 'planets' moving around 'that ravishing Conscent and Harmony of the whole family' at the 'immovable' centre. Later in the text Evelyn further specifies this centre as 'Love':

> In the first place by Love is signified that sweet Condiment and *Vehiculum* of all the rest; It is an affection diffusing it selfe from the Centre even to all the Circumfrence: nether defatigated by *Labour* nor discouraged by difficulties; extending itself to it selfe and to others.[24]

In Evelyn's microcosmic metaphors, communal virtues take pride of place over the position of any individual or group. Love and harmony are placed at the centre, similarly 'Veritie' is the insubstantial and transcendent 'soule' of the household whereas the husband and wife are merely physical body parts, albeit the exalted body parts – the head and heart.[25]

There is little space here to unfold the nuances of Evelyn's idea of love, which he developed consciously within the traditions of Christian Neoplatonism.[26] To outline some of his ideas briefly, during the course of the 1650s, with the help of Plato's *Symposium*, we find Evelyn contemplating love in the context of his commentary on the classical author, Lucretius's poem *De Rerum Natura*. Here Evelyn describes three distinct 'love' personifications,

> the one very ancient, daughter of the Heavens, *Urania*, or *Coelestis*; intimating the brightness and refulgency of the Divinity together with a most secret affection which she produceth, endeavouring to attract our souls, and unite them to the Essence of God.[27]

The other is the 'more carnal and voluptuous Pandemia'. Finally, there is 'that universal Appetite of procreating its like ... which (saith Cicero) is by Nature diffused into all creatures'.[28] Love in its various forms then, encompasses human, divine and natural worlds. All are necessary, but the love represented by 'Venus Urania of the Platonists [who] made love only to the soul', is the superior – in this last quotation he is writing to Robert Boyle, in a letter composed at the end of the 1650s.[29]

Evelyn's letter is a long 'thank you' for Boyle's gift of a copy of his recent and highly successful book, *Some Motives and Incentives to the Love of God*. The topic of both Evelyn's letter and Boyle's book was the benefits of devotional friendship, the sort of ideal 'Platonic' friendship that became known as 'Seraphick love', following Boyle's own introduction of the phrase.[30] In a 'Seraphick' friendship the participants would meet to pray, discourse, give each other counsel and, through their mutual support and devotion, hope to reach higher levels of spiritual experience, than was possible alone.[31] Approaching God this way they aspired to burn with divine love, like the Seraphim. I stated at the outset of this chapter that in this period the relationship between man and wife was beginning to be cast as an ideal form of intellectual and spiritual companionship. Certainly, in his letter to Boyle, Evelyn was at pains to defend both the virtue of women and the idea that friendship may take place within marriage (Boyle was all for celibacy and the superior love of men). In practice, however, Evelyn always defended his right to forge Seraphick friendships with other women, outside his marriage.[32] He saw these as important to his spiritual life. His wife acquiesced, even supporting him in these emotionally passionate, though physically 'chaste', relationships.

Evelyn saw some intrinsic limitations in the marriage relationship, limitations that were due on the one hand to its intrinsic carnality and, on the other, to its contractual nature. Both of these characteristics set limits to the purity – the 'sublimity' – of love between man and wife. Married love, he argued, could not be equal, because it was not free. His reservations on this count increased over the years, finding full expression in a second tract on domestic economy that he wrote for his last and most passionate Seraphick love – the beautiful young Margaret Godolphin, on the occasion of her marriage.[33] His point to Margaret was that in friendship no such compromising concerns need exist. Freely given and appropriately constrained from 'carnal and voluptuous' impulses, a loving friendship between equals, a friendship such as theirs, could, he thought, reach angelic heights. She should think carefully before marrying. She did think, she doubted, but she did marry and shortly thereafter, died in childbirth. Evelyn assuaged his passionate grief by composing a hagiographic tract – his 'Life of Mrs. Godolphin'.[34] The memory of the dear departed perhaps more perfect and sublime than the living embodiment?

But what of the little world of the domestic œconomie? Where can we place the everyday 'love' of the household in this scheme? If the love of man and wife was compromised by the legal bond, surely this 'defect', coupled with the greater inequality of master and servant, also compromised any love between the members of the household. Or did it?

In case it needs explicit statement, Evelyn was a passionately devout Christian, who developed his practices within the, at that time, exiled and persecuted Anglican Church. This culture developed a set of practices and beliefs, commonly referred to as 'holy living'. The idea was, quite simple, that spiritual practice is not an end in itself, sublime experiences notwithstanding. On the contrary, spiritual attainments should be registered in 'improvement of life'. The ideal state is expressed by Jeremy Taylor, Evelyn's spiritual advisor in these terms:

> There are some persons in whom the Spirit of God hath breathed so bright a flame of love, that they do al [sic] their acts of vertue by perfect choice, and without objection … if love has filled all the corners of our soul, it alone is able to do the work of God.[35]

Sack cloth and fasting are only neccessary for other, less blessed souls, who had to work at it. Whatever the route to illumination, this 'bright flame' was surely the 'Love', 'nether defatigated by *Labour* nor discouraged by difficulties' of which Evelyn writes in the 'Instructions'. The fact that such a love had inevitably to overcome the acknowledged 'difficulties' and fatigues of legally instituted inequalities, by no means invalidates the sincerity of his attempts to embed this transcendent virtue in the heart of the household. For Evelyn, God's love had no limits and to God all the world was but one house. The human world, on the other hand, was (and is) replete with boundaries – customary, legal, physical. Who is beyond the pale? Who may enter the garden? If duties, labours and even justice can be instituted, love – if it is to be love – cannot be instituted, it must always be free. It must be able to jump the fence, though a safe enclosure may be necessary for its cultivation.

Notes

1 John Evelyn, 'Evelyn Archive' at the British Library, Add MS 78628, fol. A; John Evelyn, 'Instructions Œconomique', 'Evelyn Archive' at the British Library, Add MS 78430.
2 Frances Harris, *Transformations of Love: The Friendship of John Evelyn and Margaret Godolphin* (Oxford: Oxford University Press, 2003), pp. 17–24; Mark Laird, 'Parterre, Grove, and Flower Garden: European Horticulture and Planting Design in John Evelyn's Time', in *John Evelyn's 'Elysium Britannicum' and European Gardening*, eds Therese O'Malley and Joachim Wolschke-Bulmahn (Washington, DC: Dumbarton Oaks Research Library and Collection, 1998), pp. 171–221; Prudence Leith-Ross, 'The Garden of John Evelyn at Deptford', *Garden History*, 25 (1997), pp. 138–152.
3 Harris, pp. 42–45.
4 John Evelyn, *Fumifugium: Or the Inconvenience of the Aer and Smoak of London Dissipated. Together with Some Remedies Humbly Proposed by J. E. Esq; to His Sacred Majestie, and to the Parliament Now Assembled, Etc.* (London: Gabriel Bedel and Thomas Collins, 1661); Roland Fréart sieur de Chambray, … translated by John Evelyn, *A Parallel of the Antient Architecture with the Modern*; … with L. B. Alberti's *Treatise of Statues* (London, 1664).
5 John Evelyn, *Sylva, or a Discourse of Forest-Trees, and the Propagation of Timber in His Majesties Dominions…* (London: printed by Jo. Martyn & Ja. Allestry, 1664); for general

introduction, Gillian Darley, *John Evelyn: Living for Ingenuity* (New Haven, CT; London: Yale University Press, 2006).
6 Margo Todd, *Christian Humanism and the Puritan Social Order* (*Ideas in Context*) (Cambridge: Cambridge University Press, 1987); Edward Shorter, *The Making of the Modern Family* (New York: Basic Books, 1975); Jonathan Goldberg, *James I and the Politics of Literature* (Baltimore, MD; London: John Hopkins University Press, 1983).
7 Todd, *Christian Humanism and the Puritan Social Order*, pp. 96–98, 117.
8 'Instructions Œconomique', fol. 20v.
9 John Evelyn, *The History of Religion: A Rational Account of the True Religion*, edited by R. M. Evanson (London: Henry Colburn, 1850), vol. 1, pp. 69, 114.
10 'Instructions Œconomique', fol. 20.
11 Much of 'Instructions Œconomique', Add 78430 is badly water damaged and illegible. On the role of the wife see a later tract, Evelyn, Add MS 78386, 'Œconomics to a newly married friend' 1676, fol. 19.
12 Jean d'Espagnet, *Enchyridion Physicae Restitutae, or, the Summary of Physicks Recovered Wherein the True Harmony of Nature is Explained*, trs Dr Everard (London, 1651), occurs in a 'List of Writers of Chymistry' which prefaces one of Evelyn's chemical notebooks from the early 1650s. Here he annotates the entry with the thought 'as elegant a piece as was ever written in any tongue whatsoever'. Evelyn, 'Evelyn Archive', at the British Library, Add MS 78335, fol. 5v.
13 Jean d'Espagnet, pp. 106–107.
14 'Instructions Œconomique', fol. 13.
15 Juliet Odgers, 'Scales of Reference: John Evelyn and Caruso St. John Architects', *Made at WSA* (2013); Odgers, 'Resemblance and Figure in Garden and Laboratory: Gaffarel's Influence on John Evelyn', *Jacques Gaffarel: Between Magic and Science*, ed. Hiro Hirai (Rome; Pisa: Serra, 2014), pp. 85–109.
16 'Instructions Œconomique', fol. 20.
17 Walter E. Houghton, Jr., 'The English Virtuoso in the Seventeenth Century: Part I', *Journal of the History of Ideas* 3 (1942), pp. 51–73; and 'Part II', *Journal of the History of Ideas* 3 (1942), pp. 190–219; Darley, p. 69; Anthony Griffiths, 'The Etchings of John Evelyn', *Art and Patronage in the Caroline Courts: Essays in Honour of Sir Oliver Millar*, ed. David Howarth (Cambridge: Cambridge University Press, 1993), pp. 51–67; Mark Laird, 'Parterre, Grove, and Flower Garden: European Horticulture and Planting Design in John Evelyn's Time', *John Evelyn's 'Elysium Britannicum' and European Gardening*, eds Therese O'Malley and Joachim Wolschke-Bulmahn (Washington, DC: Dumbarton Oaks Research Library and Collection, 1998), pp. 171–221. John Dixon Hunt, *Garden and Grove: The Italian Renaissance Garden and the English Imagination 1600–1750* (London: Dent, 1986), pp. 73–82.
18 For a transcription of the key to Evelyn's plan of Sayes Court, see Leith-Ross.
19 'Instructions Œconomique', fol. 18.
20 'Instructions Œconomique', fol. 17.
21 'Instructions Œconomique', fol. 20.
22 d'Espagnet, p. 62.
23 For an example from Evelyn's milieu see Henry Peacham, *The Compleat Gentleman, Fashioning Him Absolute in the Most Necessary & Commendable Qualities Concerning Minde or Bodie, Etc.* (London: F. Constable, 1622), p. 58. Peacham was tutor to the sons of Evelyn's early mentor Thomas Howard, the Earl of Arundel.
24 'Instructions Œconomique', fol. 20.
25 On the discourse of body and soul, form and matter in the period see Stevenson in this volume.
26 See Harris; Harriet Sampson, 'Introduction', in John Evelyn, *The Life of Mrs Godolphin*, ed. Harriet Sampson (London: Oxford University Press, 1939).
27 John Evelyn, *An Essay on the First Book of T. Lucretius Carus De Rerum Natura. Interpreted and Made English Verse by J. Evelyn Esq*, Thomason Tract 199:E.1572[2] (London: Printed for Gabriel Bedel and Thomas Collins, 1656), p. 99.

28 Evelyn, 1656, p. 98.
29 John Evelyn, 'To the Honourable Robert Boyle Says-Court', 29 September 1659, in Henry Benjamin Wheatley (ed.), *Diary of John Evelyn* (London: Bickers & Son, 1906), vol. iii, pp. 267–274.
30 Robert Boyle, *Some Motives and Incentives to the Love of God: Pathetically Discours'd of, in a Letter to a Friend* (London: Henry Herringman, 1659), p. 9.
31 Harris, p. 156.
32 Evelyn to Boyle; Harris, Chapter 3 'Nuptial Love', pp. 64–90, 77.
33 John Evelyn, at the British Library, Add MS 78386. EVELYN PAPERS. Vol. CCXIX. 'Œconomics to a newly married friend', 1676.
34 John Evelyn, *The Life of Mrs Godolphin*, ed. Harriet Sampson (London: Oxford University Press, 1939).
35 Jeremy Taylor, 'The Epistle Dedicatory', *Holy Living in Which are Described the Means and Instruments of Obtaining Every Virtue, and the Remedies against Every Vice, and Considerations Serving to the Resisting All Temptations* (London: Printed for Richard Royston, 1651).

PART 2
Negotiating value

If economy implies exchange there must of course be a place of negotiation amongst the participants. In this section the chapters address the issue of how architectural values are established as the actors in the *oikos* find and execute their roles, framing stories that sustain the architecture they profess. Some of the chapters address familiar troubles encountered within architectural practice – both historically and in the contemporary situation; others concern themselves with the way in which our accounts of architecture and our stories of dwelling support or distort architectural values. The emphasis here is on language.

We open with an account of the disagreements between architect and client in **Christine Stevenson**'s presentation of the disputes between the Duchess of Marlborough and Sir John Vanbrugh. The questions here concerned the architectural embellishments Vanbrugh proposed for Blenheim Palace – were they unnecessary 'extravagance' or cheap-at-the-price (and highly desirable) 'magnificence'? Stevenson's argument develops into a discussion of the matter of building and how it is variously framed by the competing authorities involved in a project. Drawing on the example of George Dance's St Luke's Hospital in London to amplify her discussion, Stevenson shows us how the materials of the building – the bricks, the deal floorboards, the expensive stone – become 'slippery' commodities as they are made to dance to the tune of a virtuous modesty, or an elevated 'form' by the various players.

Given the increasing difficulty that architects have nowadays in persuading future clients that they are worthy of hire on any grounds (only 10 per cent of UK construction has the input of an architect) we may mourn a situation in which 'magnificence' was a quality that might readily seduce a client. This testing situation is addressed by **Flora Samuel** in her discussion of ongoing research through the 'Cultural Value of Architecture in Homes and Neighbourhoods Project'. Why, she asks, are so few people in England able or willing to engage with, or simply to engage, architects? The situation is after all very different in other parts of the EU – in Denmark for example. Maybe the problem is that whilst architects see their creativity as their defining asset, what the clients of the English speaking world want is not creativity by low risk.[1] This piece is not a lament, it is a call for action.

Architectural values are debated not only in the practical arena of building procurement, they are, of course, also continuously argued amongst architects and architectural commentators, not least in the architectural press. Adam Sharr and Chris Smith take material from this domain, variously identifying competing discursive economies and arguing for a nearer relation between built work, image and text. **Adam Sharr** details the terrain through a discussion of the 'Technical' section of the *RIBA Journal*, and its treatment of a 'limited-edition' prefabricated villa designed for 'luxury real estate specialist Christies Estates' by 'starchitect' Daniel Libeskind. Here Libeskind's proposal is situated between four economies of architecture. The first understands rational, functional construction technology in a logical continuum with development finance. The second presents the house as a thing-unto-itself, an architectural object, the physical location of which becomes inconsequential. The third is the self-referential economy of shape-forms that has come to characterise Studio Libeskind's architecture. The fourth is the economy of art-historical architectural journalism that promotes the idea of the hero-genius-author. The jarring collision of these four economies in the text is examined as a mirror of contemporary architectural culture.

Chris Smith takes us into the territory of libidinal pleasure in his discussion of fetishistic attachment to architectural surface, which he proposes as a species of commodification. Building on the work of the philosopher and literary theorist Jean-François Lyotard he critiques the sensual membrane structures of Michael Hensel and Achim Menges, presented by these designers when they guest edited an issue of *AD* entitled 'Versatility and Vicissitude', from 2008. Smith uses the idea of a libidinal economy to examine the problematic architectural desire for surface, hinting at more significant exchanges that lie beyond the surface, exchanges that reject the reductive commodification of architecture and engage the free and explicit experience of pleasure.

We finish this section with a return to Ancient Greece as **Lisa Landrum** argues through the Homeric account of the threatened *oikos*, that it is precisely through the telling and retelling of stories that we establish and sustain our disciplinary understanding. In the *Odyssey*, Odysseus negotiates his return to his ordinary household in Ithaca through his telling of extraordinary stories about aberrant living situations – the stories of the Cyclops, Circe, Calypso and others. Whether intended for an audience of architects, or for the wider *oikos*, the tales we tell about architecture are both a vital economy of their own and an important informant of the mutual cultural and social understanding of architecture, without which architecture is surely under threat.

Note

1 Jennifer Mueller, Shimul Melwani and Jack Goncalo, 'The Bias Against Creativity: Why People Desire but Reject Creative Ideas', 2010, http://digitalcommons.ilr.cornell.edu/cgi/viewcontent.cgi?article=1457&context=articles (accessed 01/12/2014).

6
ARCHITECTURAL HUSBANDRY

Christine Stevenson

Something that intrigued me when I was researching a book about eighteenth-century hospitals in Britain and France was the way that, quite suddenly, in the 1770s physicians and journalists on both sides of the Channel began to accuse these buildings' architects of privileging ostentation over function. Historians including Michel Foucault attributed this disparagement to the growing involvement of medical science in hospital design, but this is just another way of saying the same thing, which is, that architects are incapable of sacrificing their vanity for the sake of user needs, as we would now call them.[1] At the time these complaints were framed in terms of modern and competing claims to professional authority. Richard Wittman situates them within broader indictments of architecture itself as a practice of 'conspicuous consumption that aimed to express social or political power'.[2] They are however structured by a much older philosophical dualism that seems almost hard-wired in human beings: that between container and content, matter and form, body and soul.

Largely because it feeds on this opposition, the image of the architect childishly greedy for gratification and taking patrons with him was already old in the eighteenth century and has had a vibrant career since. When, for example, a *Daily Telegraph* columnist complains that such new museums as David Chipperfield Architects' Turner Contemporary in Margate (opened 2011) are being 'touted to us, their audiences, on the merit of their shiny new architecture' as opposed to their contents, she is deploying a dualism that has dominated Western thought since antiquity.[3] Buildings are, that is, only carcasses without their animating spirits, or souls: fine permanent collections, in the museums' case, and at the hospitals, users whose needs are being met.

The construction histories of Blenheim Palace, Oxfordshire (1705–25) and St Luke's Hospital in London (1782–89) dramatize the issues of architectural authority, and economy, with peculiar vividness, and I will use them to advance two more claims. The first is, that it is in the social gap between the roles of building designer, on the one hand, and the patron–owner, on the other, that can we find a powerful structure for 'attitudes about the … purpose and value' of architecture, attitudes that 'finally [reshape] … the meaning' of built form itself.[4] 'Roles', not designers and patrons themselves: in eighteenth-century England and Scotland, proprietors designed, and professional architects were often from the landowning classes. Second, within the discourses occupying that gap, the raw materials of construction are strangely slippery. We have matter-as-rubbish, merely physical and passive, but which acquires value through the architect's imposition of what John Vanbrugh called 'form'. Like the painter who turns pigments into a portrait, the architect translates brick and stone, and in that way accumulates what Pierre Bourdieu calls 'cultural capital', or authority.[5] The good architect gives 'lustre to the vilest Materials', wrote William Chambers; 'Materials in Architecture are like words in Phraseology; which singly have little or no power'.[6]

Such claims had their own distinct place in English eighteenth-century architecture culture, but despite authors' best efforts it never grew very big. For it is not in totalizing treatises like Chambers's but in minute-books and correspondences that we find the structures for architectural value. In these contingent and local negotiations, building materials switch back and forth between base corporeality, or pure potential, on the one hand, and on the other something in itself complete, endowed with specific 'powers' (Chambers) expressive of restraint, usefulness and generosity: good husbandry. It is this conceptual slipperiness that enabled the display of economy in construction, a representation of virtue that formed a major part of the negotiations between the architect's and the patron's roles.

Blenheim

In 1705 Queen Anne's Parliament gave the royal estate of Woodstock near Oxford to the Duke of Marlborough and his heirs in perpetuity. The Duke's victory at Blenheim in Bavaria the previous year marked a turning-point in the war with France, and the gift was a mark of Anne's esteem for her general as well as her love for the Duchess of Marlborough, Sarah Churchill. The Queen also determined to build a new house for them at Treasury expense, but to protect the Marlboroughs this promise was unrecorded, an informality that was soon causing trouble for the architect, Vanbrugh.[7] The first estimate was £90–100,000, but by June 1710 Vanbrugh was reckoning on £250,000 (£20 million or so in today's money), 'Tho' I find', he wrote, that 'I shall have the Satisfaction of Peoples thinking it has Cost Double that Summ'.[8]

The boast that he can achieve this effect, this kind of pure externality, runs through Vanbrugh's letters to the Marlboroughs and other patrons: 'a few Shillings worth of distinction', he called one tiny adjustment to his remodelling of Nottingham Castle.[9] In this context economy did not mean avoiding ostentation, and certainly not the kind of artful thematization of stringency that later architects could pursue. The aim was to extract maximum advantage, the biggest possible splash, out of the money that you *did* spend.

The Duke wanted to build fast, before the Treasury funding dried up. His wife was more cautious, worrying (with reason, as it turned out) that at some point they would end up liable for the cost of finishing what she called 'that wild unmercifull hous[e]'.[10] When she died in 1744, Sarah Churchill was by far the wealthiest woman in her own right in England, the owner of twenty-seven estates,[11] who throughout her long career as a builder and property-investor proclaimed her dislike and distrust of architects and architectural display. Among the great patrons of her period, she was therefore unusual for equating (at least publicly) economy with an appearance of plainness, and not with the practice of directing the available budget to the greatest possible display. One can see her problem with Blenheim.

From the beginning, visitors to Blenheim were bemused as they tried to reconcile their impressions of great weight with a complexity whose resistance to close description was evidently irritating. In 1716 the poet Alexander Pope called Blenheim (which, with its courtyards, covers seven acres) an 'expensive absurdity ... a great quarry of stones above ground'.[12] The perception was a function, not just of the house's size, but of such extraordinary devices as the three-dimensional split pediment rearing above the portico, made by bringing the sides of the hall's clerestory forward almost to the portico's front plane (Figure 6.1).[13]

FIGURE 6.1 Blenheim Palace, Oxfordshire. Entrance (north) front portico, designed 1705–1707

Here the stone seems irreducible to a mere realization of preconceived form, the Albertian 'lineament', which we can define (in Tim Ingold's words) as comprising a 'precise and complete specification for the form and appearance of the building, as conceived by the intellect … in advance of the work of construction'.[14] The fiction of the lineament was then becoming a powerful one. Some buildings lend themselves to it more readily than others, the garden front of Burley-on-the-Hill, Rutland (1694–1700) with its sketch of a temple-front, being a good example (Figure 6.2). It was, however, at idiosyncratic Blenheim that Vanbrugh was prompted for a renewed definition of what he called 'Forme'.

In July 1708, Vanbrugh wrote a letter to the Duchess in which he defended his conduct of the works, and in particular the cost of the great lateral courtyards that he had just persuaded the Duke to add to the design. That 'ridiculous Court', she called the Kitchen Court (Figure 16.3).[15] Her suspicions forced Vanbrugh, in this letter, to define his role as an architect (which he called 'Surveyor') in terms he thought she would appreciate: those of husbandry, of good household management.[16] This was not because Sarah Churchill was a woman, but because she was rich and powerful: 'households' were still the major economic units in England. Vanbrugh wrote that,

FIGURE 6.2 Burley-on-the-Hill, Rutland, 1694–1700. Garden (south) front

Architectural husbandry 77

FIGURE 6.3 Blenheim Kitchen Court, designed 1707–1708, built 1716

Source: Photograph by Vaughan Hart.

> the good Husbandry of the Money ... lys as entirely upon the Surveyor, as [does] the Designing of the Building ... in so casting things in the Execution ... And disposing the Materialls that nothing may be Superfluous, or Improperly Apply'd; But that the Appearance of every thing may exceed the Cost.

– the familiar claim. 'Tis upon this that a Surveyor is to be reckond frugall or Lavish ... The Case is exactly Paral[l]ell to that of keeping a Frugall and yet a Creditable Table'.[17] This household or site expenditure was running at £40,000 a year, making Blenheim by far the most expensive construction project in the country, and one of its biggest industrial operations of any sort. He soon used the analogy again, in trying to persuade the Duchess to let him pay extra for the carriage of colossal stones from the quarries:

> And as to the Expence it will Appear at last, That there has been such Husbandry in the design (which is the Chief Concern) as well as in the Execution, That the Whole will by all People be judg'd to have Cost full twice as much as will be paid for't.[18]

One of Vanbrugh's innovations as a domestic planner was to turn service blocks into part of the display.[19] Yet this kind of husbandry ran the risk of violating the principle of decorum, defined as the due conformity between architectural appearances and the status of the occupants, or users: kitchen courts are used by servants. A long letter of June 1709 presents a comprehensive answer to the Duchess's ongoing objections to the indecorousness, and cost, of this court: Vanbrugh admitted that he was proposing to use freestone, that is, relatively expensive fine-grained limestone, but only that already on site but unsuitable for the main block (and there is some evidence that the Kitchen Court stone is not as good as the rest).[20] At that, he wrote, this waste stone would be finished only with the axe, 'not Smooth'd and Cleansd as in other places'. 'And if upon this whole it makes a better Appearance than such Courts do in other Houses; tis only owing to its Forme, not its Workmanship or Ornaments.'[21] This is an important claim, and one we cannot separate from Vanbrugh's explanation, a year earlier, of what it is that an architect does. He is the form-giver, and form, identified this way, is to be distinguished from the workmanship and ornaments that, along with the choice of materials, were traditional markers of hierarchy, or decorum.

The final justification:

> if any thing gives that back Court ... a more than Ordinary Appearance, 'tis those Corridores [the covered galleries] being open'd to it with Arches, which had been much less expensive, than if the Wall had been quite close [solid]. And tis by such kind of things as these, that for the same expence, One house may be made to look incomparably better than Another.[22]

'Form' is implicit in the 'such kind of things as these'. That good design saves materials was then a commonplace, which Vanbrugh was representing, even dramatizing – he was also a successful playwright – with his arch-shaped voids. Verbally, he was claiming something more, that the absence of stone made the galleries not only relatively cheap, but beautiful (or at least 'more than Ordinary'): as far as we know, this understanding of beauty as potentially generated by economical form was unprecedented in English. It was one he immediately began to offer to other clients.[23]

There is no denying the beauty of those arches with their double reveals, and of merlons sitting on the parapets like marzipan on a cake, another of Blenheim's unique devices, but the economy argument is dubious. Vanbrugh had already reported (in the same letter!) that the stone was waste and already on site: any saving in its volume must have been offset by the cost of carving the openings. Seven years later, the stone became grand, instead: 'The Kitchen court Madam look'd fine and great only from the Manner of Building, being all of fine Stone, but there is not one superfluous Office.'[24] Matter's value is always relative, or contingent, but value itself is where you find it, or where a hostile and clever patron forces you to find it.

Gentlemen and players

If the social gap between the roles of architect and proprietor offers a place where the value of built form is shaped, early eighteenth-century Britain was productive for that gap, just because building design was still more 'an ad-hoc ... activity dictated by opportunity' than it was a profession.[25] Vanbrugh tried to explain to Sarah Churchill what an architect is partly because it was not self-evident. The various activities involved in designing a building and supervising its construction were not yet tethered to professional roles, and the proprietor, or owner, might actively perform any of them. Not to have done so might even have been regarded as an abnegation of duty under the terms of a patriarchal ideal then being reinforced, in a very modern way, by the many advertisements for books and mathematical instruments that claimed they were essential to the sound management of one's estate. On the other hand, late seventeenth- and early eighteenth-century Britain was distinctive for the number of gentlemen turned professional, in the sense of designing for money, Vanbrugh (knighted in 1714) being one of them. In so doing they were encouraged by the practice's prestigious ideological and intellectual underpinnings in, first, the political myth of patriarchy, and second in the mathematics, specifically geometry, that was supposed to be part of the gentleman's accomplishments.

The end of the seventeenth century saw the first sustained exploration of the economic (in the modern sense) benefits of construction: Nicholas Barbon's *An Apology for the Builder*[26] argues for the national benefits of property speculation in London. More to the point in this context, however, is the way in which the construction of big houses was made to exemplify household management in one particular sense: as an extension of the non-institutionalized and non-monetary forms of charity that were the duty and privilege of any landowner. A memorial sermon to the 1st Duke of Devonshire (1707) referred to the work of rebuilding Chatsworth House in Derbyshire that had 'made many an ignorant Man a knowing Artist, and upheld a sinking and poor Neighbourhood'.[27] The preacher had a point, though in practice, contractors, suppliers, and workmen often went unpaid; Vanbrugh became furious about their treatment at Blenheim, where well over a thousand men could be at work at any one time.[28] Building sites so populous that they constituted the largest industrial operations of their day were in this way configured as the products of the patriarchal imperative, as household economy becomes a real political economy.

Building or renovating one's house was also presented as an obligation to one's heirs. Daniel Finch, the 2nd Earl of Nottingham, who seems to have designed his own house at Burley-on-the-Hill (see Figure 6.2), in 1695 instructed his executors to keep building in the event of his death, for he would 'not have my eldest son under the temptation of living in town [i.e., in London] for want of an house nor of being too extravagant in building one'.[29] Yet Finch junior might have preferred to take the money, the upwards of £30,000 that Burley cost, and build his own house. Again and again we read descriptions of the country house as a lasting monument to the builder, a form of self-fashioning that included shaping the minds and habits of one's children, by keeping them away from metropolitan fleshpots, for example, or by encouraging the heir to (as Finch also wrote) 'mind his own affairs and estate, which is part of a gentleman's calling'.[30] What place did the architect's role have in this Oedipal family drama, let alone the wider constellation of myths about why and how the landowner builds? According to the Duchess of Marlborough, Vanbrugh was at Blenheim thinking of his own posterity, not the Duke's:

> I think I owe it to him & to my family to prevent ... having a great estate thrown away ... for no reason that I, or any body else can see, but to have it said here after that Sir John Vanbrugh did that thing which never was don[e] before.[31]

This is the context for Vanbrugh's justifications for his presence at, and his designs for, Blenheim. Before her own fall from favour, the Duchess's offices as Queen Anne's Mistress of the Robes, Groom of the Stole, Ranger of Windsor Park and Keeper of the Privy Purse (she managed the royal household, along with several of her own) gave her an annual income of over £6,000, and considerable power at court. Her straightforward equations of architects with extravagant and uncomfortable houses were public pronouncements on the part of a woman consciously adopting the role of the patriarchal landowner who builds for himself (herself), her family and tenants without the taint of luxurious craft. After Vanbrugh's resignation from the Blenheim project in 1716, the Duchess ran construction there 'with the assistance of ... a cabinet-maker named James Moore', whom she liked and trusted.[32]

The architect's social identity became more secure, or fixed, in Britain as the eighteenth century progressed. Treatises enrolled him into the service of the landowner's domestic economy by offering him as a defence against greedy contractors, ignorant workmen and not least other, lesser architects – whom the amateur Lord Burlington called 'ignorant Pretenders' with a 'proclivity toward costly Buildings'.[33] The ignorant architect, greedy for gratification, tempts us into waste at the expense of ourselves and our posterity. The result will, mortifyingly, be 'condemned by persons of Tast[e]'.[34]

As both building types and mechanisms of financing construction diversified, the old ideology of patriarchal stewardship on behalf of future generations was translated to new, more public spheres. Hospital buildings and such other new urban types as assembly rooms were managed by boards of governors, and funded on a voluntary basis by these governors and other members of the public, so the discourse between architect and proprietor became interestingly complicated by the sheer number of people occupying the latter role. Private correspondence and conversations would not do in a community that was widely dispersed and that moreover demanded a look at the accounts. British hospital governors accordingly used print media, and their publications always address architectural economy though often, crudely, in terms of 'ornament', understood as superfluity. More positively, it is remarkable how much knowledge about construction some of these publications assume their readers have, including an appreciation of the inherent virtues of particular types of materials. A pamphlet published in 1739 on behalf of the ongoing construction of the Edinburgh Royal Infirmary, designed by William Adam, for example, explains that, it is proposed to lay all the Floors of the Galleries [wards] between the Beams with Brick Arches resting on the Scantlings, to bring these to a Plain a-top with liquid Mortar, and to pave above this with unglaz'd Dutch Tile.[35]

Though more expensive than wooden floorboards, the tiles were a 'necessary useful Expence', we read, because they muffled sound, discouraged vermin, and were more fireproof and easier to clean.[36] Such demonstrations worked: the money came in.

St Luke's Hospital for Lunatics

The architect George Dance the younger was precocious; his All Hallows London Wall began construction in 1765, when he was twenty-four. The church is an aisle-less box and, as was customary, Dance set its windows high. Externally they are expressed as large lunettes sitting in the apexes of the otherwise blind and giant brick arches, above a continuous impost made by a plain horizontal band. This way of treating the wall has ancient Roman precedents, as Dance, who had just returned from studies in Italy, probably knew. Structurally, windows in a load-bearing wall turn the parts between them into isolated shafts that actually do the work, and by recessing the masonry underneath the church's windows, Dance made this transformation very clear.[37]

Dance used a variation of the device at his later St Luke's Hospital for Lunatics, whose 493 foot front along Old Street displayed three long, superimposed rows of semi-circular windows, each marking a single 'cell' (the word had not yet acquired penal overtones), above rectangular recessions. Horizontal Portland stone bands are prominent against the stock brick in photographs of the building, converted to the Bank of England's Printing Works in the 1910s and demolished in 1963, but not in a contemporary engraving which therefore gives us a clearer notion of how the thicker parts of the walls acted as shafts down through the three storeys (Figure 6.4).

Specifications for the brickwork take up twelve pages in the construction contract, dated 30 May 1782. For example, 'The Faces [reveals] of all the External Arches which form the Semicircular heads of all the Recesses are to be 1 Foot wide', and,

> The whole of the South front, & the East and West ends of the two Flank Walls of the Center building are to be in 3½ Bricks thick, except in the parts to be recessed, where the walling is to be 2½ Bricks thick

– so, one brick's worth of depth made the recessions.[38]

At this building, which inspired wide interest, the architect, who was also a governor, often occupied the proprietor's role, hosting those studying the hospital's construction and management. In December 1793 the prominent Quaker William Tuke, then collecting funds for the York Retreat, an insane asylum for

FIGURE 6.4 St Luke's Hospital, Old Street, London (1782–1789; demolished 1963), south front as illustrated (1784) in the *European Magazine*

the Society of Friends, asked the Retreat's future architect John Bevans, himself a Quaker, to study St Luke's. Bevans wrote to Tuke the following February with much close detail about the hospital's construction and services that he had clearly obtained from Dance and his draftsmen: the cisterns, the water closets, the lining of the cell walls ('deal framing', he wrote, 'in small pannels & what we call bead & flush – this is as high as the springing of Arch, the arch whited'), their semi-circular windows ('have no glass but a Shutter that is hung at the Bottom, as per sketch'), and so on. Both galleries and cells were floored in softwood, Bevans wrote, and not tile or stone; he had been told that this was for patients' safety ('for some times they strive one with another & are thrown down with violence').[39]

'The Arches in the front of [the] Wings', wrote Bevans, 'are introduced for two purposes, firstly to save Brickwork as the External walls would be too thin without these additional piers that form these arches, & to fill up the whole solid is not necessary'.[40] In other words, economy was again achieved through omission, as with the arcades of Blenheim's Kitchen Court, though in this instance the claim is more credible: the estimate finally agreed was £17,300, or less than one-twentieth of a Blenheim. There and elsewhere Vanbrugh imagined economical ostentation, but it is clear from St Lukes's publicity that ostentatious economy, a kind of rhetorically heightened pragmatism, was what its governors wanted, their hope being that the public would infer that the same good management extended to the care and cure of the insane.[41] The other reason for the recessions, wrote Bevans, was the smallness of the cell windows.

> The plain surface of walls would look heavy & gloomy, which these breaks will measurably take off, and which ought to be studied … for … if the outside appears heavy & Prison-like it has a considerable Effect upon the Imagination & particularly on those who may have any near connections in such places.[42]

Again, as with Blenheim's Kitchen Court, the economy achieved through omission, and here the depth of a single brick, is presented as offering a positive value. In this case it was not the beauty that Vanbrugh claimed for the Kitchen Court's arcades, but an architectural character that was not heavy, and that would not terrify the inmates' families with the appearance of a prison. This idea of 'character', in the sense of the central informing identity of a building made visible and as such presumed to be capable of affecting spectators' sensibilities, their thoughts and emotions, by means of association, was about to embark on a brilliant though brief flowering in England, with this building's help. A slightly later commentator even described the treatment of the wall as representing the protective barriers put up between St Luke's inmates and a harsh world outside.[43]

I have offered this rather episodic history of eighteenth-century British architecture to support my suggestion that the gap between the proprietor's and the designer's roles offers a structure, a space, for working out the value of built form. We can trace these workings-out in a variety of interactions, of which the *least* interesting are the treatises that today mislead us into thinking that some kind of turn away from the material was an inevitable result of the valorization of form, the 'economy and apparatus of the line', in Catherine Ingraham's words, through which 'architecture initially presents itself'.[44] The Dutch tiles at Edinburgh and the deal floorboards of St Luke's were celebrated for their unique virtues, though sometimes, admittedly, what was celebrated were absences, the shapes that matter surrounds. Even so, one might conclude that in the final analysis it is indeed part of the architect's role to persuade patrons to spend, by projecting not just buildings but buildings with value, however defined: the vanity, in short, with which I began. Yet that risks turning patrons, like materials, into passive and undifferentiated stuff. It is the interactions between them that make virtues out of necessities – the recessions under St Luke's windows – and even necessities out of virtues – the arcading of Blenheim's Kitchen Court.

Notes

1 Christine Stevenson, *Medicine and Magnificence: British Hospital and Asylum Architecture, 1660–1815* (New Haven, CT; London: Yale University Press, 2000), pp. 4–8, 195–212.
2 Richard Wittman, *Architecture, Print Culture, and the Public Sphere in Eighteenth-Century France* (New York: Routledge, 2007), pp. 196–209 (p. 196).
3 Florence Waters, 'The British Museum leads the way'. Accessed 21 June 2011 at www.telegraph.co.uk/culture/art/art-news/8580514/The-British-Museum-leads-the-way.html.
4 An 'understanding of how social position structures attitudes about the very purpose and value of poetry finally reshapes the meaning of the verse itself': John Huntington, 'Furious Insolence: The Social Meaning of Poetic Inspiration in the 1590s', *Modern Philology*, 94 (1997), 305–26 (p. 308).
5 Pierre Bourdieu, *Distinction: A Social Critique of the Judgement of Taste*, trans. Tony Bennett (Abingdon: Routledge, 2010).
6 William Chambers, *A Treatise on Civil Architecture* ... (London: the author, 1759), p. ii.
7 Frances Harris, *A Passion for Government: The Life of Sarah, Duchess of Marlborough* (Oxford: Clarendon Press, 1991), pp. 114–15, 119–20.
8 *The Complete Works of Sir John Vanbrugh*, vol. 4, *The Letters*, ed. Geoffrey Webb (London: Nonesuch Press, 1928), p. 41 (to the Duchess, 6 June 1710); Kerry Downes, *Vanbrugh* (London: Zwemmer, 1977), pp. 64, 69.
9 Vanbrugh, *Letters*, p. 119 (to the Duke of Newcastle, September or October 1719).
10 In 1721: quoted Harris, p. 238.

11 Marcia Pointon, 'Material Manoeuvres: Sarah Churchill, Duchess of Marlborough and the Power of Artefacts', *Art History*, 32 (2009), 485–515 (p. 488); James Falkner, 'Churchill, Sarah, Duchess of Marlborough (1660–1744)', *Oxford Dictionary of National Biography*, Oxford: Oxford University Press, 2004; online edn, January 2008 [www.oxforddnb.com/view/article/5405, accessed 24 June 2011].
12 *The Works of Alexander Pope* ... ed. William Roscoe, 10 vols (London: J. Rivington [etc.], 1824), viii, p. 428; Harris, p. 120; David Cast, 'Seeing Vanbrugh and Hawksmoor', *Journal of the Society of Architectural Historians*, 43 (1984), 310–27 (pp. 310–14, 324).
13 I paraphrase Downes, p. 67.
14 Tim Ingold, 'The Textility of Making', *Cambridge Journal of Economics*, 34 (2010), 91–102 (p. 93).
15 Downes, p. 59.
16 Vanbrugh, *Letters*, p. 22 (likely to Arthur Mainwaring, 8 July 1708).
17 Vanbrugh, *Letters*, p. 23 (to the Duchess, 8 July 1708).
18 Vanbrugh, *Letters*, p. 27 (to the Duchess, 14 September 1708).
19 Vanbrugh, *Letters*, pp. 34–5 (18 July 1709).
20 W. J. Arkell, 'The Building-Stones of Blenheim Palace, Cornbury Park, Glympton Park and Heythrop House, Oxfordshire', *Oxoniensia* 13 (1948), 49–54 (p. 49); Vanbrugh, *Letters*, p. 31 (to the Duchess, 11 June 1709).
21 Vanbrugh, *Letters*, p. 31 (to the Duchess, 11 June 1709).
22 Vanbrugh, *Letters*, p. 31 (to the Duchess, 11 June 1709).
23 Vanbrugh, *Letters*, p. 15 (to the Earl of Manchester, 9 September 1709).
24 Vanbrugh, *Letters*, p. 71 (to the Duchess, 10 July 1716).
25 Hentie Louw, 'The "Mechanick Artist" in Late Seventeenth-Century English and French Architecture: The Work of Robert Hooke, Christopher Wren and Claude Perrault Compared as Products of an Interactive Science/Architecture Relationship', in *Robert Hooke: Tercentennial Studies*, ed. Michael Cooper and Michael Hunter (Aldershot: Ashgate, 2006), 181–99 (p. 181).
26 Nicholas Barbon, *An Apology for the Builder, or, a Discourse Shewing the Cause and Effects of the Increase of Building* (London: Cave Pullen, 1685).
27 Charles Saumarez Smith, *The Building of Castle Howard* (London: Faber & Faber, 1990), p. 24.
28 Douglas Knoop and G. P. Jones, *The London Mason in the Seventeenth Century* (Manchester: Manchester University Press, 1935), pp. 49–54; Downes, p. 60.
29 H. J. Habakkuk, 'Daniel Finch, 2nd Earl of Nottingham: His House and Estate', *Studies in Social History: A Tribute to G. M. Trevelyan*, ed. J. H. Plumb (London: Longmans, Green, 1955), 139–78 (p. 147).
30 In writing to his executors again, in 1705; Habakkuk, p. 172.
31 In a letter of 1716; Harris, p. 213.
32 Downes, p. 57.
33 From the introduction to the *Fabbriche antiche disegnate da Andrea Palladio* (dated 1730 but probably published between 1736 and 1740), Joseph M. Levine, *Between the Ancients and Moderns: Baroque Culture in Restoration England* (New Haven, CT; London: Yale University Press, 1999), p. 268, n. 143.
34 James Gibbs, *A Book of Architecture* ... (1728) (New York: Benjamin Blom, repr. 1968), p. ii.
35 'Philasthenes', *A Letter from a Gentleman in Town, to His Friend in the Country, Relating to the Royal Infirmary of Edinburgh* (1739), p. 9.
36 Stevenson, p. 196.
37 Harold D. Kalman, 'The Architecture of Mercantilism: Commercial Buildings by George Dance the Younger', *The Triumph of Culture: 18th Century Perspectives*, ed. Paul Fritz and David Williams (Toronto: A. M. Hakkert, 1972), pp. 69–96 (p. 89).
38 Sir John Soane's Museum, London: AL 5D; Jill Lever, *Catalogue of the Drawings of George Dance the Younger (1741–1825) and George Dance the Elder (1695–1768) from the Collections of Sir John Soane's Museum* (London: Sir John Soane's Museum, 2003), p. 118.

39 York University, Borthwick Institute for Archives, RET 2/1/1 (8.) and (13.), letters from Tuke to Bevans (probably December 1793) and from Bevans to Tuke (26 February 1794); quotations from the latter; Lever, pp. 122–3.
40 Borthwick Institute, RET 2/1/1 (13.).
41 Stevenson, pp. 92–4; cf. Mario Carpo, 'The Architectural Principles of Temperate Classicism: Merchant Dwellings in Sebastiano Serlio's Sixth Book', *RES: Anthropology and Aesthetics*, no. 22 (1992), pp. 135–51 on the '*show of plainness*' (p. 144). 'Rhetorically heightened pragmatism' is Leslie Topp's coinage, for which I thank her.
42 RET 2/1/1 (13.), letter to Tuke, 26 February 1794.
43 Stevenson, pp. 104–5.
44 Catherine Ingraham, 'Lines and Linearity: Problems in Architectural Theory', *Drawing/Building/Text: Essays in Architectural Theory*, ed. Andrea Kahn (New York: Princeton Architectural Press, 1991), pp. 63–84 (p. 66).

7
HOME ECONOMICS

Flora Samuel

What is the value of architecture in the economy of homes and neighbourhoods? What ultimately is the value of architecture at all? In 2007 I embarked on a series of interviews of home owners in Cardiff on the reasons why they chose not to employ architects to assist them with the design of their house extensions. My findings gave me a profound sense of uneasiness about public perceptions of the architect in the United Kingdom. When I became the Head of a highly ranked School of Architecture my discomfort continued. Was what we were teaching fit for purpose? The unease led me to set up the Royal Institute of British Architects (RIBA) Student Destinations survey, a longitudinal study of seven schools to find out where architecture students were employed and how our graduates thought we could improve education. It also led to the instigation of the Arts and Humanities Research Council (AHRC) funded Home Improvements project which was about supporting practitioners in doing research and creating an evidence base for the value of their work, and the Cultural Value of Architecture project developed with Nishat Awan, Carolyn Butterworth, Sophie Handler and Jo Lintonbon, which is the focus of this chapter. This is an account of my warping journey through the weft of architectural culture in pursuit of value. Through the action of darning I shall try to make good some of the holes in what we know.

It is not an objective account. As the daughter of two architects I am well stocked in what Pierre Bourdieu would call 'cultural capital' and am likely to react against architecture, just as a belligerent teenager rebels against her parents. I am trying to see architecture from both within and without the profession in Francesca Hughes' terms. Quantitative methods and simple definitions are often treated with suspicion but, as Lisanne Gibson argues, there is a case for instrumental value discussions when organizations are internally divided and persist in paying lip service to the political imperative of being more inclusive.[1] I argue that architecture – notorious for its exclusivity in terms of gender, race and class – is a case in point, and it is time for the field to see its own impact, or lack of impact, expressed in stark, rigorous, instrumental terms. Such sentiments have their origin in feminist concerns with articulating unrepresented voices. In this chapter I seek to make definitions, to name, to categorize, to make diagrams and to measure. We must name things in order to see them and make them understood. Once they are acknowledged, once they are absorbed they can be dismantled. I take courage from Kim Dovey's observation that it is the tacit nature of architecture that makes it so open to colonization from others.[2] It is our inability to state what it actually is that we do, the value that we add to the world, that is contributing to the architectural profession's drift towards obscurity in the UK at least.

The word value is tainted for many by the idea that those who are evaluating are making crude economic judgements. It is highly political as value is the language of exclusion. A quick foray into, for example, the UK Government's Homes and Communities Agency's *Additionality Guide* – a guide to the value benefits added by a development – quickly reveals that models of economic value are not really so objective as they might at first seem and that it is time we engaged with their critique.[3] Even within economics there is a recognition of a diversity of approaches, within the field of 'behavioural economics', a version that gives value to the social and the cultural as well as the financial, the work of Daniel Fujiwara on the wellbeing cost of housing being a good example.[4] There is also a recognition of the need to work in a more interdisciplinary way.[5] I will borrow some economic terminology, in a manner that is part playful and part purposeful, creating slippages between it and the language of architecture. I will also borrow from the tools and language of marketing. As Anna Klingmann notes in her book *Brandscapes* it is time to use marketing and branding as a force for wellbeing, in other words good.[6]

This chapter begins with a brief summary of value types followed by a description of the context and evidence base for my proposal – an action plan for communicating the value of architecture in homes and neighbourhoods to non-architects.

Context

Value is of course highly culturally specific. Architects are valued differently in China to how they are valued in the United Kingdom but it seems that the malaise that I am about to write about has spread well into Europe, yet Copenhagen – the most 'livable city in the world' – is a testament to what is possible when architecture is understood and valued.[7] The underlying cultural and political willingness to engage with architects in Denmark is strong. In England the situation is very different. Architects generally describe their main asset as creativity but research from the University of Pennsylvania shows that people do not want creativity – they want low risk.[8]

The figures speak for themselves. In the UK fee levels have dropped 40 per cent in six years. It is estimated that only 10 per cent of UK construction has the input of an Architect (capital A indicates ARB/RIBA qualification). The average median lifetime pay of an architect is £36K.[9] Owing to new forms of building contract most Architects are now employed by building contractors and have little say over the quality of outputs achieved. Architects have become extremely marginal, a situation not helped by negative perceptions of the profession.[10] Things are little better in the US where, in 2012, 40 per cent of architectural practices revenue had been wiped out since 2008, and almost one-third of the profession had been laid off.[11] It is well known that the construction industry goes in booms and busts but the overall trajectory for Architects seems to be down, damaged by the worst recession in recent years.

If you are interested in wellbeing then you will be interested in 'social' and 'cultural' value but the differences between them are subtle. Social values are wider values about accepted ways of being, while cultural values are shared codes belonging to a particular cultural group within society.

Cost effectiveness analysis (evidence base)

Value is a complex philosophical question. It is therefore unsurprising that most of the discussions of value in architecture have foundered at the first hurdle within the depths of theory.[12] Whilst acknowledging the importance of these issues we have had to set them to one side. The history of value, though called by other names, goes back to the very beginnings of architecture and is asserted through its canon. Our work develops out of Sebastian Macmillan's recent history of value in the UK, a cautionary tale of failed but worthy ventures.[13] There are of course many different types of value well summarized by Macmillan in *The Value Handbook* produced for the now largely defunct Commission for Architecture and the Built Environment (CABE), created for the promotion of design by the New Labour government.[14]

The evidence for this chapter is the 'Cultural Value of Architecture in Homes and Neighbourhoods Project' (CVoA). This was part of a wider AHRC Cultural Value of the Arts project and has also contributed to the development of the three year RIBA Value project to be completed in 2016. CVoA consisted of two work packages. The first, the focus of this chapter, a critical review of 'grey literature' on value comprising 120 reports and documents produced by industry, charities and others since 2000 – the year that RIBA first really turned its attention to the issue of value. The second work package took the form of a series of consultations with both industry experts and the general public. A detailed project report can be found at www.culturalvalueofarchitecture.org. Less than a year after its completion the project has been influential on two other reviews of architectural value, one in Ireland and one in Canada, suggesting that this is a live issue.

Weightings

The central finding of the critical review was that past studies have placed too much weight on the final built artifact. A building or place is the result of a huge interdisciplinary team and is not a commodity. Tracing the value of the architect's input once construction is completed is extremely difficult. Much is written about the value of 'design' but it is not clear whether it was actually an Architect who did the design, making the pursuit of architectural value very difficult. The preoccupation with built fabric reaches an extreme form in the CABE report *Physical Capital* which tried to create a built environment parallel to the term social capital.[15] It is our firm belief that the discussion must move away from produce to process, to the benefits of working with Architects. Alain de Botton observes that:

> The advantage of shifting the focus of discussion away from the strictly visual towards the values promoted by buildings is that we become able to handle talk about the appearance of works of architecture rather as we do wider debates about people, ideas and political agendas.[16]

The most convincing research that we reviewed focused on the 'actions of architects, planners and developers in creating places where people are genuinely happy to live', rather than buildings.[17] It is for this reason I focus on the skills of architecture, rather than the things that they produce, architecture as verb not noun.

Defining the skills of the Architect

Architecture is a notoriously inward looking profession. A 2012 survey found that 'the majority of British adults have little idea what architects do'.[18] This must, in part, be because we in the profession are so poor at communication to non-architect audiences. Our review of 'grey literature' revealed very considerable confusion as to what it is an Architect does. One of the problems with Architecture is that it contains several different value systems that can often appear to be at odds with one another, sending a mixed message out to its potential audience.

Our audience is non-architects which is why we have set out to express ourselves so simply. In the language of marketing we need to 'segment' the market to make our values and audience more clear. I therefore propose three different categories of architect: social, cultural and commercial. These categories are not mutually exclusive as all architects need to be income generating and all architects need to hit sustainability targets, but suggest priority values. I have tried to express these types in Figure 7.1. Each of these architect types has a particular skillset that adds value within its economy.

Skillset of social architects

- Transforming mental and physical states – creating environments that change the way we feel and think.
- Changing networks and communities – creating built, and other, frameworks for community interaction.

90 Flora Samuel

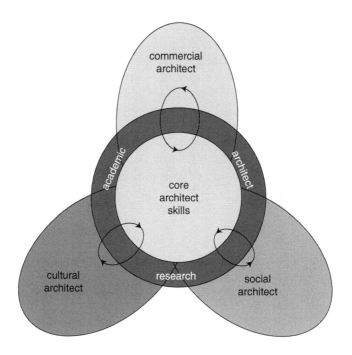

FIGURE 7.1 Architect types

Source: Agency Spring/CVoA.

- Identity, belonging, heritage and social labelling – co-designing curation/branding of place to positively impact on resident's feelings about the value of their place in the world.
- Making transformations through the design process itself – facilitating fulfilling learning through co-design, also architecture as part of experience economy.
- Rigorous recording and representation of events – mapping and representation of space in use, networks and events, in doing so providing important evidence of impact.

Skillset of commercial architects

- Appraisal of financial viability – translation of construction knowledge into language of banks and business, often at a global level.
- Maximise investment potential – the planning, design and implementation of a development, redevelopment or regeneration project with multiple uses or a single prime use, the success of which is predicated on demonstrating financial viability.

- Efficient business practice – leadership and planning to reduce risk to client.
- Conversant with patterns of mass consumption – projects are based on current state of knowledge in retail, marketing, real estate and related fields.
- Regulatory and planning compliance – maintaining standards while maximizing value.

Skillset of cultural architects

- Strong conceptual framework – cultural currency often comes from art and performance practice.
- Cultural capital conferred to client and project through practice brand resulting in 'iconic' projects.
- Experience economy – the experience of working with the practice is carefully choreographed giving added value to the client.
- Marketing – the practice and its work inspire debate and media coverage.
- Innovation in technology and representation – this is harnessed to brand identity.

These skills are not discrete. They reinforce one another. These are the skillsets that are increasingly being taught in architectural academia, whether practice sees itself in this form is another matter. The actions of architecture can be positive or negative so we need a sliding scale that shows this differentiation.

Evidence

Only once we have definitions in place is it possible to start collecting evidence of the value of the different skillsets of Architects. Unfortunately a cultural shift within the profession towards nuanced forms of post-occupancy evaluation is needed before we have any chance of completing this, or any similar, matrix. I have begun this exercise with reference to the skillset of the social architect using the review of grey literature as evidence; however a systematic review of refereed academic literature is urgently needed.

Transforming mental and physical states

Architects and planners have an important role to play in taking the strategic overview of neighbourhoods and communities – 87 per cent of the public believe better quality buildings and public spaces improve their lives.[19] It has been found that large open spaces do not promote positive community feelings as much as smaller natural areas close to housing. This sense of community cohesion can be further promoted by providing a range of uses including private and public activities keeping the area animated throughout the day for the enjoyment of a wide range of users.[20] It is time that the value of the architectural skillset in promoting health was set out in a systematic way.

Changing networks and communities

It is common sense that the layout of housing can impact on the way in which communities develop, but increasingly architects are becoming more involved in development of digital communities and also in facilitating the induction of new residents into a community and the development of community activities. David Halpern notes that 'the form of the built environment can strongly influence friendship and group formation'.[21] Choreographing the degree of privacy between neighbours is a complex issue particularly in high density settings.[22] It too can contribute strongly to wellbeing. Ted Rosenblatt *et al.* write that 'people will only engage in civic and community activity if it connects with their "projects" or biographies of selective belonging that relate to their specific needs or predispositions'.[23] Participatory architectural practitioners are well used to teasing out of communities the best way in which this might be done.[24]

Crime and perceptions of safety are extremely important for communities. Rachel Armitage has set out with great clarity the importance of design for the minimization of crime.[25] Design against crime works at different scales, from the layout of streets to the design of front doors, all impact on this issue.

There has over recent years been a drive towards mixed development.[26] While mixed use may create diverse communities it does not necessarily foster social inclusiveness.[27] The choreography of the mix takes considerable skill.

Identity, belonging, heritage and social labelling

The impact of the form and look of housing is not to be underestimated. Clare Cooper Marcus' and Wendy Sarkissian's *Housing as if People Mattered* research based on nearly 100 post occupancy evaluations in the UK and elsewhere came to the, perhaps obvious, conclusion that the overall impression of homes had a considerable impact on the way that people felt about them.[28] 'How residents feel about their neighbourhood, and how they perceive others to view their neighbourhood are related to both their perceptions of home quality, and their feelings of status and control.'[29] Research has shown the importance of building distinctive features into housing, a sense of identity being important for neighbourhood satisfaction, hence wellbeing.[30]

Anecdotal evidence from property developer Martyn Evans of the Cathedral Group suggests that a distinctive narrative, sometimes involving the reuse and inclusion of old buildings, is extremely important for sales. 'Property development' he says 'is all about storytelling'.[31] The University of Bristol carried out a survey of 600 households on a large suburban housing estate with little or no distinctive design quality. The researchers found that these residents exhibited more difficulties in selling and experienced more negative equity than those living on more distinctively designed developments.[32]

CABE found that 'Beauty is regarded as a positive experience strongly related to bringing about happiness and wellbeing in individuals lives'.[33] Beauty in the built environment was seen as being important for civic pride and for attracting people to an area. 'History and memory can play an important role in making a place feel beautiful. There tends to be a preference for older buildings over newer ones – for a variety of reasons that go beyond purely visual taste.'[34] People's overall ability to appreciate beauty is affected by whether they feel comfortable, safe and included in a place. Hence when there is a shared history, feeling of community and pride in a place, people are more likely to say they experience beauty there. These findings were echoed in a New Economics Foundation project based in Peckham in London:

> The use of local designers and artists in the development of the streetscape in the Bellenden neighbourhood roused curiosity in residents and bestowed the place with a uniqueness and distinctiveness, features which are thought to be important for a shared sense of belonging.[35]

It is important to use creative means to counter negative perceptions of ageing within neighbourhoods. It is surely here that architects can make a real difference.[36] This, we argue, is the territory of architects, the curation of lifestyle and branding of place being a much underrated aspect of their work. Peter Hall has written of the impact of 'branding' on some of the newer neighbourhoods in the Netherlands.

> The idea of 'branding' different neighbourhoods, as with manufactured goods, seems a powerful one. It has helped create a much broader market for new homes than in the UK, as new homes offer a distinctly better product than many of the old apartments.[37]

Hall has also noted the importance of using 'architects or other building professionals able to act as catalysts or enablers' to facilitate the adoption of sustainability. In Freiburg it has been found that although better architecture and construction can add 8–14 per cent to the cost of new homes, it is more than repaid through energy savings.[38]

'Visioning' is another underexplored aspect of architecture. John Punter writes that 'visioning has become an integral part of corporate governance in the UK, a key feature of civic entrepreneurialism and place-marketing'. Further, 'it has a particularly important role to play in conveying desirable urban futures and building public consensus to deliver them'.[39] The architecture/planning practice Urbed provide an excellent exemplar of a practice that focuses on participatory work and the 'visioning' of community. There is however remarkably little evidence that 'visioning' actually has a positive impact on communities. Architects rarely have the time or money to measure the effects of what they do.

Making transformations through the design process itself

One of the most resoundingly powerful messages emerging from this review is the importance of participatory practice for wellbeing. This, argues CABE, should be compulsory training for all Built Environment professionals and is a key part of the Architect's role which is barely acknowledged by RIBA's criteria for the validation of Architecture schools.[40]

The New Economics Foundation study revealed that,

> the way in which a development or regeneration project is delivered on the ground matters, influencing the extent to which all stakeholders feel part of the place shaping and place making process and the connections which are fostered between people within the neighbourhood.[41]

They advocate a 'co-production approach' in which professionals share information and experiences with local people. They recommend the financing of this from the earliest stage in the process to make it 'genuinely useful'. They found that 'being actively involved in the development process through choosing street-level designs or helping to manage community gardens was important for stimulating social interaction and strengthening social networks'. In other words the very act of co-design had a positive impact. 'This sense of "neighbourliness" was sustained long after the renewal work ceased and was identified as one of the core neighbourhood assets that supported people's individual well-being.' Further they recognise the need for a 'new skills base within the sector in engagement and coaching techniques'. These skills reside within Architecture but are not widely recognised and need to be more universally available.

Another example is a £2.2 million housing redevelopment project for the Shoreditch Trust in north London where savings caused through community engagement were estimated to be in the region of £500,000. Compared to other projects, there were fewer delays and associated costs caused by responding to residents' complaints, reworking designs at a late stage to meet user needs and on-site events such as vandalism and crime.[42]

There is a very large body of evidence that proves the efficacy of community art practice on health.[43] It seems likely that fruitful comparisons can be drawn between the potential wellbeing benefits derived from working together on arts projects and wellbeing derived from working together on the built environment. Again there is a profound lack of evidence in this area. The lack of exploration of the therapeutic potential of the built environment is notable.[44]

Rigorous recording and representation of cultural changes

The mapping of human activity has been pioneered through the public space studies of the architect Jan Gehl[45] and has also been the focus of 'Space Syntax' methodologies developed at University College London by Bill Hillier and his team.[46] Architects have taken mapping to new heights with the use of digital technologies.[47] Tools of mapping are invaluable to make manifest aspects of spatial experience no other discipline can collect.[48] The research practice 00:/ suggest that unlocking dormant assets requires a wide awareness of what is there already. Collaboratively 'mapping' the assets of places (both physical spaces and hidden talents and learning dreams) is a process that could bring policy-makers and service providers together with the wider public, creating platforms for genuine discussion about the shared aspirations for places.[49] Clearly a mapping of the existing situation is also needed to demonstrate the value of any intervention, before and after.

Conclusion

This brief exploration into the economy of the 'social architect's' skills in homes and neighbourhoods promoting wellbeing shows just how frail the evidence base is. There is within these documents a suggestion of great value but we cannot say with any authority what it is. Another issue that quickly becomes apparent is the lack of interconnectedness between disciplinary areas – why is so much known about the impact of community art when so little is known about the impact of community Architecture?

If Architects want to increase their influence upon the built environment they must express their value in terms of convincing non-architects. In order to do this they need to gather evidence and learn to communicate that evidence in simple legible terms. This can only be done by developing architectural research in practice and by making post-occupancy evaluation the norm.[50] Further, forms of building evaluation need to take on board the subtle issues of identity and community that are so very key to the social architect's skillset.

I began this chapter with my concerns about the value of Architectural education. RIBA is currently undertaking a wide ranging review of the structure of architectural education in the UK in the light of sudden and dramatic increases in student fees. The universities are under new pressure to deliver value, in terms of employability, in terms of potential earnings and in terms of innovation and impact. RIBA statistics show that only one in 14.5 first-year architecture students ever makes it to qualification. It is rarely acknowledged that architecture is a generalist subject that delivers a good range of transferable skills, many of which are described above. Architectural education is likely to be good value for the 13.5 who leave the profession as long as they are able to articulate what it is that they know. Architectural education will also be good value for the one that enters and becomes an Architect if we, the profession, make a cultural shift towards the evidencing of value, but we can only evidence value with any success by developing architectural research practice and business skills. I am aware how dry this must sound, a flashback to the scientific models of architectural knowledge promoted by Leslie Martin and others in the 1960s, but I am proposing something very different. Research methodologies and critical thinking have progressed immeasurably since Martin's time and can encompass the nuances of the most qualitative of experiences and atmospheres. The framework that we suggest omits none of the profession's splendours; it is just a tool for the communication of their value.

Acknowledgements

Nishat Awan, Jo Lintonbon, Sophie Handler, Carolyn Butterworth were all Co-Is on the Cultural Value of Architecture in Homes and Neighbourhoods project. Anne Dye, Director of Technical Research at RIBA, Elanor Warwick, Director of Research at Affinity Sutton Housing and Paul Iddon of Kernel Simpatico marketing assisted greatly with the diagrams and thought.

Notes

1. Lisanne Gibson, 'In Defence of Instrumentality', *Cultural Trends*, 17 (2008), 247–57.
2. Ceridwen Owen and Kim Dovey, 'Fields of Sustainable Architecture', *The Journal of Architecture*, 13 (2008), 9–21.
3. HCA, *Additionality Guide, Fourth Edition, 2014*, https://www.homesandcommunities.co.uk/sites/default/files/aboutus/additionality_guide_2014_full.pdf [accessed 11 May 2014].
4. Daniel Fujiwara, *The Social Impact of Housing Providers* (HACT, 2014), www.hact.org.uk/sites/default/files/uploads/Archives/2013/02/The%20Social%20Impact%20of%20Housing%20Providers%20report2013.pdf [accessed 25 March 2014].
5. Craig Watkins and Robert McMaster, 'The Behavioural Turn in Housing Economics: Reflections on the Theoretical and Operational Challenges', *Housing, Theory and Society*, 28 (2011), 281–7.
6. Anna Klingmann, *Brandscapes: Architecture in the Experience Economy* (Cambridge, MA; London: MIT Press, 2010).
7. Puay-Peng Ho, 'Consuming Art in Middle Class China', *Patterns of Middle Class Consumption in India and China* (London: Sage, 2008), pp. 277–91.
8. Jennifer Mueller, Shimul Melwani and Jack Goncalo, 'The Bias Against Creativity: Why People Desire but Reject Creative Ideas', 2010, http://digitalcommons.ilr.cornell.edu/cgi/viewcontent.cgi?article=1457&context=articles [accessed 5 June 2014].
9. Bruce Tether, 'Top 100', *Architects' Journal Top 100*, 23 May 2014, 148–59.
10. Sebastian Conran, 'Design and the Creative Economy' (presented at the AHRC Creative Economy Showcase, King's Place London, 2014) www.youtube.com/watch?v=gJuuukHAv4g [accessed 15 July 2014].
11. Elliot Blair Smith, 'American Dream Fades for Generation Y Professionals', *Bloomberg*, 2012, www.bloomberg.com/news/2012-12-21/american-dream-fades-for-generation-y-professionals.html [accessed 15 July 2014].
12. *Center/10 Value*, ed. by Michael Benedikt (Austin, TX: Center for American Architecture and Design, 1997).
13. Sebastian Macmillan, *Designing Better Buildings: Quality and Value in the Built Environment* (New York: Spon, 2004); Richard Saxon, 'The Future of the Architectural Profession: A Question of Values' (unpublished Milo Lecture presented at the Milo, RIBA, London, 2006).
14. CABE, *The Value Handbook: Getting the Most from Your Buildings and Spaces* (London: CABE, 2006), http://webarchive.nationalarchives.gov.uk/20110118095356/www.cabe.org.uk/files/the-value-handbook.pdf#page=1&zoom=auto,36,643 [accessed 27 March 2014].
15. CABE, *Physical Capital: How Great Places Boost Public Value* (London: CABE, 2005).
16. Alain De Botton, *The Architecture of Happiness* (London: Hamish Hamilton, 2006).
17. Ipsos Mori and CABE, *People and Place: Public Attitudes to Beauty* (London: CABE, 2010), p. 1, http://webarchive.nationalarchives.gov.uk/20110118095356/http:/www.cabe.org.uk/publications/people-and-places [accessed 5 February 2014].
18. YouGov, *An Archi-What?*, 9 March 2012, http://yougov.co.uk/news/2012/09/03/archi-what [accessed 16 January 2014].

19 Ipsos Mori and CABE.
20 Rachel Kaplan, 'Nature at the Doorstep: Residential Satisfaction and the Nearby Environment', *Journal of Architectural and Planning Research*, 2 (1985), 115–27.
21 David Halpern, *Mental Health and the Built Environment: More than Bricks and Mortar?* (London; Bristol, PA: Taylor & Francis, 1995), p. 119.
22 CABE, *What Homebuyers Want* (London: CABE, 2005), http://webarchive.national archives.gov.uk/20110118095356/http:/www.cabe.org.uk/publications/what-home-buyers-want [accessed 29 April 2014].
23 Ted Rosenblatt, Lynda Cheshire and Geoffrey Lawrence, 'Social Interaction and Sense of Community in a Master Planned Community', *Housing, Theory and Society*, 26 (2009), 122–42.
24 Paul Jenkins and Leslie Forsyth, *Architecture, Participation and Society* (London; New York: Routledge, 2010).
25 Rachel Armitage, *Crime Prevention Through Housing Design: Policy and Practice* (Basingstoke: Palgrave Macmillan, 2013).
26 Mark Joseph and Robert Chaskin, 'Living in a Mixed-Income Development: Resident Perceptions of the Benefits and Disadvantages of Two Developments in Chicago', *Urban Studies*, 47 (2010), 2347–66.
27 URBED, 'Living Places: Urban Renaissance in the SE, URBED and UCL', 2000, www.rudi.net/books/10433 [accessed 19 February 2014].
28 Clare Cooper-Marcuse and Wendy Sarkissian, *Housing as if People Mattered* (Berkeley: University of California Press, 1986).
29 Julie Clark and Ade Kearns, 'Housing Improvements, Perceived Housing Quality and Psychosocial Benefits from the Home', *Housing Studies*, 27 (2012), 915–39.
30 CABE, *What its like to Live There: The View of Residents on the Design of New Housing* (London: CABE, 2005) http://webarchive.nationalarchives.gov.uk/20110118095356/http:/www.cabe.org.uk/publications/what-its-like-to-live-there [accessed 29 April 2014].
31 Martyn Evans, Twentieth Century Society Impact Event, London, 28 April 2014.
32 Ray Forrest, Tricia Kennett and Phil Leather, *Home Owners on New Estates in the 1990s* (York: Joseph Rowntree Foundation, 1997) www.jrf.org.uk/publications/home-owners-new-estates-1990s [accessed 17 February 2014].
33 Ipsos Mori and CABE.
34 Ibid., p. 5.
35 NEF, *Good Foundations: Towards a Low Carbon, High Well-Being Built Environment* (London: New Economics Foundation, 2012).
36 Ilan Wiesel, 'Can Ageing Improve Neighbourhoods? Revisiting Neighbourhood Life-Cycle Theory', *Housing, Theory and Society*, 29 (2012), 145–56.
37 Peter Hall, *Good Cities, Better Lives: How Europe Discovered the Lost Art of Urbanism* (London: Routledge, 2013), p. 170.
38 John Punter, 'Urban Design and the English Urban Renaissance 1999–2009: A Review and Preliminary Evaluation', *Journal of Urban Design*, 16 (2011), 1–41.
39 Ibid.
40 CABE, *Ordinary Places* (London: CABE, 2010) http://webarchive.nationalarchives.gov.uk/20110118095356/http:/www.cabe.org.uk/publications/ordinary-places [accessed 29 April 2014].
41 NEF, p. 3.
42 Patricia Kaszynska and James Parkinson, *Re-thinking Neighbourhood Planning* (London: RIBA and ResPublica, 2012), www.architecture.com/Files/RIBAHoldings/PolicyAndInternationalRelations/Policy/RIBAResPublica-Re-thinkingNeighbourhoodPlanning.pdf [accessed 19 May 2014].
43 Hannah Macpherson, Angie Hart and Becky Heaver, *Building Resilience through Collaborative Community Arts Practice* (Swindon: AHRC, 2012), p. 3, www.ahrc.ac.uk/Funding-Opportunities/Research-funding/Connected-Communities/Scoping-studies-and-reviews/Documents/Building%20resilience%20through%20collaborative%20community%20arts%20practice.pdf [accessed 8 May 2014].

44 Katerina Alexiou, Theodore Zamenopoulos and Giota Alevizou, *Valuing Community-Led Design* (Swindon: AHRC, 2012), pp. 1–13.
45 Jan Gehl and Birgitte Svarre, *How to Study Public Life* (London: Island Press, 2013).
46 Bill Hillier and Julienne Hanson, *The Social Logic of Space* (Cambridge; New York: Cambridge University Press, 1984).
47 Albena Yaneva, *Mapping Controversies in Architecture* (Burlington: Ashgate, 2012).
48 Nishat Awan and Phil Langley, 'Mapping Migrant Territories as Topological Deformations of Space', *Space and Culture*, 16 (2013), 229–45.
49 Alexiou, Zamenopoulos and Alevizou, p. 8.
50 Flora Samuel, Laura Coucill, Anne Dye and Alex Tait, *RIBA Home Improvements: Report on Research in Housing Practice* (London: RIBA, 2013), www.architecture.com/Files/RIBAProfessionalServices/ResearchAndDevelopment/Publications/HomeImprovementsMethodologyandData.pdf [accessed 14 March 2014].

8

FOUR ECONOMIES OF ARCHITECTURE

Adam Sharr

This chapter is about a 'limited edition' prefabricated house marketed under the Daniel Libeskind brand and an account of it in the architectural press. Claiming that the house and its depiction in the media offer an insight into contemporary architectural culture, I will propose that four economies of architecture are at work in the Libeskind house's physical and intellectual construction.[1] The fact that these economies can be discerned as separate, I will argue, indicates that contemporary architectural production can be characterised by the radical compartmentalisation of multiple economies.

In summer 2010, an issue of the *RIBA Journal* addressed the merits of prefabricated construction (Figure 8.1). It was headlined 'Prefabulous: Or Not?' by the magazine's punning headline writer. A short article near the back, titled 'One Foot in the Past: Bespoke Prefabrication', recounted a modular luxury house designed for 'limited-edition production' by 'starchitect' Daniel Libeskind.[2] The piece is called 'One Foot in the Past' because – as the staff journalist puts it – while 'Daniel Libeskind has entered the prefab market with a designer vision … only traditional skills can build it'. Appearing in the 'Technical' section of the journal, the text recounts the production of the so-called 'Libeskind Villa' for 'luxury real estate specialist Christies Estates' in the technocratic language of building procurement, real estate marketing and construction technology.

David Leatherbarrow has described the origins of the word 'economy' in relation to the ancient idea of the villa.[3] In his explanation, the community of the villa – its inhabitants and staff – lived in intimate connection with the locality. Their cultivation of the land and consumption of its fruits were balanced carefully in an almost autonomous system. The villa, in association with its community and locale, is advanced here as being *sustainable* in the broadest sense of that word. It is not the sustainability of eco-gadgets and energy calculations but rather the sustainability of self-sufficiency; where enough is sufficient. Agriculture supplies the food it can; stone and trees provide a

FIGURE 8.1 'One foot in the past'

Source: page spread from *RIBA Journal*, July/August 2010.

certain amount of building material; every possible use is made of animals for food, leather, gelatine and fur and little is wasted. Economy is understood here as a harmony in which supply and demand, consumer and consumed, residents and place, and architecture and site are balanced healthily in a match that is negotiated and re-negotiated over time. This idea of the ancient villa is a powerful imaginary – albeit one that is freighted with overtones of authenticity and class, and idealising a past that may or may not have really existed – and it serves to characterise contemporary Western culture as obsessed by excessive consumption, both in architecture and beyond. This idea of the villa and its economy is not so much about competition according to free market forces as it is about the reasonable exercise of wisdom, cunning and care in balancing need and sufficiency. Thus defined, an 'economy' is a largely autonomous, self-sustaining, self-referential system. It is this definition of 'economy' that underpins the following argument about the 'Libeskind Villa'.

I will explore how the *RIBA Journal* story about Libeskind's 'limited-edition' prefab situates the house both within and between four economies of architecture – as defined here in terms of largely self-referential and self-sustaining systems. First, it is situated unquestioningly in the economy that understands construction to be logically continuous with financial markets and development finance. Second, the house is discussed as a thing-unto-itself, an architectural object whose material location in the world is inconsequential. Third, it is presented as part of the self-referential economy of shape-forms that characterises Studio Libeskind's architecture. Fourth, its manner of presentation highlights the economy of art-historical architectural journalism that promotes the idea of the architect as a hero-genius-author. My aim here is to review the awkward conjunction of these four economies pertaining to the Libeskind house, as presented in the *RIBA Journal* article, and their implications for contemporary architectural culture.

Economy #1

The first economy I want to address with respect to the Libeskind prefab is the most conventional: the economy of the financial markets in which corporations, financiers, developers and professionals operate; the global economy where to prosper is to make profit.

The *RIBA Journal* article primarily locates the Libeskind house in this economy; and it is here that its designers seem to have imagined it. As the journal's Jan-Carlos Kucharek explains,

> developer Proportion has been set up to commission and market the Libeskind Villa, a zinc and glass complex crystal form of timber frame and solid panel construction, using the latest ground source heating and cooling, with very high thermal performance, and rainwater harvesting. This comes hand-in-hand with high specification – the house is equipped with en suite bedrooms, games room, wine cellar and a sauna, and Libeskind has personally designed and/or specified all the fixtures and fittings.[4]

The house is understood here as a designer object like a Rolex watch or a Maserati sports car, not just a home but also the totem of a lifestyle that is imagined to cement the prestige of its purchaser in society. With its wine cellar, sauna, games room and the latest environmental gadgets, it is envisaged as a status symbol where the architect's signature serves to assure the rank of the consumer. It is portrayed as a 'high end' designer product that belongs with private shoppers, private jets and elite parties, with the ownership and perpetuation of financial capital.

In this economy, profit is assured by minimising cost, time and risk. To financiers, project managers and quantity surveyors, such ambitions are comforting. The article confirms that the project team shared the same concerns. The developer is quoted as saying: 'We were looking at how we could minimise on-site construction risk, and optimise the build and finishes quality', priorities with which, Kucharek shows, the architect concurs:

> 'Our notion of prefabrication carries with it industrial baggage, compromised both in quality and cost', explains Daniel Libeskind Studio principal Yama Karim. 'But the Libeskind Villa is about creating a custom fabricated house that can be duplicated many times. In this case, the use of prefabrication should not be seen as a compromise but as a means of assuring higher quality and control' he says.[5]

Mass production is not associated here with any idea about the loss of individuality but is portrayed instead as a productive mechanism for effective quality management. The article goes on to detail the technical problems of specification and assembly that were negotiated in order to achieve the trademark Libeskind shape in a reliably repeatable fashion. We are informed that 'detailed planning was required to guarantee dimensional accuracy to ensure the successful prefabrication of the 53 separate wall elements, the smallest of which is 1.3 by 3m and the biggest 12m by 5m'. But, we are reminded, 'the idea did not make the leap to investigate new methods of production to optimise the buildability of the design, so the house was built using traditional crafts rather than according to modern methods of construction (MMC)'.

The *RIBA Journal* article's account of the so-called Libeskind Villa is fascinating in numerous ways. First, because it assumes that regular building has become 'traditional', waiting to be supplanted by mechanised, industrialised component production like car manufacturing; an imminent future that nevertheless predates Reyner Banham's exhortations of the 1960s and 1970s. Second, because it assumes that success in architecture equates to accuracy and control in construction; thinking that locates architectural quality in the regularisation of process rather than in the experience of the built building.[6] Third, because it suggests that the priorities of the architect are immediately and uncritically aligned with those of profit-driven financiers, developers and marketeers.

Philosopher Fred Dallmayr has characterised this mainstream contemporary Western economy – in which Villa Libeskind has been procured, marketed and distributed – as a 'currency of equivalence'.[7] Such a 'currency of equivalence', he has argued, equates the free flow of capital with ideas of freedom and technical rationality. Financial capital here consolidates its power through a universalising positivist rhetoric. This rhetoric – Dallmayr suggests – constructs a continuity between the technocracy of the military-industrial complex, the utilitarian bureaucracy of (conventional) management theory, the rational authority of the professional expert and supposedly universal ideas about (a certain kind of) democracy. In this economy, technocratic precision in construction, quality management procedures, ideas of constructional efficiency and the notion of the free market are conceived as a seamless whole.

Economy #2

The second economy evident in the *RIBA Journal* article finds the Libeskind Villa to be a thing-unto-itself – an architectural object whose actual physical location in the world remains inconsequential.

As a prefab, the house can, supposedly, be built anywhere. It is simultaneously siteless and potentially pervasive. Unlike the ancient villa from which the word 'economy' derives, it begins without place, without climate, populated in the designers' imagination only by generic 'users'. It is hardly engaged with rhythms of season, of planting and harvest, of sun and rain, of life and death. It can contain such rhythms in the most basic ways but it pays little concern to their situation in the social and material specificity of the world. This is in contrast to the ancient villa, in Leatherbarrow's romantic idea of its ancient conception, which is only ever in engaged, sustaining harmony with its residents, the place and the fruits of the land. While its autonomy is always already located, Villa Libeskind, on the other hand, is so radically autonomous that its site can only ever be incidental.

So does this mean that – while being named a 'villa' – the house is, in fact, nothing of the sort, no economy in the ancient sense of the word? When constructed, it is, of course, connected, plugged-in to all the mains services expected by contemporary Western housebuyers: electricity, gas, running water, telephone, television, broadband internet. Italo Calvino's invisible city of Armilla springs to mind, where – long abandoned – the houses have rotted away to leave a network of pipes hanging in mid-air, their washbasins and WC pans still attached, glinting in the sunlight.[8] Calvino's Armilla anticipated the idea of the house as a terminal in the network society – where, rather than cables and pipes being hidden in walls and ceilings, walls and ceilings are instead conceived primarily as containers for services. Rather than the house discreetly servicing its residents, house-users become components of the networks into which they are plugged. Just because the prefab is radically autonomous, it does not mean that this is a house unplugged. Instead, it comprises a connected system of services, in service of the service economy.

If Villa Libeskind is grounded in a site, then it is the site where the house was imagined: the scalar drafting plane of the 'Rhino' CAD package. Rhino's coordinates are mathematical; measured in equal increments on x, y and z axes. This is the grid of Cartesian space: boundless and infinitely zoomable, simultaneously everywhere and nowhere. The house was drawn in two and three dimensions, delineated in plan and section and visualised in perspective and axonometric while remaining in a curious relationship with the fourth dimension: time. In this digital site, it seems both timeless and out-of-time; incapable of weathering, of accepting the traces of inhabitation, of really becoming a home rather than a house.

Somehow, the structure's material reality – as depicted in the illustrations accompanying the *RIBA Journal* article – looks like a pale imitation of the Rhino file. It is flat and shadowless but without any of the artificial sparkle of digital images. Its built appearance appears, curiously, like a bad print of the digital rendering. If this is an economy, then, it is an everywhere economy, simultaneously plugged-in to the world and disconnected from it. It is more than self-sufficient, set-up to consume services, resources and leisure 'on demand'. But it is also less than self-sufficient: its conception permitting endless repetition and consumption rather than striving towards any idea of balance; its material and temporal reality unable to live up to its representation in the digitally perfect, conceptually timeless, space of software.

Economy #3

This leads to the third economy that I would like to address: the self-referential economy of shape-forms that has come to characterise Studio Libeskind's architecture.

It was the Jewish Museum in Berlin that first brought Daniel Libeskind to media fame as a 'starchitect'. Politically and architecturally, this project was exceptional, commemorating the trauma and mass-murder of the Holocaust so boldly in the city where that genocide was planned. The coordinates of the jagged shapes were derived, in Libeskind's account, from the addresses of murdered and deported Jews.[9] The Museum's form rejects the expectation that architecture should be comfortable. It unsettles visitors, dislocating them from the city into the vicarious experience of trauma. The emphasis on sloping floors, awkward angles, truncated routes and diagonal cuts can be understood, in Berlin, as a clear consequence of the design's distinctive *schema*.

Following the success of this project, Studio Libeskind has repeated the same distinctive family of shape-forms that won it fame in multiple projects, on multiple sites and with multiple programmes; understandably, perhaps, in projects that also deal with trauma such as the Jewish Museum in Copenhagen and Imperial War Museum North in Salford, UK. But this formal repetition is less immediately understandable in other projects such as the Graduate Centre for London Metropolitan University or at the shopping mall on the outskirts of Bern in Switzerland. Instantly, their shape-forms allow these buildings to be identified as products of Studio Libeskind. But, somehow, their existence seems to undermine that architectural vocabulary's origins in the particularities of Berlin. What was once redolent and provocative could be seen to have become a visual trope for the marketing and sustenance of a global architecture brand. Somehow, this architectural idiom seems jarring on the occasions when it operates blatantly in service of the first economy outlined here, the economy of financial markets, utilitarian bureaucracy and the technocratic expert.

In their frequent repetition, the shape-forms of Studio Libeskind's architecture have become a kind of economy following the definition proposed above. They comprise a self-referential system in which individual projects repeatedly quote and re-quote each other. Could it be that Libeskind is living Adorno's suggestion that 'to write poetry after Auschwitz is barbaric',[10] accepting that the Holocaust terminated the Enlightenment project of beauty and reason, arguing that all architecture can only ever be architecture-after-the-Holocaust? Or is this over-interpretation? Is it instead the logic of branded, globalised consumption where super-rich clients buy a Libeskind as they would buy a Picasso or a yacht? If the latter interpretation is more accurate, then the prefabricated villa could be seen as the ultimate commission for brand Libeskind. Being siteless, the awkward particularities of climate and location that could disrupt the self-referential logic of its brand forms are negated. The house is freed from necessities of site to indulge in the cultural capital of the studio's own visual economy.

Economy #4

The fourth economy indicated by the *RIBA Journal* article is that of art-historical architectural journalism, an economy that prefers to promote the idea of the genius author. As if to affirm the authorial agency of the hero architect; the magazine piece includes a photographic portrait of Libeskind, striking a thoughtful pose, next to a business-suited portrait of the developer Michael Merz, a pairing that in this context apparently underscores their commercial and ideological alliance. In this economy, the designer – and the brand of their respected practice – assures the developer high-end value.

Designer brands such as that of Libeskind owe their reputation to the distinctive vocabulary of art connoisseurship that is sustained by books, journals, newspapers and magazines where fame is itself constructed by famous critics and historians. In the sociologist Pierre Bourdieu's interpretation, this constellation creates and sustains 'cultural capital': a canon and a language of high art, where cultural value might or might not relate directly to financial value. Bourdieu has shown how the super-rich consume art capital to establish more serious public credentials, whereas artists and critics articulate power through the fine nuances of their knowing judgement. As a largely self-referential system, the vocabulary and demeanour learnt and practised by connoisseur-critics can be described as an economy.

The Sunday newspaper architecture columns are, perhaps, one of the barometers of this economy. Their accounts are frequently characterised by aesthetic judgements: by the rhetoric of fine details and rich composition, of novelty and daring, of (supposed) refusal to compromise in the face of society's presumed banality and philistinism. When it is written about, Libeskind's architecture is most often accounted for in such terms. What is surprising and striking about the *RIBA Journal* article about the Libeskind Villa is that it presents an unusually striking conjunction of this vocabulary with the vocabulary of technical delivery, process and profit. Most often, these vocabularies are kept separate: building, management, surveying and engineering journals establishing the terms of technocratic delivery; art and architecture journals and newspaper columns consolidating the priorities of aesthetic merit. It remains – arguably – in the interests of the critic and the brand-name designer that the connections between these two discourses remain largely implicit because it permits a certain mystery to be maintained around artistic credibility, a mystery that is necessary to sustain the marketable idea of the hero genius.

It is in the interests of the professional media to maintain an image of critical distance from the architects they write about and the construction industry of which they are a part. But the economy of art-historical criticism is, in the end, essential to – and indivisible from – the idea of the hero genius, and therefore the idea of the genius' personal design brand, and therefore the economy of financial markets and development finance in which it generates and sustains 'high-end' value.

Four economies

I have argued that four economies are apparent here in and around the Libeskind Villa and the *RIBA Journal*'s account of it: first, the economy of technical efficiency and commercial profit; second, the autonomous economy of the house itself as a siteless, timeless network terminal; third, the shape-economy of Libeskind-branded architecture; and, fourth, the connoisseur's economy of cultural capital. While there are connections, these economies are each largely autonomous, self-referential systems. The *RIBA Journal* article highlights their points of disconnection, their jarring collision in the text mirroring their jarring collision in architectural high culture.

The journal article records the effective separation of developer, builder, designer and connoisseur – and for that matter inhabitant, client, engineer and surveyor – in professionalised contemporary construction. It displays multiple, awkwardly overlaid, economies, each with their own specialised habits, values and vocabularies. It is, perhaps, for this reason that architects often find themselves sideways-on to the construction industry. Engineers, surveyors and developers, for the most part, operate within a single economy, with little doubt about the primary motives of profit, efficiency and technical rationality. Architects – with their implicit duties to the 'end-users' of buildings as well as developers, and to the cultures and histories of the topographies in which they work, finding their designs discussed according to the vocabulary of art connoisseurs as well as that of financiers – inevitably perceive themselves to be in a more complex situation. More frequently than their professional colleagues, architects operate across and between multiple value systems, across multiple economies.

The idea of the ancient villa relies on the notion of a singular economy; a single self-sustaining set of values to which its community can subscribe. The Libeskind

Villa, however, derives from multiple, intersecting economies. In more multivalent times, this is perhaps hardly surprising. However, the house's awkwardness stems not from the multivalence that it reflects but instead from the compartmentalisation of its multiple economies. The article throws into sharp focus how separate architectural production has become from architectural appreciation, how separate architectural brands, and brand-name architecture, have become from the specific needs of sites and inhabitants. While the rhetoric of its sustainable values remains appealing, the idea of the ancient villa economy – singularly conceived, with everything in its place and everyone knowing their place – may no longer be desirable as a model. But nor is the radical compartmentalisation of multiple economies to which Villa Libeskind attests. That house and its description are valuable, though, because of their capacity to characterise the problems of contemporary architectural production, and to characterise some of the problems of being an architect in contemporary Western culture.

Notes

1. Title with apologies to Reyner Banham. Banham's novel analysis of Los Angeles, published as *Four Ecologies of Architecture* in 1971, proposed 'four ecologies' of that city in relation to its beach, freeways, flatlands and foothills, treating the city as a whole architectural object and revelling in its informal and temporary structures as much as its more conventionally 'architected' ones, paying attention to objects that, at that time, were not considered to be proper objects of historians' attention. This chapter is not derived directly from Banham's work but it does, similarly, aim to think about things – specifically the media constructions of architects and commercial architectural culture – which mainstream art-historical architectural scholarship tends to pay less attention to.
2. Jan-Carlos Kucharek, 'One Foot in the Past: Bespoke Prefabrication', *RIBA Journal*, July/August 2010, pp. 47–50.
3. David Leatherbarrow in conversation, on the occasion of his visit to the Welsh School of Architecture in Cardiff in May 2009.
4. Kucharek, 'One Foot in the Past', p. 47.
5. Kucharek, 'One Foot in the Past', p. 50.
6. See Allison Dutoit, Juliet Odgers and Adam Sharr eds, *Quality Out of Control: Standards for Measuring Architecture* (London: Routledge, 2010).
7. Fred Dallmayr, 'Exit from Orientalism', in A.L. Macfie, *Orientalism: A Reader* (Edinburgh: Edinburgh University Press, 2000) pp.365–368, p.366.
8. Italo Calvino, *Invisible Cities* (New York: Harcourt Brace, 1978).
9. Daniel Libeskind, 'Between the Lines: Extension to the Berlin Museum, with the Jewish Museum', *Assemblage*, 12, August (1990), pp. 18–57.
10. Theodor W. Adorno, 'Cultural Criticism and Society', *Prisms*, trans. Samuel and Shierry Weber (Cambridge, MA: MIT Press, 1967), p.19.

9
THE LIBIDINAL ECONOMY OF ARCHITECTURE

Skin, membranes and other surfaces of desire

Chris L. Smith

Introduction

This chapter focuses on the most perverse and intense of economies. It is the economy introduced by the philosopher and literary theorist Jean-François Lyotard: the *libidinal economy*. The reason is simply stated: one of architecture's key exchanges is libidinal. It is a simple stated reason but not so simply demonstrated; and it is a demonstration that I seek to undertake in this chapter.

In turning to the work of Lyotard, I do so as someone for whom the spatial, the material, the tectonic and the architectural are key concerns. And Lyotard's text of 1974, *Economie Libidinale*, is ripe for this reading.[1] Lyotard begins his text not with a discussion of economy in any traditional sense, but rather with the spatiality and materiality of the body. The body described by Lyotard is neither sanctified as *subject* nor reified as *object*; nor is it particularly personalised. Lyotard starts rather with the body as corpse – disposed to the anatomist's knife. He commences with a clinical description of the dissection of a female body. He opens this body with the gentle slide of a scalpel that cuts a plane – a section – that makes the body sectional. The organs of the body, including the skin, are likewise neither engaged as objects nor as functional elements of a subject but rather as mobile surfaces to be traced. The dissection cuts through the skin and then unfolds the interior as a surface confounding interior/exterior dialectics and simultaneously allowing Lyotard to attest the visceral immediacy of the act of negotiating any surface. Lyotard asks that we rupture, break, lose, open, spread, undo or disconnect the skin as a way to open other possibilities for negotiating the body and for understanding the self. His concern is not only the architectures of the body, but also that which extends from it. In this sense we undo the body as we know it for the same reason that we undo architecture as we know it; so that we may know it in other ways.

Lyotard describes *Libidinal Economy* as 'a piece of shamelessness, immodesty and provocation'.[2] I want, in this chapter, to pose the libidinal economy – the shameless, immodest and provocative libidinal economy – as a means of thinking about another surface, that of the architectural membrane. The architectural surface is the object of much contemporary architectural investment and it will be explored specifically herein with reference to the 2008 edition of the journal *AD* guest-edited by Michael Hensel and Achim Menges. The edition is titled 'Versatility and Vicissitude'. The present chapter will explore the discourse primarily related to the 2005–8 work of Hensel and Menges focused on membrane systems developed through work at the Rotterdam Academy of Architecture and Urban Design; the Architectural Association; and London Metropolitan University.[3] Lyotard's consideration of the libidinal economy as a negotiation of the surface is explored in this chapter for its potential to at once facilitate and problematise the architectural desire for surface.

The libidinal economy

In the second chapter of *Libidinal Economy*, Lyotard departs from the work of Sigmund Freud and extends the work of the artist, writer and translator, Pierre Klossowski in radicalising the libido. Klossowski is best known for his work on the most gratuitous of commodifiers of sex: the Marquis de Sade. Klossowski's essay of 1967 *Sade My Neighbour*, turns to the rationalist linguistic and numeric systems established by Sade as a play between economic commodification and the intensities of sexual pleasures and excess.[4] One of the most terrifying and yet entrancing characteristics of the work of Sade is the manner by which the text slides from monetary economics to the intensities of sex and sexual violence. Sade introduces the context of his *The 120 Days of Sodom*: 'as one of the periods in the history of the French Empire when one saw the emergence of the greatest number of these mysterious fortunes whose origins are as obscure as the lust and debauchery that accompany them.'[5]

In Sade, representative money fulfils the promise of the economy of the 'gift' in a placing of a unit or value (a dollar) on all objects and subjects that makes the most incongruous of trades possible. Sexual acts, bodies, property, servitudes and titles are all traded – and often for each other. Representative money makes congruity from the incongruous. It creates a liquidity and a politics of exchange – what Lyotard refers to as 'political economy'. There is a clear correspondence between the fetishism of the libido and of the commodity; of the body and of economy. According to Laura Mulvey, the film theorist known for operating at the intersections of feminism and psychoanalysis: 'The concept of fetishism, as an inappropriate attribution of value to an object, emerged alongside and in conjunction with the emergent articulation of the commodity form.'[6] The fetish would seem to exist alongside the habits of thought we might generally call economics. This dual emergence of sexuality and monetary systems is also a departure point for Lyotard's libidinal economy as that which rages alongside the political economy and that which invests in aberrations. This convertibility between the numerabilities of monetary value and the singularities of pleasure parallels the convertibility of Sade's (bourgeois inflected) Enlightenment language and gratuitous sexual violence.[7] Sade uses clinical and neutral descriptors to describe the most intense of violent and erotic acts. The rationalism by which Sade elaborates his 'clandestine commerce'[8] is posed by Klossowski in intense, tense and poignant difference to the depraved acts and violations engaged.

Not surprisingly then, Lyotard turns to Klossowski first by performing in poststructuralism's key arena – that of finding fault in representation. The discourse is one with which we are all today familiar: representation is concerned with the instilment of something that stands in place of another thing. The word 'horse' that stands in place of that which does the galloping; the love letter that stands in place of love; the blue velvet that stands in the place of mother's dress; mother's dress that stands in place of the phallus; the architect's blueprint that stands in place of architecture. In the representation of linguistics the *word* stands in place of the *thing* and for Lyotard, as for his contemporaries, 'signification is always deferred, meaning is never present in flesh and blood'.[9] (There is only text in *The 120 Days of Sodom*; not flesh.) The poststructuralist critique is that which signifies; that which stands in place of; mediates, moderates, inflects, infects.[10] Representation *masks* and in masking suggests that there is that which stands behind the mask – the original, the real, the subject or object. (There is no real sodomy behind *The 120 Days of Sodom*.)

In Sade the incommensurability of life is disguised under value systems (economics and language) which imply the exchangeability of all. For Lyotard the political economy is reliant upon this same form of representation. What representative money, currency, the dollar, does is to operate as the denominator for all forms of qualities and characters. It signifies value. It devalues. It masks the incompossibility of life. It gives currency to the exchangeability of all. It is only through the dollar that I can imagine converting the otherwise incompossible elements of: a reading of Sade; writing a chapter; wine; cheese; and a pair of nice shoes. And the tautological inversion here is that the exchangeability of all implies that there *must* be a common denominator to exchanges.

For Lyotard, the political economy does not, cannot, deal with singularities, intensities. It cannot deal with the singularity of pleasure. It cannot deal with X getting pleasure from giving to Y. Anchored in loss and negation the political economy cannot but replace one object for another. It cannot but repress intensity under value – the value that stands in place of the exchange itself, as in the negotiations between a sex worker and a client establishing the dollar value of different sex acts.

From the mediations of signification, Lyotard turns to the intense immediacy and mobility of signs: for him the sign is 'indissociably, singular and vain intensities in exodus';[11] and from the *from X to Y* exchanges of the political economy he suggests that in any exchange, there is simulacra; an XY intensity. Thus alongside the political economy Lyotard excites the libidinal economy: the unmediated exchange; the exchange without loss; the exchange without negation. The libidinal economy is the economy of the singular exchange of intensity, as in the singular intensities of sex acts. Lyotard's libidinal economy is an economy of affirmation and connection. It is an economy for which all are gifted: gifted in the immediacy and simultaneity of connection: When I touch you, both you and I are pleasured. Lyotard suggests that of any exchange 'we hope to be set in motion'.[12] In place of the object and subjects of exchange (in place of the you and I and of the gift that passes from one to the other) Lyotard invokes a 'pulsional machinery'.[13] For Lyotard the libidinal economy is the 'pulsional machinery' of death and eros together. The machinery is in constant motion, displaceable, non-denumerable, incomposible. It flows but not under a common unit or measure. It wreaks havoc but not under a hierarchy or as an organisation.[14] For even organs are not organised in the libidinal economy but rather fragmented, dissimilated, played multiple, metamorphosed, constructed, engorged and erected. The libidinal economy thus focuses not on the interiorisation of selves and organs and their common denominators or currencies but rather on their exteriorisation. The libidinal economy is, in this regard, *incomposible*. It is an exchange that is not about the you and the not you; the self and that which is exterior to the self; the self and the other – but rather the exchange of the libidinal economy is based on the exteriorisation of the ever-other; the complete exteriorisation.[15] The bodies of the libidinal economy are all surface, continuously transmissive surface. The singular libidinal skin absorbs the dichotomies of inside and out.

The membrane

It is almost by definition that architectural membranes negotiate this same dichotomy of inside and outside; of interior and exterior. Complicating the relations between interiors and exteriors has been an ongoing point of fixation in architecture and the singular architectural membrane lends itself to a very particular kind of complication. This is because the architectural membrane tends towards a homeomorphism whereby the negotiation of interiors and exteriors is not a matter of arrangement of multiple elements but rather a matter of performance: of stretching, of bending and of folding. Such performative spatial manoeuvres have been made all the more pliant with the aid of contemporary digital technologies. The 'Emergent Technologies and Design Group' of the Architectural Association and the international research network *Ocean* has operated at the forefront of experimental engagements with the architectural skin. The 'Emergent Technologies and Design Group' is directed by Hensel, Menges and Michael Weinstock. *Ocean* was also formed at the Architectural Association in London and established in 1994 by Hensel, Ulrich Königs, Tom Verebes and Bostjan Vuga.[16]

In order to briefly trace the libidinal economy of the architectural membrane I will concentrate on one particular journal edition guest-edited by Hensel and Menges: the March/April 2008 'Versatility and Vicissitude' edition of *AD*.[17] *AD* is a London-based, bi-monthly journal. This is the third edition of *AD* that has been guest-edited by Hensel and Menges.[18] Helen Castle, the usual editor of

AD, offers a page long introductory 'Editorial' to the edition and refers to the 'Versatility and Vicissitude' title as 'curiously Jane Austen-like'; however goes on to say that '[t]he approach of the title is analogous to Hensel's and Menges' approach to architecture. It requires a level of serious engagement. There is no all encompassing soundbite to sum it up.'[19] Castle generously ends the editorial suggesting that in this edition of *AD*, 'the new emphasis on performance in a dynamic architectural context casts architecture not only potentially as part of a greater natural ecology, but starts to suggest what this might offer the end user in terms of "intensified spatial experiences"'.[20] It is argued below that whilst there is something entirely intense in the spatial experiences prompted by Hensel and Menges, regrettably the key trope of the discourse is entirely 'Jane Austen-like'.

Courtly love

Hensel and Menges offer 'Versatility and Vicissitude' as a way of rethinking ideas of sustainability as 'an ever greater division of exterior and interior space'.[21] The key point being made here is that much architectural design associated with sustainability has centred upon the use of wall thickness (and insulation) as a key means of controlling climate and maintaining interior comfort. In place of this technique that extends the 'division' of the interior/exterior dualism, Hensel and Menges offer the architectural membrane as part of a wider package of architectural technologies that fit under the banner of 'performance-oriented design'. It is with some regret that Hensel and Menges then define the membrane as 'a thin, synthetic or natural pliable material that separates two environments and constitutes the lightest environmental modulation in architectural design'.[22] It would seem that the dualism would persist, but just at a reduced dimension of 'division'. Though in the edition Hensel and Menges describe a separation of interiors and exteriors in the architectural projects concerned with membranes, the interiors and exteriors of the membrane projects are configured solely as matters of surface: curvatures, flex and inflections; and it is to the disjunction between the text and images of this work that the present chapter turns.

That which is described as a dualism of interiors and exteriors in the text appear incompossible in the spatial experiments of Hensel and Menges. The work of the 'Membrane Spaces'; 'Membrane Arrays' and 'Layered Membranes and Arrayed Membrane Features' studios is intense (Figure 9.1).

It is intense in the sense that the surfaces generated are charged with an erotic energy: libidinally charged. These intense surfaces fold and infold in sweeping manoeuvres. You cannot look at these surfaces without finding your eyes moving, sliding from taut surfaces to swooning curves and seamlessly from surfaces that open to surfaces that enclose. The eye traces these surfaces in a manner by which it might trace a lover's body. This is not merely because one is seduced by the images themselves but because there is something intensely bodily about these surfaces. The aesthetic at play here is one of taut curvature. The same aesthetic focus we find in much erotic photography and in much pornography.

The libidinal economy of architecture 113

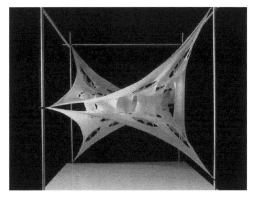

FIGURE 9.1 'Membrane Interaction'

Source: Ralph Doggen, Rotterdam Academy of Architecture, 2005.

FIGURE 9.2 'Membrane Arrays'

Source: Pavlos Sideris, AA London, 2005–2006.

There is pleasure here. In the 'Membrane Arrays' project by Pavlos Sideris at the Architectural Association there is a repetition of nearly similar membranes ('patches') strung taut in a cable-net (Figure 9.2).

The elements slide across the space in which they are framed. There is a curvature to each membrane that reminds us of the torsos that used to decorate the beaches of our late teen years; and those that we used to have and hold in our early twenties. There is an intensity in the formal repetitions of this surface across the cable-net that the eye bounces along as if one were flicking pages in *Playboy* magazine. However, you will not locate any pleasure in the economy that Hensel and Menges engage to describe the projects. Of this project they write:

Once the interaction between cable-net and arrayed membrane patches is established in a series of physical tests, it is possible to elaborate the differentiated assembly through continuous variation in a parametric associative modelling environment, utilising a dynamic relaxation function that through an iterative mathematical process approaches the minimal surface geometry of form-active tension systems. The output of this process was subsequently evaluated and ranked through advanced digital analysis (computer fluid dynamics) with regard to the modulation of airflow.[23]

There is something of political economy in Hensel and Menges' account of the architectural membrane. The aversion to dealing with aesthetics and the intensities of the work leaves Hensel and Menges with descriptions of the work that are a banal accountancy of forces and formal correspondences – systems, functions, modelling and evaluations rather than pleasures. It is not that systems, functions, modelling and evaluation are not libidinal; it is that the descriptions of the projects leave one imagining that the eroticisms of the work are entirely coincidental and that they are the accident of an economy whereby pleasure has either no place or is aberrant. One is reminded of the work of Jane Austen. There is something intensely sensual, romantic, erotic in the outcomes of the endeavours described by Austen and yet there is not a single torso in the discourse. No lips, no labia, no-one kisses. In *Pride and Prejudice* at the high point of what would be intensely erotic in life, the text breaks off prior to libidinal exchanges, giving way to the following report of Mr Darcy: 'He expressed himself on the occasion as sensibly and as warmly as a man violently in love can be supposed to do.'[24] When my eye runs joyously over the membranes of Hensel and Menges I imagine they may be equally violently in love.

Tension

The key exchange in the architectural surfaces of Hensel and Menges would appear to be an exchange of *force*. There is nothing inherently banal about force unless we reify it by removing from it intensity; that is, where the idea of force becomes not a force *of*, or applied *to*, but rather a tension without intensity. Force in this way operates like representative money in a placing of a unit or value (a Newton) on all objects and subjects and all exchanges between, making congruity from the incongruous. When we deal with force as a quantity, as a tension and a corresponding compression without *touch* we run the risk of removing the surface, the membrane, from its key economy of pleasure.

There is, in the images of the membranes of the 'Versatility and Vicissitude' issue something forcefully poised. Something in tension. The images speak of a particular force applied to a particular membrane in order to achieve a particular pleasure, a particular aesthetic. This *poise* is not a balance nor an equilibrium but a dynamic tension. Indeed it is like the pulsional machinery of which Lyotard spoke, 'in its unpredictable displaceability'.[25] There is also something of bondage in the architectural membrane (Figure 9.3).

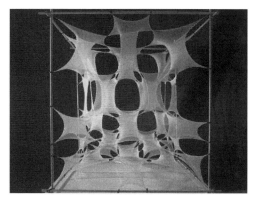

FIGURE 9.3 'Membrane Interaction'

Source: Ralph Doggen, Rotterdam Academy of Architecture, 2005.

There is here something of a surface suspended in space and time, something of (what Menges and Hensel refer to as) 'specifically chosen control points', something of the tension and forces applied to achieve a prolongation and an exhaustion of the surface, something of the delayed climax. Indeed the images of the work of Hensel and Menges could well excite a masochist.

In the text of Hensel and Menges, however, we are left with a reduction of the surface to what Didier Deleule and François Guéry might call 'a machinery, and the intellectual forces of production, the head, the brain, whose present state is the *software* of the information scientist'.[26] Perhaps the key to this reduction is the idea of equilibrium which populates the descriptors of Hensel and Menges. An equilibrium is the implied 'balance' of forces that constitute their membrane systems:

> In order for a membrane to be in tension and thus structurally active, there needs to be equilibrium of tensile forces throughout the system: if this is not the case, the membrane will typically show flat or wrinkled regions. This implies that the membrane's shape and extent must be established as part of the solution, and specifically that membrane systems must be form-found, utilising the self-organisation behaviour of membranes under extrinsic influences such as by applying tensile forces, and by constraining the membrane via specifically chosen control points.[27]

The descriptors of the work of Hensel and Menges occur as a pseudo-scientific negotiation of unitised measures:[28] of *this* tension relating to *that* tautness. The descriptors might also occur as Platonisms: of this system 'directly correlated' to that 'form'. There is a fixation here on the membrane at rest. On forces in equilibrium and forms locked in ('found') by force. These equilibriums are the balances of the political economy – of trading a tension for a compression, of placing a body at rest by a quaint exchange. The act of giving is secondary – it is that you have or

116 Chris L. Smith

have not that matters in the political economy. The balancing of an account. There is little pulsional machinery to the descriptors of Hensel and Menges and in spite of the intensity of the architectural membrane itself there is nothing in the text 'which moves us'. Again, the language of equilibriums belies the intensities involved and one is reminded of Austen's account of the intensity between her heroine Emma Woodhouse and her suitor Mr Knightley:

> Emma understood him; and as soon as she could recover from the flutter of pleasure excited by such tender consideration, replied: 'You are very kind – but you are mistaken – and I must set you right – I am not in want of that sort of compassion.'[29]

The heart flutters with pleasure in the libidinal economy of the architectural membrane; and yet when architects lean in close to your ear too often they whisper a story of accountancy. Of equilibriums, of tender flesh, of chest without cleavage, of cleavage without nipple, of nipple without clamp.

Conclusion

Pleasure, desire and titillation are all qualities of architecture and yet so much of the manner by which architecture trades and is traded reduces it to the more banal economies of the dollar; the economy of the gift; the political economy of ideology and investment; and an economy of equilibrium and balance. The way we write about architecture seems often inept in engaging with its actuality. The images that the text accompanies often bare only tenuous resemblance to the written descriptions. The work itself, the architecture, is often unrecognisable. It is the intention of this chapter to reinvigorate an interest in another economy that surges through architecture and that might better speak of architecture's pleasures: a libidinal economy. The architectural membrane is a particularly poignant site for an exploration of this economy. This is because the membrane is a surface upon which so many of the dualisms with which we battle collapse. The interior/exterior dialectic mean little to the geometries of the membrane. The object/subject dialectic too is displaced like blue velvet in a sweaty palm. The architectural membrane is also a particularly poignant site for an exploration of the libidinal economy because of its singular intensity. That is, it operates as a dispositif of so many images, imaginings and material intensities. So many pleasures, so many triggers. Like skin, the architectural membrane is a surface of sensual immediacy. A surface of desire.

Notes

1 Jean-Francois Lyotard, *Libidinal Economy* (London: Continuum, 2004). Translation of *Economie Libidinale* (Paris: Les Editions De Minuit, 1974) by Iain Hamilton Grant.
2 Ibid., p. xix.
3 'Membrane Spaces'; 'Membrane Arrays' and 'Layered Membranes and Arrayed Membrane Features': 'Membrane Spaces', GPA 02 Studio (Michael Hensel and Achim

Menges), Rotterdam Academy of Architecture and Urban Design, The Netherlands, 2005; 'Membrane Arrays', Diploma Unit 4 (Michael Hensel and Achim Menges), Architectural Association, London, 2005–6; 'Layered Membranes and Arrayed Membrane Features', LMU Diploma Unit 9 (Michael Hensel, Daniel Coll I Capdevila and Mattia Gambardella), London Metropolitan University, 2006–7.
4 Pierre Klossowski, *Sade My Neighbor* (Evanston, IL: Northwestern University Press, 1991). Translation of *Sade mon prochain* (Seuil: Paris, 1947) by Alphonso Lingis.
5 Marquis de Sade, *The 120 Days of Sodom and Other Writings* (New York: Grove Press, 1987), p. 191. Translated by Austryn Wainhouse and Richard Seaver.
6 Laura Mulvey, *Fetishism and curiosity* (Bloomington: Indiana University Press, 1996), p. 125.
7 Refer to Jean-François Lyotard and Iain Hamilton Grant, 'Libidinal economy in Sade and Klossowski', *Sade and the Narrative of Transgression*, (Stony Brook: State University of New York, 1995), pp. 62–75.
8 Sade, *The 120 Days of Sodom*, p. 193.
9 Lyotard, *Libidinal Economy*, p. 43.
10 Lyotard does not linger in what he refers to as the 'nihilism' of semiotic exchanges but instead looks to an alternate economy; the economy of intensity. 'To remain in semiotic thought', Lyotard writes, 'is to languish in religious melancholy and to subordinate every intense emotion to a lack and every force to a finitude.' Lyotard, *Libidinal Economy*, p. 48.
11 Lyotard, *Libidinal Economy*, p. 49.
12 Lyotard, *Libidinal Economy*, p. 50.
13 Lyotard, *Libidinal Economy*, p. 51–2. Reference here to Dora is to the Freudian Case Study: 'Fragments of an Analysis of a Case of Hysteria' (1905 [1901], *Standard Edition* (Vol. 7): pp. 1–122).
14 Or as Lyotard suggests, 'the libido circulates and invests over the organic body, in its unpredictable displaceability'. Lyotard, *Libidinal Economy*, p. 52.
15 Ibid., p. 13.
16 Michael Hensel and Birger R. Sevaldson (web editors), www.ocean-designresearch.net. Accessed 2 August 2011.
17 Michael Hensel and Achim Menges eds, 'Versatility and Vicissitude: Performance in Morpho-Ecological Design', *AD* (2/78, March/April 2008).
18 The earlier two editions were guest-edited by Hensel and Menges with Michael Weinstock. Weinstock along with Hensel and Menges is a director of the 'Emergent Technologies in Design' MSc/MArch program at the Architectural Association, London. Michael Hensel, Achim Menges and Michael Weinstock eds, 'Emergence: Morphogenetic Design Strategies', *AD* (3/74, May/June 2004); Michael Hensel, Achim Menges and Michael Weinstock eds, 'Techniques and Technologies in Morphogenetic Design', *AD* (2/76, March/April 2006).
19 Castle, Helen, 'Editorial', *AD* (2/78, March/April 2008), p. 5.
20 Ibid.
21 Hensel and Menges, 'Versatility and Vicissitude', p. 7.
22 Ibid., p. 10.
23 Ibid., p. 77.
24 Jane Austen, *Pride and Prejudice*, ed. R.W. Chapman. 3rd edn (London: Oxford University Press, 1966), p. 366.
25 Lyotard, *Libidinal Economy*, pp. 51–2.
26 Didier Deleule and François Guéry, *Le Corps Productif* (Paris: Mame, 1972), p. 39. Quoted in Lyotard, *Libidinal Economy*, p. 118, original emphasis.
27 Hensel and Menges, 'Versatility and Vicissitude', p. 75.
28 It must be noted, however, that the aversion to the language of libidinal and aesthetic intensities does not in the above quote stop that same aesthetics and libidinal investment from surging. Indeed in the text itself there is a note as to what Hensel and Menges do not want from a membrane space: 'flat or wrinkled regions'.
29 Jane Austen, *Emma* (Oxford: Clarendon Press, 1923 [1916]), p. 426.

10
ARCHITECTURAL RENEWAL AND POETIC PERSISTENCE

Investing in an economy of stories

Lisa Landrum

In its original Greek sense *oikonomia* referred to the art of managing households, and the first household described in Western literature is that of Odysseus in Homer's *Odyssey*. Although the word *oikonomia* does not appear in this epic poem, Odysseus' 'household' (*oikos*) and the problem of its management (*nemein*) figure prominently throughout. Thus, the overall story of the *Odyssey* is said to be framed by an 'economic crisis'.[1] This crisis will be considered here insofar as its imagery implicates architectural concerns. The primary purpose is neither to speculate on the design of Homeric palaces, nor to investigate how domestic economies actually functioned in archaic Greece.[2] Rather, the aim is to show how Odysseus' storied approach to household management can help us understand architectural value as narratively construed. For Odysseus restores order to his troubled *oikos* largely by recalling, adjusting, and exchanging stories about radically diverse yet comparable dwelling situations. It is this poetic and discursive way of 'managing households', wherein situational and narrative practices are productively intertwined, that this chapter seeks to recover. For sure, the pre-monetary society depicted in the *Odyssey* is radically remote from our own, but its narrative economy still speaks to our perennial obligation to discursively find value in architecture – a disciplinary 'household', if you will, perhaps no less troubled than Odysseus was when his story began. How, then, did his story begin?

Odysseus' economic crisis

As presented in the opening to the *Odyssey*, during his twenty-year absence from Ithaca (ten years fighting in Troy and ten more wandering at sea), Odysseus' household has fallen into utter disarray. Presuming the hero would never return, eager opportunists have moved into his territory, vying for possession of his wife and property. These greedy suitors have made themselves at home in Odysseus' great hall, devouring his estate's food, wine, and other resources as if these were in infinite supply. As Odysseus' son Telemachus despairingly exclaims, these suitors will 'consume' the *oikos* and 'devour' its livelihood.[3] This frequently repeated portrayal of the suitors gorging themselves on Odysseus' *oikos* links their improper behaviour to that of the Cyclops who, likewise, 'devours' Odysseus' crew.[4] But before his household is completely wasted Odysseus does return, and through an elaborate scheme – as violent as it is cunning – he overcomes these Cyclopean suitors and begins to renew the household that has long occupied his mind.

Throughout this economic crisis, Odysseus' property and resources figure prominently as tangible measures of his changing fortune. The dwindling resources of his *oikos* in Ithaca are paralleled by his diminishing situation at sea, entailing the gradual loss of his fleet, his entire crew, his own ship, and, with it, his cargo of Trojan spoils. Even his clothing is consumed by Poseidon. However, in spite of these devastating losses, Odysseus, it is said, will return with 'countless gifts', with 'many rich treasures', and with so much wealth as 'to feed his children up to the tenth generation'.[5] Sure enough, Odysseus returns to Ithaca with many valuable treasures given to him by Alcinous, the hospitable Phaeacian King. But Alcinous, we must recall, gives Odysseus these valuables (together with an escort home) in gratitude specifically for his fitting speech and enchanting stories.[6] With this exchange, Odysseus' stories appear to garner direct remuneration, prefiguring practices of later fifth-century poets such as Simonides, who 'composed poems for a price', and Pindar, who literally and metaphorically trafficked in praise.[7] Though ambivalently associated with trade and commerce, Odysseus' stories also participate in an economy of gift exchange, an institution in which value is measured not solely by material worth or usefulness, but more by a gift's cultural and symbolic meaning: by its appropriateness to a situation of exchange; by its provenance, or history of illustrious (or infamous) affiliations; and by the social bonds of reciprocal friendship that such diplomatic exchanges secure and sustain.[8] As if to prove these points, soon after arriving on the shore of Ithaca, the Phaeacian gifts are hidden in a cave, since material wealth is of no use to Odysseus, who must resolve his economic crisis through more situationally discursive (if deceptive) means.

And, so, while it is true that Odysseus' material property and resources reflect his changing fortunes, they also perform as symbols of those less tangible kinds of wealth he accumulates during his perilous travels, including a wealth of ethical knowledge acquired through experiencing diverse dwelling situations, and a treasury of paradigmatic stories by which those situations are remembered, interpreted, and conveyed. It is by drawing on this discursive sort of wealth – ethical and situational knowledge, and persuasively paradigmatic stories – that Odysseus resolves his economic crisis and renews his household.

To see how this discursive economy bears tectonic and architectural significance, it is sufficient to consider three episodes of the *Odyssey*: when Odysseus makes his raft (in book five); when he recounts his extraordinary stories (in books nine through twelve); and when, having overcome the suitors, he recalls the story of building his marriage bed at the centre of his *oikos* (in book twenty-three). First the raft.

Valuable (and vulnerable) cargo

The imagery of a narrative economy is made tangible in book five, where we witness Odysseus building his raft. This pivotal act inaugurates his release from Calypso's island and his return to Ithaca. The Homeric poet narrates this transformative advancement of the plot in great detail: describing the tools with which Odysseus works; the careful actions by which he transforms natural materials into a means for human transport; and the adjustable devices with which he plans to navigate the sea and steer his homeward course (5.233–61). But that is not all. The poet also names a model after which Odysseus makes his raft: a large cargo-bearing ship, like those used by Phoenician merchants. This model is introduced with a telling simile: 'as a man well-skilled in carpentry marks-out the hull of a cargo ship, broad of beam, just so wide did Odysseus make his raft' (5.249–51). Beyond conjuring a vessel suitably scaled to a momentous journey, this otherwise incongruous image of a modest one-man raft being laid out as a deep-hulled cargo ship sets up a manifold comparison linking Odysseus' 'skilled' manner of making his vessel to his analogous manner of making stories, while further casting these stories as valuable cargo to be conveyed in the imagined hull of his ship.

As Carol Dougherty has convincingly shown, Odysseus' work of making his raft (in book five) closely prefigures his composition of stories (in books nine through twelve).[9] This correspondence is suggested, in part, by specific vocabulary: Odysseus 'knowingly' prepares his timbers, just as he 'knowingly' tells his tales;[10] and he skilfully fabricates each as a 'carpenter', or *tekton*.[11] The link is further supported by a variety of dispersed metaphors establishing a 'common figurative alliance of ships and songs'.[12] Yet, the correspondence also plays out dramatically through narrative events. Right from the start, Odysseus doubts that a wooden raft could withstand the turbulent sea. Indeed, soon after fitting it so well together this raft is shattered to pieces by Poseidon. In spite of its total destruction, Odysseus arrives to the Phaeacian shore with his most valuable cargo preserved and his *technē* for 'fitting-together' and 'steering' narrative events fully intact. For following this shipwreck, Odysseus goes on to compose stories with well-shaped verses, and these stories he assembles in a way that, unlike the raft, hold together and endure. Moreover, these well-composed and well-conveyed stories gain for Odysseus precisely what the raft had not: a return home, since the Phaeacians, moved by his 'wondrous' stories, convey him to Ithaca in one of their own 'wondrous' ships. The symmetry of this exchange, reinforced by the link between wonder-inducing modes of transport (stories and ships), further confirms that by making his raft in the way that he did – with *tekton*-like attention to its connections, performativity, and adjustability – Odysseus was, in a sense, rehearsing the fabrication of stories that would ultimately bring him home. Put differently, Odysseus' provisional work in wood models, in manifold ways, the well-made tales he goes on to tell – tales that advance his return to Ithaca, where further discursive work awaits him.

Letting go of the raft, what, then, are the tales Odysseus tells, and how do these narratives contribute to renewing households?

Paradigmatic stories offered profitably in exchange

Having hosted Odysseus with elaborate feasts, athletic games, dancing, and songs, the Phaeacian King then urges him to reveal his identity and to share his stories. With genuine ethical curiosity, he says 'tell me of the people and of their populous cities, both of those who are cruel and wild and unjust, and of those who are kind to strangers and fear the gods in their thoughts' (8.574–6).[13] Odysseus responds by telling of the widely diverse people, places, and practices he encountered during his difficult years at sea, including his encounter with Polyphemus, a giant one-eyed cannibal, residing amid his sheep in an isolated cave; with Aeolus, the fickle keeper of winds, living with his incestuous family upon a floating island of bronze; with Circe, a treacherous witch, singing and weaving with her attendants in enchanting halls of stone; with the blind seer Teiresias (and other spirits of the dead), bearing heavy counsel at the dank mouth of Hades; and with Calypso, an immortal nymph, singing, weaving, and dwelling in a realm of alluringly manifold sensuality. While each encounter entails urgencies complicating the overall plot, the narration advances with, what Norman Austin has called, 'unhurried care', for Odysseus and the Homeric poet linger descriptively over situational details in ways that craft meticulous interconnections between various kinds and levels of order: synthetically linking the configuration of physical settings with patterns of individual conduct, social exchange, and natural and cosmic rhythms.[14] As Austin emphasizes, Odysseus' survival throughout these episodic trials depends on his capacity to discern such rhythms (at both micro and macro scales), and to act in agile accordance with these.

While each incredible story on its own provides diverting entertainment, when considered collectively in relation to Odysseus' 'economic crisis' and model 'cargo-ship', these stories should be received as valuable intellectual goods being offered not simply in direct exchange (for an escort home), but in discursive and interpretive exchange whereby 'understanding' may be brought home.[15] For, against each account of an extraordinary dwelling situation, one may profitably compare and contrast the troubled situation in Ithaca, thus gaining a greater comprehension of its crisis while envisioning – alongside Odysseus – a scheme for its re-ordering. In other words, the mythic households of Polyphemus, Aeolus, Circe, Teiresias, Calypso, and others, serve as reflective grounds for interpreting the crises and potentialities of Odysseus' own *oikos*. By the same token, Odysseus' various schemes for enduring and ultimately escaping these troubled domains rehearse possibilities for analogous transformative action in Ithaca.

Strikingly, Odysseus' experience in the land of the Cyclops, a story from which we might least expect to learn the art of 'managing households', shows best how this narrative exchange performs.

Lessons from the land of the Cyclops

Thanks to its monstrous inhabitant, the land of the Cyclops looms large in popular imagination. But in the eyes of Odysseus, this land was most remarkable for what it lacked, since the Cyclopes lacked institutions essential to viable households. They lacked ships and ship-builders, together with the corresponding institution of foreign trade (9.125–8); they lacked agricultural practices, together with the synchronization of social life with seasonal rhythms (9.107–9); and they lacked assemblies for counsel, together with customary laws, discursive skills, and the capacities for judgement and tolerant co-habitation that such 'assemblies' (*agorae*) would foster (9.112). Odysseus recognizes what the Cyclopean land lacks by direct observation but also by regarding it in relation to the neighbouring island where he initially beaches his ship (at a safe distance). According to Odysseus, this nearby island possesses a natural harbour, pleasant meadows, level fields with rich soil, freshwater springs, flourishing vines, innumerable goats, and countless poplar trees – that is, all the environmental preconditions from which resourceful 'artisans' (*tektones*) might fashion a settlement that is 'well-arranged' (9.130). Since this special epithet, 'well-arranged', often qualifies his own *oikos* in Ithaca,[16] it would seem that while regarding the deficiencies of the Cyclopean land and untapped potentialities of its adjacent island, Odysseus has his own home situation simultaneously in mind.

These juxtapositions, inviting interpretive comparison, are compounded by the situation in which Odysseus tells his tales: the land of the Phaeacians, with its exemplary orchards, vineyards, meadows, and groves; with its city walls, harbours, ships, and ship-builders; and with its inviting halls, temples, assembly places, and dancing floors – all of which Odysseus beholds with 'wonder' just prior to sharing his wonder-inducing stories.[17] By gathering these comparative passages, the epistemological and ethical value of the diverse situations conveyed through Odysseus' stories becomes more apparent. As marvellous, monstrous, and mythic as these situations are, they play critical roles in delimiting what a common 'household' might be, what it ought to be, and what it is not. Thus, these extraordinary stories help Odysseus (and his audiences) recognize and re-imagine cultural conditions and constraints at home.[18]

There are many practical lessons Odysseus learns in the land of the Cyclops, such as how and when to exercise his cunning, to conceal and reveal his identity, to curb his curiosity, and to check his hubris. But the valuation of social practices is paramount, and of these practices the most at risk in the *Odyssey* is hospitality (*xenia*). It is the negation and perversion of this custom that plays out in both the *oikos* of Odysseus and the cave of Polyphemus. While the Cyclopean situation is not completely devoid of order (Polyphemus pens his sheep 'separately' by age, milks his ewes and goats 'in due order', and drives his flocks to pasture with regularity),[19] this limited orderliness falls short of *nemein* since it does not extend to hosting (and learning from) others. This absence is all the more significant because *nemein* (the root verb of *oikonomia*), though usually translated as 'managing', most often refers in Homeric poetry to acts of 'distributing' equitable portions of meat and wine during practices of hospitality and sacrifice.[20] In other words, the institution of *xenia*, which propitiates social order and harmony among mortals and gods, is a practice requisite to the 'management' of households.

Renewing households by recalling founding stories

Whereas the stories Odysseus shares in the Phaeacian palace extend to mythic and magical dwelling situations, the storied scenes in Ithaca gather more common domains, each exemplifying forms of life integral to viable households. These include the well-tended property of the loyal swineherd Eumaeus; the flourishing orchards of Odysseus' father Laertes; the well-kept storeroom of the trusty maid Eurycleia; the room of Telemachus with its broad outlook; as well as the threatened harbour, ailing assembly space, and vexed reception halls. In these local settings, Odysseus' stories – his so-called Cretan lies told while in disguise – play an operative role in advancing his scheme of transformation, enabling him to conceal his identity, gather information, earn trust, test loyalties, and procure the resources he needs to reform and renew the *oikos*. But the stories Odysseus tells in Ithaca are not entirely deceptive, for they also include true recollections by which he gradually and selectively reveals his identity to loyal servants and family members in ways that recall and renew intimate bonds. With such bonds in mind, we turn now to briefly consider one further episode of the *Odyssey*: the climactic event of recognition and renewal with Penelope in book twenty-three.

By this point in the epic, Odysseus has already overcome the suitors through cunning and violent scheming, but he has neither fully resolved his 'economic crisis' nor completely restored his 'household' until he renews his marriage bond with Penelope. Like his return to Ithaca, his return to Penelope is accomplished with a story. For Penelope recognizes Odysseus neither by his rejuvenated appearance nor by his distinguishing scar, but only when he tells the story of how he had made their marriage bed, thus recalling the origins of their 'well-founded' household (23.184–204). With details comparable to those invoked when making his raft, Odysseus describes the tools with which he worked and the 'knowing' manner by which he transformed natural materials. But most significantly, and in a way that both counters and complements the adjustable devices of the roving raft, Odysseus emphasizes the immovable centre round which he had made this bed: a rooted olive tree. In anchoring the bed to the land, this olive tree – with its invisible but tenacious roots – stands as an enduring symbol of fidelity: binding Odysseus to Penelope, the house to the land, and the *oikos* to Athena (the olive tree being her special emblem of perennial vitality). And, so, Odysseus founds his household anew by recalling a story of architectural beginnings rooted within shared memory, in the shared *logos* of myth, the ground of his culture.

Bringing Odysseus home

In conclusion, I will begin the task of bringing this Odyssean discussion home: that is, back to the disciplinary 'household' of architecture and to a renewed understanding of its paradigmatic stories and challenges.

Aside from recovering a narrative approach to construing architectural value, Odysseus' story, as told here, yields three disciplinary topics. First, there is the topic of exotic travel for architects and of understanding the motives for and benefits of such travel: be it actual travel (such as Inigo Jones to Italy, Bernini to France, Loos to America, Wright to Japan, Le Corbusier to the East, Sverre Fehn to Morocco, or Jean Nouvel to Abu Dhabi); or more hypothetical travel, as exemplified by Leon Battista Alberti, who travelled far and wide through diverse works of literature so as to better understand his local situation and to better orient others (in the future) when interpreting theirs. Travel for the purpose of discursive exchange was integral to the early Greek sense of *theōria*. Before Plato appropriated *theōria* as a special form of philosophical speculation, the term named a social custom of travelling to engage other peoples, places, ways of living, and modes of thought.[21] Yet, learning through travel brings with it twin problems we cannot ignore. On the one hand, there is the Heraclitian impossibility of return; since encountering others can lead to such personal change that one's home may no longer be recognized as an ideal destination. On the other hand, the premise that one can profit culturally through travel is contingent on the continued existence of meaningful diversity in the world. Such 'poetry of diversity', to borrow an expression of Martha Nussbaum, is in jeopardy from our global economy, which tends to homogenize the very situations we ought to learn from.[22]

Second, Odysseus' story addresses the challenge of defining, acquiring, and sustaining those 'properties and resources' that would not go down with our disciplinary ship. In his treatise *On Architecture*, Vitruvius posed this very challenge in the form of a story about the shipwrecked philosopher Aristippus, who (not unlike Odysseus) washed up on the shore of a strange land with his discursive capabilities and ethical curiosity intact. When these capabilities allowed him to adapt to (and profit from) his new situation, Aristippus concluded, 'that children ought to be provided with property and resources that could swim with them even out of a shipwreck. For these' – Vitruvius added for emphasis – 'are indeed the true supports of life'.[23] More than Odysseus, Aristippus desired encounters with strangers. Whereas Odysseus endeavoured to return and reform his homeland, Aristippus abandoned the idea of return, choosing instead to offer advice from foreign shores and to engage others in more nomadic forms of *oikonomia*.

Lastly, a third topic raised by Odysseus' 'economic crisis' concerns a necessary confrontation with what we may cheekily call architecture's Cyclopean suitors – those exploitive agents threatening to 'devour' the discipline's livelihood. The agorae of architecture schools have become host to arbitrary commercial and technical opportunists, seeking to appropriate the presumed prestige of the architectural title without bothering to interpret the vast treasury of stories that its disciplinary history and theory provide. Instead, other stories are peddled, full of promises of an imminent future where novel but deterministic technologies will liberate the designer from the limiting burdens and unruly influence of human labour; from basic but fallible materials; and from inconvenient situational and temporal contingencies. All the poetic cargo and narrative imagination in the world may not be enough to counter the ongoing erosion of genuine cultural and natural diversity. But there is a possibility that continued investment in the related *technēs* of *mythos* and *logos* will keep the regenerative arts of storytelling and interpretation afloat.

Notes

1 Richard Seaford, *Money and the Early Greek Mind. Homer, Philosophy, Tragedy* (Cambridge: Cambridge University Press, 2004), p. 71. See also James M. Redfield, 'The Economic Man', *Approaches to Homer*, ed. by Carl A. Rubino and Cynthia W. Shelmerdine (Austin: University of Texas Press, 1983), pp. 218–47.
2 On these topics, see Bradley A. Ault, '*Oikos* and *Oikonomia*: Greek Houses, Households and the Domestic Economy', *Building Communities: House, Settlement and Society in the Aegean*, ed. by R. Westgate, N. Fisher, and J. Whitley (*Studies of the British School of Archaeology at Athens*, 15 (2007)), pp. 259–65; Walter Donlan, 'The Homeric Economy', *A New Companion to Homer*, ed. by Ian Morris and Barry Powell (Leiden: Brill, 1997), pp. 649–67; and Robin Osborne, 'Archaic Greece', *The Cambridge Economic History of the Greco-Roman World*, ed. by Walter Scheidel, Ian Morris and Richard Saller (Cambridge: Cambridge University Press, 2007), pp. 277–301.
3 *Odyssey* 1.250–1; 1.160. All translations are those of A. T. Murray, *Homer: Odyssey*, 2 vols, revised by George E. Dimock (Cambridge, MA: Harvard University Press, 1995).
4 Redfield, p. 243.
5 Odysseus himself utters these predictions (while in disguise): 14.323–6; 19.272, 282–6, 293; 24.272–9. Cf. 5.39.
6 *Odyssey* 7.226–7; 11.333–4; 13.1–2; 13.47–8.
7 Anne Carson, *Economy of the Unlost: Reading Simonides of Keos with Paul Celan* (Princeton, NJ: Princeton University Press, 1999), p. 15; Leslie Kurke, *The Traffic in Praise: Pindar and the Poetics of Social Economy* (Ithaca, NY; London: Cornell University Press, 1991).
8 On the significance of gift exchange to archaic Greek society, see Sitta von Reden, *Exchange in Ancient Greece* (London: Gerald Duckworth & Co., 1995), pp. 13–44, 58–76.
9 Carol Dougherty, *The Raft of Odysseus: The Ethnographic Imagination of Homer's Odyssey* (Oxford: Oxford University Press, 2001), esp. pp. 77–8.
10 *Odyssey* 5.245; 11.368. Cf. 21.406; 23.197. 'Knowingly' here is *epistamenōs*.
11 *Odyssey* 5.250; 14.131.
12 Dougherty, pp. 13, 19–37. See also M. L West, *Indo-European Poetry and Myth* (Oxford: Oxford University Press, 2007), pp. 35–43.
13 Odysseus himself poses the same question on three occasions: when he sets out opportunistically to explore the island of the Cyclops (9.175–6); when, years later, he washes up spent on the shore of the Phaeacians (6.120–1); and when he awakes in disbelief in Ithaca (13.201–2). At each pivotal juncture – before engaging the Cyclops, the Phaeacians, and the Ithacans – he wonders aloud 'to the land of what mortals have I now come? Are they cruel, and wild, and unjust? Or are they kind to strangers and fear the gods in their thoughts?' The repetition not only relates Odysseus' ethical curiosity to that of the Phaeacian King, but also echoes that of the Homeric poet who, in the opening lines of the epic, asks his Muse to tell of 'that man' and the many 'cities he saw and minds he learned' (1.1–3).
14 Norman Austin, *Archery at the Dark of the Moon: Poetic Problems in Homer's Odyssey* (Berkeley: University of California Press, 1975), p. 130. My interpretation of these episodes is indebted to Austin's chapter, 'Intimations of Order', pp. 130–78.
15 With reference to Odysseus and the concept of *oeconomia,* Latin philosophers from Cicero to Erasmus described the event of understanding as a kind of 'homecoming'. See Kathy Eden, *Hermeneutics and the Rhetorical Tradition: Chapters in the Ancient Legacy*

and its Humanist Reception (New Haven, CT; London: Yale University Press, 1997), pp. 27–36.

16 *Odyssey* 6.315; 9.533; 15.129; 22.52; 23.259; 24.226, 336, 377. The *oikos* of Nestor and of Menelaus, where Telemachus is hosted during sacrificial and nuptial celebrations, are also 'well-arranged' (*euktimenēn*, 3.4, 4.476). On the significance of this epithet to nascent city-states evidenced in Homeric poetry, see Stephen Scully, *Homer and the Sacred City* (Ithaca, NY: Cornell University Press, 1990).

17 *Odyssey* 6.262–315; 7.43–5; 81–135.

18 Dougherty, p. 77. The *Odyssey*, Dougherty contends, would have helped the Greeks interpret their mythic past and 'imagine a new world', p. 176.

19 *Odyssey* 9.221–7, 245, 309–12, 438, with Austin, pp. 143–4.

20 Seaford, pp. 49–50.

21 A. W. Nightingale, *Spectacles of Truth in Classical Greek Philosophy: Theōria in its Cultural Context* (Cambridge: Cambridge University Press, 2004). See also Lisa Landrum, 'Performing *Theōria*: Architectural Acts in Aristophanes' *Peace*', *Architecture as a Performing Art*, ed. by Marcia Feuerstein and Gray Read (Farnham and Burlington, VT: Ashgate, 2013), pp. 27–43.

22 Martha C. Nussbaum, *Political Emotions: Why Love Matters for Justice* (Cambridge, MA: Belknap Press of Harvard University Press, 2013), p. 297.

23 Morris Hicky Morgan, trans. *The Ten Books on Architecture* (New York: Dover, 1960), p. 6, pref. 1–2.

PART 3
Managing production

The role and value of the professionalised architect in the context of a market economy is examined further in this third section. Here it is suggested that one of architecture's key dependencies is economics and the essays presented examine relationships between architecture and 'scarcity.' At one level this issue is treated as a question of the survival of the professional architect. It is argued that if unable to engage creatively with economics, the role of professional architect is under threat of total eclipse, a threat that was already present in the mid-nineteenth century as the fragmentation and specialisation of an economically driven building industry left architects struggling to define their value and place. At the extremities of the relationship between architects and scarcity, informal economies globally produce informal architectures using what is to hand, driven by need and initiative, and developing an 'instant urbanity' with little or no input from the architectural profession. The central question addressed by this section is: must a creative approach to economy and its conceptual frameworks be a part of architects' attempts to reconcile their design ambitions with the financial pressures that so strongly influence contemporary architectural practice?

Jeremy Till, a key thinker on scarcity and creativity, opens this section by relating the production of architecture to economy through concepts of scarcity. Focusing on three key historical moments in economic theory – Malthus in 1792; Robbins in 1932; and the Club of Rome in 1972 – Till relates each to a concurrent architectural discourse, respectively Sir John Soane's search for a universal architectural language; modernist approaches to mass housing; and a sustainability agenda framed by constraint. Rather than suggesting a causal link between each economic and architectural moment, Till instead contextualises the architectural discourses within the wider implications of economic debates. Economic definitions of scarcity as an abstracted and necessary inevitability, as a detached science, and as a means of imposing and regulating constraints are revealed to frame, and,

Till argues, limit architectural agendas. Contemporary constructs of scarcity that challenge such historical definitions may, Till concludes, similarly offer more fruitful possibilities for re-imagining architecture's role in a post-growth society.

Sergison Bates architects is a practice noted for the experiential richness it achieves through modest means and for a deep concern with the everyday. **Jonathan Sergison** offers a stark viewpoint from within architectural practice by examining connections between the building industry and broader financial contexts in differing European cultures, specifically the UK and Switzerland. The diminishing role of the architect in a UK building culture defined by risk management and sub-consulting to numerous building industry specialists – strategies adopted by the building industry to control costs – are here demonstrated to increase costs while arguably diminishing quality. Sergison's experiences suggest that where the architect still controls building work, as in Switzerland, projects achieve better value for money. Architects inescapably operate within the context of economic situations over which they have little or no control, but acknowledging this through a creative and informed response to financial pressures may permit a better project. Economy should always be considered, Sergison concludes: the design of buildings can and should be informed by the financial circumstances in which it is proposed.

Often, the pressures categorised by Sergison make architectural value seem little more than an 'optional extra'. **Mhairi McVicar**'s review of the design, construction of and reaction to the 1856 'Brompton Boilers' at what would become the Victoria and Albert Museum highlights a specific moment in the late nineteenth century in which the value of the architectural profession was significantly challenged by the pressures of an economically driven context. The relegation of architecture *per se* to a one line item in a specification – an optional 'architectural front' to be omitted if costs did not permit, in a significant civic project procured without architectural services – is linked here to concurrent architectural discourses that argued that architecture was necessarily embedded throughout all aspects of construction, and could not be distilled to façade treatment alone. The mid-nineteenth-century pressures upon architects to quantify the value of architecture within an economically minded context remain present in twenty-first century practice, highlighted by Caruso St John Architects' economic justification for the decorative civic façade in their 2006 entrance addition to the relocated Brompton Boilers at the Museum of Childhood in Bethnal Green.

The ongoing pressures for the architectural profession to quantify the value of architectural design amidst financial pressures are captured by **Silke Ötsch** in her analysis of professional architectural practices across Austria, France, the UK and the USA. Surveying the architectural profession through the lens of financial capitalism, Ötsch poses the question of whether the architectural profession itself will disappear through the misalignment of professional criteria with the expectations of financialisation. Observing that most of the architects surveyed in this research reported increasing financial pressures regarding costs, Ötsch highlights a subtle erosion of professional criteria, in which the criteria held dear to many architects

– design quality – is increasingly less financially rewarded, particularly within a weakening public sector. In a financialised economy, Ötsch suggests, the profession of the architect disappears or diversifies.

The first four chapters in this section consider the role, past and future, of the architectural profession in response to the pressures of a financialised economy. In the final paper here, the architect disappears altogether in the context of the rapidly evolving conditions of informal border economies. **Cristian Suau** discusses the instant urbanity generated by post-Fordist economies of production along the Pan-American highway, focusing on the US-Mexico and Peru-Chile borders. The conventional role of the architect or urban planner has no mention in 'instant urbanities' which adapt and change to evolving economic constraints and opportunities, seasonally, daily or even hourly. Neither residual not marginal, Suau suggests, these informal conditions in border towns and trans-urban corridors are the most dynamic sector of fast-growing economies in these regions, demanding similarly agile responses from design professions, if they are to participate at all.

11

SCARCITY CONSTRUCTS

Jeremy Till

When I first delivered a version of this chapter at the Economy and Architecture conference in Cardiff in July 2011, we had not had riots in London and other metropolitan centres, Greece had not yet defaulted and there were 'only' 100 food banks in the UK (against 400 in 2014). By the time you read this, a new collection of conditions that we had taken for granted as stable will have been dismantled and passed into the turbulence of contemporary society. There are of course innumerable factors that underlie this melting, but common to many of them of them are conditions of scarcity – of resources, of equity, of capital and so on. If the previous decade of the 2000s was defined by tales of abundance – or, as it turned out, false abundance – it is likely that the present one will be shaped by our response to conditions of scarcity. You might try to ignore it, or fight it – as Sartre says, 'the whole of human existence, at least up to now, has been a bitter struggle against scarcity'[1] – but increasingly scarcity is always going to be there. This suggests that in order to understand the conditions under which the built environment is produced, we are going to need a better understanding of scarcity, or more particularly the construction of scarcity.[2]

The discussion of scarcity is directly related to a collection of essays on economy because much economic thought has been based around conceptions of scarcity. As Andrew Simms of the New Economics Foundation notes: 'In the absence of scarcity no difficult choices would need to be made. No prices would have to be attached to anything. The study of economics would be rendered entirely unnecessary.'[3] Scarcity is entangled with economics, which in turn entangles architecture, and so in the age of scarcity we need to understand the operations of scarcity in order to understand the potential operations of architecture. To help in this, the chapter will focus on three key moments in the discussion of scarcity and economics: 1792 with Malthus, 1932 with Lionel Robbins and 1972 with the Club of Rome. Each of these three moments will be set against a contemporaneous episode in architecture. The idea is not to formulate causal links between the two, as if an economic theory of scarcity had a direct effect on the direction of architectural culture. The point is to suggest that in the conjunction of these economic and architectural episodes one can find analogies as to the way that methods, values and priorities are played out and spatialised as part of architecture's dialectical relationship with other societal forces. Through a better understanding of this relationship, the chapter ends with a speculation around how the contemporary constructions of scarcity might inform new spatial formations and agencies.

Episode 1: Malthus and Soane

Prior to the modern era, scarcity was a time-bound phenomenon in which cycles of seasons, weather and wars led to particular forms of lack. Scarcity was indeed experienced in terms of dearth, but as a localised, temporal and contingent condition it was very different from the essentialist formulations of scarcity that arose out of modernity.[4] The text that most definitively throws down the gauntlet of scarcity as an essential condition of modern life is the Reverend Thomas Malthus' *An Essay on the Principle of Population*.[5] Malthus' argument is straightforward: population grows at a geometric rate, food supply at an arithmetic rate; at a certain moment (the Malthusian point), population demand will exceed supply and the resulting scarcity will lead to famine; population growth must therefore be restricted in the face of the spectre of scarcity. In the first edition of the essay in particular, this argument was made more on the basis of hunch than empirical evidence, but nonetheless Malthus presented it as premise founded on evidence and logic. He tries hard throughout to distinguish his work from that of William Godwin, whose utopian views of equitable society Malthus was specifically targeting, 'pitting "facts" against "speculation", "science" against "fantasy"'.[6] Malthus thus gives his construction of scarcity a hard edge, one apparently based on reality, and this grants it both authority and objectivity. After Malthus, scarcity is accepted as an unavoidable fact, and one that has a profound effect on what became known as neo-classical economics.[7] Malthus can claim to be the world's first professional economist, with his appointment in 1805 to the Chair of Political Economy at the East India Company College.[8] Although in a later book, *Political Economy*, Malthus argues that he does not consider economics as a form of absolute knowledge, he does present it as a science. And within that science, scarcity is posited as something inevitable. He *naturalises* scarcity by lifting it out of human history and into crude formulae.

For the purposes of this essay what is of interest is less the specifics of the economic arguments and more the abstraction that Malthus initiates, and the shadows that hide beneath this abstraction. What we find behind the veil of logic and so-called objectivity is a deeply ideological text, which was to have direct political consequences. Malthus' rationalisation in favour of population restraint brings with it some unedifying arguments in relation to the poor. If one attempts to alleviate poverty, as was being proposed in the contemporaneous Poor Laws, then (he argued) population growth will follow, which in turn will lead to scarcities. Malthus' solution is to leave the poor alone: 'The poor are the arbiters of their own destiny', he writes, 'and what others can do for them is like dust in the balance compared to what they can do for themselves'.[9] Let scarcity regulate poverty, it is both the origin of poverty and the effective instrument against any population growth that might arise out of the alleviation of poverty. As David Harvey notes, for Malthus 'the only valid policy with respect to the lowest classes in society is one of "benign neglect"'.[10] This laissez-faire attitude to the poor, worrying enough in its own way, is also a lever for the exploitation of the poor because, as Malthus recognised, the poverty arising out of scarcity 'made the working class more willing to submit to wage labour'.[11] As Perelman notes, this association with the rise of capital and its exploitation of the working class, is hidden behind a stance of empirically grounded reason. 'Abstract principles allowed him to adopt a cover of scientific objectivity while his actual policy recommendations were tailored to the more immediate needs of capital.'[12] The immediate political consequences of Malthus' essay were very direct. The Poor Laws, which he had argued contributed to 'carelessness' among the poor, and a 'want of frugality', were repealed under the Malthusian threat of the population growth of a fecund proletariat.

The point is not to dwell here on this particular effect of Malthusian scarcity, but rather to identify how, under the cover of founding a discipline on apparently law-like principles, the political consequences and underlying ideologies are neatly masked. As Larry Lohmann puts it: 'Malthus's dry mathematics acted as a ritual denial of the discrimination in the terror myths and of the persecution that they both gilded and sanctioned.'[13] The framing of economics within a purportedly objective method, with an accompanying suppression of the political and human consequences, is the first Malthusian legacy, and one in which the frame becomes ever tighter with the rise of neo-classical economics. The second legacy is his naturalisation of scarcity as something that exists as a given and, as the harbinger of crisis, a fearful one at that. Human progress from now on is in thrall to scarcity, which is left unchallenged as a term. Both legacies are with us today. The first most clearly in the acceptance of neo-liberal principles of growth and market freedom as necessary conditions, the second in the way that scarcity as threat is used to drive environmental and political discussions.

We will return later to these Malthusian legacies, and their effect on the production of the built environment, but now need to turn to architecture, or more specifically to the architecture of John Soane. The aim is not to find causal links between Soane and Malthus (though it is tempting to draw implications from the presence of Malthus' *Essay* in Soane's library, one of only a very few books on economics or politics in a very extensive collection[14]), but to suggest how each are representative of, and to a certain extent responsible for, a particular tendency in their disciplines. Soane is a natural partner to Malthus for reasons over and above the convenient overlapping of their lives (Soane 1753–1837, Malthus 1766–1834) and of their great works (The Bank of England 1788–1833 and the six editions of the *Essay* 1798–1826); more it is their association with the neo-classical, not merely as a name but as the designation of the search for underlying and universal principles that can regulate and evaluate their respective disciplines.[15] In the case of economics, it is the rules of supply and demand within the context of scarce resources that become embedded in the core and ideology of mainstream economics. In the case of architecture, the basic tenets of proportional rules, standard relationships and a limited range of formal elements create a new 'language' of architecture. As David Watkin shows convincingly: 'Soane ... was more preoccupied than any other British architect with the ideals of ... the French Enlightenment'[16] – the context within which notions of the universal based on reason and nature were most clearly developed.

What is central to the understanding of these neoclassical tendencies is their universalising urge, lifting them above the specifics of historical or social contingency. Marx's critique of Malthus was based on exactly his dehistoricising of the conditions of scarcity; in essentialising scarcity Malthus had disconnected it from its conditions of production – from, as Perelman notes, 'the historically specific set of relations and forces of production, distribution, consumption, and so forth'.[17] In Soane's case, at least in the version of the man described by John Summerson, we get a proto-modern version of abstraction. 'Soane is remembered', Summerson argued, 'for his personal and unique mode of abstraction from neo-classicism'.[18] We have seen how Malthus used his abstracting approach to hide a deeply political agenda – Marx famously described him as 'a shameless sycophant of the ruling classes' – under the premise of a logic founded on empirical evidence. It would be wrong to find in Soane and his English architectural contemporaries quite such overt political associations, but what their mode of abstracted neo-classicism does is to initiate the removal of architecture from the immediate historical and therefore political conditions of its production. In the concentration on architecture as a form of universal language with a strong appeal to the internal senses, one can develop the discipline away from the contingencies of the external world, believing in architecture's completeness as an internalised discipline. But, as I have argued elsewhere,[19] this removal only operates conceptually; in reality politics are immanent to architecture, and in the case of the neo-classical it is easy to see how the politics of space are embedded in the architectural codes in the form of spatial control and power.

The obvious building to illustrate these analogous tendencies of Malthus and Soane is the Bank of England. Is there any building that better spatialises the machinations of early capital? A blind wall keeping innocent or prying eyes away from the internal workings, away from the high games of profit and loss, games hidden from public accountability. Within these walls nationhood is established on the principles of lucre rather than God, and Soane creates a mythical land of perfected antiquity to spatialise this financial heart of capital. Economics, partly thanks to the Reverend Malthus, is now established as a science, and this building is the laboratory where financiers experiment with the systems of money and Soane with the systems of architecture. And if Joseph Gandy's famous vision of the Bank of England as a ruin is intended to glorify Soane's masterpiece by situating it in the canon of the great ruins of antiquity, doesn't it also presciently suggest what happens when the experiments of capital get out of hand?

The clearest lesson that can be learnt from this first episode concerns the implications of abstraction. If the identification of the Malthusian point leads to the regulation of the scarcity through the abandonment of the poor and population control, then so be it; what the 'rules' produce emerges as a de facto truth that has overriding authority. The same can be seen in the identification of Soane as a proto-modernist, 'obsessed by the fundamentals of architecture, by the origins of architectural language and by the attempt to separate the essentials of architecture from the accidents of style'.[20] In the application of universal principles, the neoclassicist, architect and economist alike, relegate any particular social consequences beneath the quest for truth.

Episode 2: Robbins and Existenzminimum

We now move forward a century to the publication in 1932 of Lord Robbins' classic text *An Essay on the Nature and Significance of Economic Science*. In this essay, Robbins attempts once and for all to, in his words, 'arrive at precise notions concerning the subject matter of Economic Science'. Its first task, he says, 'is to *delimit* the subject matter of Economics'.[21] The word delimit is telling here, because its reductive stress draws a still tighter circle around the issues that economics can and cannot address.[22] Robbins arrives at his famous definition of economics in relation to scarcity early in the essay, and the rest is spent justifying his definition against others. 'Economics … is concerned with that aspect of behaviour which arises from the scarcity of means to achieve given ends. It follows that Economics is entirely neutral between ends.'[23] There is something shocking in the nonchalance of this conclusion, which sets out a very particular path in terms of the establishment of economics as a detached science. Robbins drives the point home later with his claim that, given this neutrality, the 'economist is not concerned with ends as such. He is concerned with the way in which the attainment of ends is limited'.[24] Again we have the disavowal of the consequences of economists' actions in their concentration on the operations of the economy, and not on the ends themselves. Such a disavowal was all too apparent during the build-up to the 2008 financial crisis, in which the complexity of the machinery of the banking system completely blinded its operators to taking into account the very human consequences of their actions. Bankers piled ever more complex financial instruments on top of one another, each with a peculiar logic of its own, but in combination hiding the fatal weakness of the impossibility of endless growth masking endless debt.

While it would be completely wrong to blame Robbins for setting the course towards economic collapse, he does establish a particular relationship of economics to scarcity, defining the former through the latter. Robbins' version of scarcity is relative, rather than the absolute one of Malthus.[25] By stating that the behaviour of *homo economicus* is defined by 'the relationship between ends and scarce means that have *alternative* uses', Robbins acknowledges the variable conditions of scarcity against which choices must be made. But whether absolute or relative, scarcity is, as with Malthus, naturalised as a condition, and so posited as inevitability.

It was this sense of the inevitability of lack that influenced the architectural discourse around the same time as Robbins' essay, and in particular the debate around the provision of mass housing in the 1920s and 1930s. The discussion is focused most clearly through the second CIAM congress of international architects held in Frankfurt in 1929, entitled *Die Wohnung für das Existenzminimum* (literally translated as The Subsistence Dwelling), which was subsequently recorded in a book of the same title. Faced with an unprecedented demand for housing, but against the backdrop of post-war scarcities, architects responded in two ways. First, through the development of plans for reduced space standards, and second through the employment of new industrialised technologies. As with Robbins, the scope of these investigations was delimited. Thus Karel Teige's *The Minimum Dwelling* opens with the words: 'Essentially, the housing question is a *problem of statistics and technology*, as is any question concerning the provision and satisfaction of human needs.'[26] Teige's directness is tempered in the language of other early modernists, who tied this technocratic regime into a wider project of social emancipation, but in all cases we can see parallels with the concurrent economic discourse.[27] As Siegfried Giedion notes in his opening address to the Frankfurt congress that at the first CIAM conference, 'it was settled that the prime task of the architect is to "bring himself into line with the times" ... Connection of architecture with economy could obviously not help being made the first point of the Programme.'[28] Just as Robbins' science of economics studies human behaviour in terms of need and desire in the context of scarcity, the new science of architecture takes human need in the context of imposed limits, and frames it in the quasi-scientific language that went hand-in-hand with the progressivist rhetoric of early modernism. Scarcity was seen as something that could be overcome through architectural ingenuity, rational thinking and technological advance. However, scarcity is still accepted as a given; removed from its social and political foundations it is treated as another abstracted problem for which to find another abstracted solution, as described by another of the CIAM congress speakers, the Belgian Victor Bourgeois. 'Architecture, owing to its close touch with experimental science, favours the analytical method, which proceeds from the investigation of facts to the formulation of rules.'[29] Such an attitude is shown most clearly in the diagrams of use within reduced space standards that were developed by architects such as Heinrich Leppla, Mart Stam and Johannes Van den Broek.[30] The removal of the underlying issue (scarcity) from its social and economic construction brings with it the detachment of the spatial solution from its social context. The abstraction of human existence into codes of activity might stand for social consequences in the mind of the modernist, but it is also severely reductive. This reduction is what the Brazilian architect Joan Vila implies in his droll but very precise criticism of *Existenzminimum*: 'They did the minimum and forgot the existence' – a warning that might apply equally to economics as it does to architecture.[31]

Despite this warning, one can see in this episode that an engagement with material and financial shortages was allied with attempts to find architectural values through the confrontation with scarcity. The technocratic and abstracted approaches that were used were part of a wider architectural project in which social progress, and its associated values, was allied to technical and architectural progress. Less is More, Mies van der Rohe's famous dictum, conjoins an aesthetic imperative with an economic condition to produce new forms of value. Although, as will be seen, the methods of dealing with contemporary conditions of scarcity need to be very different from Mies's, it is worth remembering the lesson that new values can be found through a constructive engagement with constraints.

Episode 3: the Club of Rome and early environmentalism

The next episode is marked by the publication of the report *Limits to Growth*, in 1972.[32] Commissioned by an informal group, The Club of Rome, as part of their 'Predicament of Mankind' project, the report was written by a group of systems dynamics experts, developing previous work done by Jay Forrester.[33] The group used very early computers to build a model called *World3*, which tracked the interaction between human and material systems. In nearly all cases, the model showed that, without adjustments to our present patterns of consumption and behaviour, the various systems would reach crisis sometime in the twenty-first century. It concluded that:

> If the present growth trends in world population, industrialisation, pollution, food production, and resource depletion continue unchanged, the limits to growth on this planet will be reached sometime within the next one hundred years. The most probable result will be a rather sudden and uncontrollable decline in both population and industrial capacity.[34]

At the time, and ever since, the report was criticised from all sides. Scientists noted mistakes in the computer modelling, systems analysts argued that the wrong data had been entered, traditional environmentalists took issue with the technocratic basis of the whole enterprise, Marxists criticised the lack of socio-economic analysis, and so on.[35] Despite these criticisms, the basic predictions made by the original authors have been shown to be impressively, and frighteningly, accurate 40 years later.[36] One criticism that does stick, however, is that the report re-introduces a Malthusian line of analysis – one of the essays criticising it is titled *Malthus with a Computer*[37] – and a Malthusian line of solution. The analysis is one of plotting growth against time, and then from the shape of the graph, predicting crisis. The solution is to impose 'deliberate constraints on growth'.[38] The authors of *Limits to Growth* do acknowledge that there will be social and political consequences arising out of those constraints, but nonetheless the overriding message is one of limit. The spectre of scarcity is raised ever higher in order to invoke systems of control, while not addressing the underlying causes of potential scarcity.

The same approach can be found in architectural approaches to environmentalism starting in the late 1960s and continuing through to today. Buildings are treated as technical instruments that can be tuned to control carbon emissions in particular. For example Alexander Pike's Autarkic House project in the early 1970s used basic computer modelling to design a house that could be completely free of mains services.[39] In the world of quantified limits presented by the Club of Rome, the only available response is one of control; buildings are reduced to their measurable aspects, technical objects isolated from wider systems. It is an approach inscribed in contemporary measures of architectural sustainability such as LEED and BREEAM, which regulate (in every sense of the word) the discourse around sustainability, and at the same time hold out the false promise that technical fixes alone will be able to mitigate underlying scarcities. This is not to argue, of course, that we should not be addressing issues of climate change as a matter of urgency, but it is to suggest that the dominant discourses around sustainability effectively essentialise scarcity, accepting it as an inevitable condition that can only be dealt with through the imposition of limits. What would have happened if, instead of following the path of technical instrumentalism, sustainability in architecture had more clearly developed the ideas and tools set out in Stewart Brand's *Whole Earth Catalog*, with its bottom-up and indeterminate approach based on cybernetic and ecological thinking?[40]

Episode 4: scarcity constructs

In all three of these briefly described episodes, what one encounters is how the conceptualisation of economics through scarcity is to a greater or lesser extent reflected in contemporaneous architectural approaches. Running through all three is the narrative that scarcity is an inevitable condition against which economic behaviour should be regulated and evaluated. This narrative has not disappeared in the dominant economic model of today, that of neo-liberal capitalism. In fact despite – or more precisely and exactly because of – the 2008 collapse, the spectre of scarcity is being used still more to establish the neo-liberal hold. The threat of scarcities, in terms of rising debt and falling collateral, is used continuously as the justification for, amongst many other things, spending cuts, with resulting growth of social inequality and the relaxation of environmental laws. Just as in Malthus' era, these deeply political acts are masked as the necessary, nay inevitable, consequence of scarcity. And just as with the Club of Rome, the spectre of scarcity is being used to sanction indiscriminate behaviour by nations and global corporations alike: oil is running out, therefore fracking is allowed, food is running out, therefore land grabs in Africa are seen as natural, and so on. And just as in Robbins, scarcity is depicted as the brake on growth and so action must be taken to take the foot off that brake in order to allow growth – the sine non qua of neo-liberal orthodoxy – to continue. And throughout all these consequences of scarcity are spatialised, as is shown so poignantly in the work of, among others, Mike Davies, David Harvey and Neil Smith, all of whom describe how the operations and effects of capital have clear spatial memes.

It is therefore the miserable pall attached to scarcity that needs to be most urgently addressed. Then, if my argument about the link of scarcity to architecture holds, new approaches and priorities for architects and designers will follow. First, scarcity has to be released from its position within neo-classical and neo-liberal economics, where it sits unchallenged as the determinant of economic decision-making. Far from being an essential and inevitable condition, scarcity must always be understood as constructed. Social, economic and political forces combine in various ways to create unequal distributions of resources and capital, and with this construct a landscape of scarcities. These scarcities are real (things really are running out) and their effects very palpable, but they arise out of human action and constructs. The implication for architects is that instead of dealing with the consequences of scarcity, mainly through limit and control, one's attention shifts to intervening in the way that scarcity is constructed. We address this in much more detail in the book *The Design of Scarcity*,[41] so for the purposes of this chapter I will conclude with some of the implications of an understanding of scarcity as constructed rather than inevitable, and the way these might impact on architecture.

The first implication of a re-described version of scarcity is a shift from exchange value to use value. When harnessed by economic thinking, scarcity is used to drive exchange value; the market controls supply and in making things scarce increases both desire and with it the economic value of commodities. The implications for the built environment are direct, with architecture seen solely as part of a system of commodity exchange, a market defined condition that it has become increasingly ensnared by. However, if scarcity is no longer defined by economics but understood as a social construction, then things, including buildings, rather than being described in terms of their exchange value, assume a livelier dynamic in terms of the way they are used and their social agency – and the mitigation of scarcity is effected not through the controls of commodity exchange, but through the way that we use things.

The second implication of scarcity as constructed is that it upsets the traditional human–nature dualism in which the natural world is seen as a standing reserve of resources that can be drawn on. In this model, pretty much the one described by the Club of Rome, future scarcity of resources is seen as inevitable. However, scarcity as constructed describes resources as more than simply fixed quantities of inert matter. In this light, oil for example may be limited, but it is only our human use of it that makes it potentially scarce. Far from a dualism, the human–nature relationship is one of interdependency, in which the use of resources in one sphere is tied in to the operation of the other sphere. Away from notions of a dualism, the built environment is now not considered as part of the unnatural sphere and therefore always the other of nature, but as part of a wider urban political ecology and sensitive to the relationships this sets up and the systems, natural and human, that it is embedded in. This is very different from the technically determined 'solutions' that are offered by some aspects of the current sustainability discourse.

The final and most obvious implication of new readings of scarcity is what it does to our understanding of growth, and in particular the neo-liberal addiction to the premise of endless growth. The age of scarcity ushers in a post-growth society in which design has to move from its default mode of just adding more stuff to the world. Architects and designers tend to define themselves through the production of the new, but as this becomes less tenable under conditions of scarcity, then one's creative attention has to shift in two directions. First to the redistribution and reinvention of what is there already, and second through the re-imagination of what is not yet there, in terms of new social and spatial configurations. Scarcity here is not seen as a shackle to the designer, but quite the opposite: it is a condition that invokes new ways of working and new creative approaches.

The three earlier episodes – the neo-classical universals and abstractions of Malthus and Soane, the limits and techniques of Robbins and the early modernists, and the neo-Malthusian tendencies of the Club of Rome and the early environmentalists – show analogies between the definitions of scarcity and the operations of architecture. In each case scarcity is defined through its relationship to economics, and so a chain from economy to architecture is established, restricting architecture to a particular set of values. My argument ends with a version of scarcity, and with it architecture, that is freed from a purely economic understanding. Only then can we find new forms of value, and with this fresh spatial thinking, that might allow us to imagine the new social formations that are so urgently needed in a post-growth society.

Notes

1. As quoted in: Nicholas Xenos, *Scarcity and Modernity* (London; New York: Routledge, 1989), p. 1.
2. The idea of the construction of scarcity is explored by Lyla Mehta in *The Limits to Scarcity: Contesting the Politics of Allocation*, ed. by Lyla Mehta (London: Earthscan, 2010).
3. Andrew Simms, *Economies of Scarcity*, Scarcity Exchanges, http://backdoorbroadcasting.net/archive/audio/2011_05_11/2011_05_11_ScarcityExchanges_AndrewSimms_talk.mp3 [accessed 22 August 2011].
4. See in particular: Xenos, Chapter 1.
5. T.R. Malthus, *An Essay on the Principle of Population* (Oxford: Oxford University Press, 1993). The essay was first published anonymously in 1798. Five years later, Malthus published a second edition under his own name, which was subsequently revised over five more editions. The difference between the first and second editions is the one most commented on: 'The basic shift was from the First Essay, a mainly deductive book of 55,000 words, to the Second Essay in which the expansion of theory and of illustrative data increased the work to 200,000 words.' W. Petersen, *Malthus* (Cambridge, MA: Harvard University Press, 1979), p. 53.
6. See Geoffrey Gilbert's introduction to: Malthus, p. x.
7. The relationship of Malthus to the development of neo-classical economics is disputed. For some the connection is direct, for others he was much less dogmatic than the eventual development of neo-classical economics, particularly in the version developed through Ricardo. Keynes famously hailed Malthus as pre-Keynesian. See Lionel Robbins, 'Malthus as an Economist', *The Economic Journal*, 77 (1967), 256–61 (p. 280); and Petersen, p. 68.
8. Petersen, p. 28.
9. This is a quote from the 1820 edition, p. 280.
10. David Harvey, 'Population, Resources, and the Ideology of Science', *Economic Geography*, 50 (1974), 256–77 (p. 260).
11. M. Perelman, 'Marx, Malthus, and the Concept of Natural Resource Scarcity', *Antipode*, 11 (1979), 80–91 (p. 81).

12 Perelman, p. 81.
13 Larry Lohmann, 'Malthusianism and the Terror of Scarcity', *Making Threats: Biofears and Environmental Anxieties*, ed. by Betsy Hartmann, Banu Subramaniam and Charles Zerner (London: Rowman & Littlefield, 2005), pp. 81–98 (p. 95).
14 Sir John Soane's Museum, *Catalogue of the Library of Sir John Soane's Museum* (London: Wyman and Sons, 1878).
15 It is, however, important to note that neither Soane nor Malthus postulated on pure universals. In Soane's case David Watkin notes:

> Soane's own position was ... self contradictory. On the one hand, he wanted to proclaim a set of universal axioms that would guarantee permanently correct proportions and on the other hand, he was deeply conscious of the contingency of our preferences conditioned, as they are, by accidents of climate and inherited assumptions.

John Soane, *The Royal Academy Lectures*, ed. by David Watkin (Cambridge: Cambridge University Press, 2000), p. 13. In Malthus' case, one of things that Keynes respected was this same tension:

> Malthus was one of the 'brave army of heretics ... who, following their intuitions, have preferred to see truth obscurely and imperfectly rather than to maintain error, reached indeed with clearness and consistency and by easy logic, but on hypothesis inappropriate to the facts'.

As quoted from *The General Theory* in Petersen, p. 86.
16 David Watkin, *Sir John Soane: Enlightenment Thought and the Royal Academy Lectures* (Cambridge: Cambridge University Press, 1996), p. 1.
17 Perelman, p. 86.
18 John Summerson, *Architecture in Britain, 1530 to 1830* (New Haven, CT: Yale University Press, 1993), pp. iii, 470.
19 Jeremy Till, *Architecture Depends* (Cambridge, MA: MIT Press, 2009).
20 Watkin, p. 10.
21 Lionel Robbins, *An Essay on the Nature and Significance of Economic Science* (London: Macmillan, 1932), p. 1, my emphasis.
22 This delimiting was one of the aspects of the essay that was subsequently criticised, and answered (not entirely satisfactorily) by Robbins in the preface to the second edition. Robbins did later recant on the dogmatism of the *Essay*, saying he had 'become the slave of theoretical constructions which ... were inappropriate ... the theory was inadequate to the facts'. As quoted in: Ben Fine, 'Economics and Scarcity', *Limits to Scarcity*, ed. by Lyla Mehta (London: Earthscan, 2010), pp. 73–91 (p. 77).
23 Lionel Robbins, p. 40.
24 Lionel Robbins, p. 41.
25 See: A. Daoud, 'Robbins and Malthus on Scarcity, Abundance, and Sufficiency', *American Journal of Economics and Sociology*, 69 (2010), 1206–29.
26 Karel Teige, *The Minimum Dwelling*, 1st edn (Cambridge, MA: MIT Press, 2002), p. 9, original emphasis.
27 Hilde Heynen is particularly good on the intersection of the social, the aesthetic and the technological within the wider context of economic crisis in the period of the *Das Neue Frankfurt*, out of which *Existenzminimum* arose. Hilde Heynen, *Architecture and Modernity: A Critique* (Cambridge, MA: MIT Press, 1999), pp. 43–50.
28 Ernst May, *Die Wohnung für das Existenzminimum* (Frankfurt: Englert & Schlosser, 1930), p. 8 (in English summary at end of book). CIAM denotes Congrès internationaux d'architecture modern, or International Congresses of Modern Architecture.
29 May, p. 8.
30 Tatjana Schneider and Jeremy Till, *Flexible Housing* (Oxford: Architectural Press, 2007), p. 16.

31 In a talk at the 4th Annual Colloquium on Housing Research, Belo Horizonte, Brazil, 14 August 2007.
32 Donella Meadows, Dennis Meadows, Jørgen Randers and William Behrens, *The Limits to Growth: A Report for the Club of Rome's Project on the Predicament of Mankind* (London: Universe Books, 1972).
33 Jay W. Forrester, *World Dynamics* (Cambridge, MA: Wright-Allen Press, 1971).
34 Meadows *et al.*, p. 23.
35 Many of the positions are included in: *Thinking about the Future: A Critique of the Limits to Growth*, ed. by H.S.D. Cole Christopher Freeman, Marie Jahonda and K.L.R. Pavitt (London: Chatto & Windus, 1973). It should be noted that the authors of the report are quite open about the limits of their own method.
36 G. Turner, *Is Global Collapse Imminent?*, MSSI Research Paper (University of Melbourne: Melbourne Sustainable Society Institute, 2014).
37 Christopher Freeman, 'Malthus with a Computer', *Futures*, 5 (1973), 5–13.
38 Meadows *et al.*, pp. 158–169.
39 John Littler and Randall Thomas, *Design with Energy: The Conservation and Use of Energy in Buildings* (Cambridge: Cambridge University Press, 1984).
40 See for one possible answer: Simon Sadler, 'An Architecture of the Whole', *Journal of Architectural Education*, 61 (2008), 108–29.
41 Jon Goodbun, Michael Klein, Andreas Rumpfhuber and Jeremy Till, *The Design of Scarcity* (Moscow: Strelka Press, 2014).

12
ECONOMY OF MEANS

Jonathan Sergison, Sergison Bates architects LLP

FIGURE 12.1 Bricklayer, Crediton Road

Source: Photograph by Emiel Koole.

For anyone involved in the building industry, the past few years have offered a stark reminder of the inextricable link between construction and the wider economic circumstances in which it operates. The causes of the last global recession were not directly attributed to the UK economy but the manner in which it affected it, and the building industry in particular, was very evident.

When we refer to a period of recession or economic prosperity the differences in production are not so wildly different. Where the impact is felt, it is in relation to numbers of people employed and salary levels achieved.

Speculation on the future economic stability of the building industry is a topic that constantly occupies the architectural press and this is understandable because, whatever part we play in this industry, our circumstances will be affected in ways we can exercise very little influence over.

This chapter will address the notion of economy in relation to two discrete and overlapping themes. In the first instance, economic factors will be considered in relation to the wider economic circumstances. It will explore the role architecture plays within an evolving building industry and will draw upon the experience of operating within different European building cultures.

Second, economy will be considered in relation to the role architects are required to play in terms of reconciling creative ambition with the financial responsibilities and pressures that are exerted upon practice as a business. This will lead to a speculation on future practice and on the forms and models that it might be compelled to adopt in the future.

Economy will also be considered at a conceptual level in terms of the manner in which the design of buildings can and should be informed by the financial circumstances in which it is situated. Consideration will be given to the way that a contemporary building should respond to the needs of the brief and clients' needs but also be aware of the local conditions of the building industry in terms of finding locally available building materials and employing known forms of construction.

Building/industry

It is sometimes difficult to understand the process of constructing buildings as an industry. The word 'industry' implies a sense of organisation, efficiency and the need for coordination between a set of complex disparate elements. Today, the process of building is messy, and rather than craft, it involves assembling prefabricated elements. The servicing of buildings is the one area where a greater degree of complexity has evolved in the past 50 years, but generally the skill level in most building trades has declined.

The role of the architect has also shifted considerably over the past 50 years: while architects are still able to generate forms and affect the appearance of buildings, their role in managing the process of building has, likewise, greatly diminished.

The emergence of other building-industry consultants, project managers, quantity surveyors, in addition to the increased role of engineers, facade consultants, interior designers and landscape architects means that aspects of the work that an architect traditionally had a competence to perform are now undertaken by other parties. Arguably, in the case of large and complex construction projects, this ever-growing structure of consultants means that responsibility is diffuse and often unclear. Experience, however, often demonstrates that this is not necessarily the case, and certainly accounting for the fees commanded by all these parties means a significant increase in the cost of building.

When I look out over London, a city that in the past 20 years has experienced a time of economic prosperity and has built at a significant scale – notwithstanding the more recent economic slowdown – what I see realised in terms of general urban and architectural quality is, frankly, quite poor. A great opportunity has been squandered, and I feel this to be true of other places, too. My numerous journeys through the United Kingdom and continental Europe lead me to the same conclusion: that contemporary buildings are infinitely worse than the building stock that predates them, particularly pre-twentieth-century buildings. And when we understand that more has been built in the world in our time than at any point in the whole of history, the scale of the problem becomes evident.

While it is clear that architects can not be expected to work in the same manner they came to enjoy at the end of the nineteenth and beginning of the twentieth century, I do attribute the lack of quality in contemporary construction to the ascendency of these other contributors to the process of building. For many of them the management of risk – be it financial or general building performance – and the achieving of often very tight programmes far outweighs all other considerations, among them design quality.

All buildings contain embodied energy and consume energy in their daily life. Experience also demonstrates that buildings tend to last considerably longer than their predicted life expectancy. The emergence of new building industry-related professions can, on occasion, have a negative impact on the quality of the built environment. In my experience, project managers often know little about construction, although their services come at a high price, with the result that, rather than save money, they significantly add to the cost of building in the UK.

Now, it is unreasonable to make such great generalisations without giving evidence to support these claims, and I will do so by drawing upon what I trust – our own experience.

In 1999 we were a young architectural practice who had built a number of one-off, somewhat prototypical projects. We were invited to work on the extension and refurbishment of a former industrial building in southwest London. Our client, an architect by training, was a very careful developer with a few successful projects to his name. Unusually, he combined an ambition to make a profit with a belief in producing good architecture. This means he was not overly influenced by what is produced by rival conservative, risk-averse volume house builders.

The greatest financial risk for this project – given its unconventional character – was the protracted planning period. Consent was eventually won through the appeal process, and this meant that our client had to invest many thousands of pounds to achieve what seemed a very uncertain outcome. This is not an unusual experience in this country: risk and uncertainty attract costs, and compel developers to consider exposure to risk carefully, often by sharing this burden with architects, among others. Uncertainty contributes to driving the overall cost of a project up, and consequently affects the price a home will be sold for.

Eventually the project in Wandsworth was developed using a traditional form of contract and project management structure. A very experienced and reasonable quantity surveyor was employed. There was no project manager. We produced a specification and a carefully coordinated set of drawings and the quantity surveyor produced a measured bill of quantities. The project cost £1,071 per m². Every flat sold before the building was completed and the developer made a very healthy profit. In this instance our client was able to support a project that was architecturally ambitious, well-built and good value for money.

More recently, in 2004, we won a bid for a site in north London together with a housing association we had previously worked with. This meant competing on the open market against other housing associations and private housing developers. The bid was successful because we were ambitious in terms of the density we believed reasonable and appropriate for this site, so that the housing association was able to make a higher bid than the parties who took a more conservative view of the site's potential.

Securing planning permission for this project, however, was not straightforward. Experiencing difficulty in obtaining planning consent is the norm rather than the exception for projects across the city, and yet London has an enormous need for new homes. From an analysis of housing statistics from the Department for Communities and Local Government (DCLG) and Greater London Authority, London Councils (the body that represents 33 local authorities) found that 526,000 new homes would need to be built between 2011 and 2021 in London just to keep up with current housing demand. Scarce supply against strong demand explains the incredible rise in house prices London has witnessed in the past 15 years. The government has a very *laissez-faire* attitude to this problem. Many developers are sitting on sites that they paid too much for, but know will be worth considerably more in the future. Foreign investors see central London as a financially lucrative market and they are buying much of the building stock. The result, however, is that these properties often remain empty, and the people who make the city work and function are unable to afford to buy or rent a home near their place of work.

In Zurich and other Swiss cities, unless you occupy a flat as your primary residence, you simply cannot buy or rent it. Zurich also has a housing shortage, but the increase in property prices is relatively low and stable. The Swiss housing market is regulated and controlled by legislation, and as a result does not follow the boom-and-bust model that is typical of the UK. The Swiss economy operates with a degree of autonomy and independence from the European Union and this attitude is applied to building and homeownership.

This point can be made most clearly by reference to attitudes to home ownership. In the UK owning a house is considered desirable, but it is also an economic necessity. To illustrate the case, suffice it to say that the average cost of a house in the UK was £58,611 in 1977, which had risen to £189,316 by 2006, and hit £250,000 in February 2014, having risen by 8.4 per cent just over the past year. Currently the increase in value year on year of a property is often greater than the salary of the people who own it.

In Zurich – as in many other continental European cities – many years have been devoted to developing an urban plan that is democratically approved. This means that it takes time to change this plan, but developers are never in any doubt as to what volume it is possible to construct on any given site, at a given moment in time. This allows them to quantify building potential, and thus the biggest element of risk is removed.

It is during the planning period that architects working in the UK have the most influence. This was certainly the case with the north London project I referred to earlier. The housing association relied on us to develop a project and make the necessary argument to secure consent with the local planning authority. Planning consultants have knowledge of planning legislation, but negotiation requires an ability to evaluate when to compromise and when to stand firm, and they cannot do this.

Once planning permission was secured, a contractor was appointed and the design-and-build contractual arrangement followed. This meant that the contractor was our client. Fortunately for us, they were inexperienced, and we were able to persuade them to build things that other contractors would not have accepted. We wanted to make a decent, well-detailed building that would last for many years.

A contractor generally manages many sub-contractors and sub-sub-contractors. The contractor for the first project I described had a workforce that they had trained themselves, and many trades were sourced through their own organisation. In the case of the second project, this was not the case. A number of surveyors and estimators were employed to get everything as cheaply as possible. In fact, the project cost £4.8 million, which represents £1,771 per m².

A smaller project in north London reinforces my point. A contractor that has been building in this part of London for almost 200 years built this project to a very high standard. Nearly all their workforce have been employed and trained by them since leaving school. The project area is 670 m², and it cost £800,000 to build, i.e. £1,194 per m².

To widen the scope of this story, I would like to draw upon our experience of working on a number of projects in continental Europe. The difficulty in using these for comparative purposes is that at today's exchange rate the pound is constantly fluctuating. Therefore, I am going to refer to the exchange rate that was applicable at the time the projects were costed.

Our recently completed project for the city library in Blankenberge, Belgium – which was very complicated in terms of its construction sequence and was built to the high standard expected for a public building – cost £1,092 per m². The only public building project we have built in the UK was in North Wales and cost £1,915 m² (and this was seen as representing very good value for money). The Nottingham Contemporary, for example, cost almost double this.

We recently completed a care home, again in Belgium, to a high specification and with high standards of workmanship at a cost of £795 per m². Standards of living in the UK and Belgium are comparable, as is the cost of raw materials, so how can it cost half as much to build something that is better quality?

With this question in mind, I would like to turn to the country whose building industry and architectural culture we know best outside of the UK, notably Switzerland. In fact, we have a studio in Zurich to help run the projects we have there. A project we completed in 2012 in Geneva includes a crèche for the local community, which is paid for by the city, and an 18-apartment housing project funded by the local equivalent of a housing association. This project is on a very tight and important urban site. It has the most complex prefabricated concrete panels we have ever proposed, and they were built with a high level of tolerance and coordination. The cost of this project was £795 per m^2. How can this be?

The answer to the questions lies in the role architects play. Swiss architects are responsible for producing cost information within a very well structured convention. In addition, they are also responsible for coordinating work on site. This means being responsible for ensuring that the different building trades are on site at the right time and that their work is well executed.

In many ways, this describes what seems a very old approach to building. The case for removing architects from this area of professional involvement was made in relation to competence, but I believe that clients are paying considerably more than they should as a result of 'hidden' management costs. In other words, clients in the UK are paying a very high price for cost and programming certainty. Our experience of working in continental Europe is that, where the architect is still controlling building work, costs are considerably reduced.

And when we look at the evidence in terms of public finance initiatives, where profit margins are typically between 7.5 and 15 per cent (compared to an industry standard of 1.5 to 2 per cent), this really is a scandal.

The UK construction industry represents about 10 per cent of the country's gross domestic product. It employs 1.9 million people and is worth a staggering £65 billion, ranking among the top 10 in the world. Taking all these factors into consideration, it is far-fetched to imagine that things are going to change for our profession. Too many other people are making too much money.

The service sector

Architectural practice is part of the largest employment category, the service sector. In the UK this represents 76.7 per cent of the total workforce. In Switzerland this figure stands at 73.2 per cent. In the UK we work the longest number of hours per week, currently an average of 42.4 hours – longer than any other country in the Western world. I do not have figures for the average working week for architects, but I am sure we contribute to distorting it.

In Switzerland this average is also quite high, 41.6 hours per week. But Switzerland is one of the world's most stable economies. The average per capita income is high, and unemployment is low.

Architects in Switzerland are well paid and their jobs are relatively secure. Inflation is stable and the graph of house price increases is almost a straight line.

If you were looking to make short-term financial gains from property and were attracted to a high-risk model, you would not find Switzerland attractive.

Swiss architects are well trained by the three federal schools of architecture: ETH Zurich, EPFL Lausanne and the Accademia di Architettura in Mendrisio. There are also a number of excellent technical schools of architecture. The competition system is well organised and flexible, so that the appropriate procedure can be applied to any given situation. Clients tend to be aware of the need to be accountable to society and recognise that something well-built will last for a very long time. In contrast to this, the British tend to consider capital costs and financial returns as a much bigger priority.

The SIA (Swiss Engineers' and Architects' Institute) has developed a very reasonable and robust fee charging structure. There are a number of factors that need to be agreed (degree of difficulty, building type and applicable hourly rates), but it is recognised that architects perform a complex and demanding role in the making of buildings, and should be remunerated accordingly.

This is a very different situation from that we encounter in the UK. The need to negotiate fees, rather than employ a standardised fee structure in this uncertain market ensures that clients get a cheap service, although not always a good one.

In our projects in other European countries we have on occasion been taken aback by the respect and expectation of leadership we have encountered. With this sense of expectation comes a great sense of responsibility. The ideas we generate and the decisions we make have a profound impact on many hundreds, sometimes thousands of people. We are very aware of this and take our responsibilities very seriously. However, it is much more pleasant to work in an environment where you are valued as a qualified practitioner with the ability to make a useful contribution to society rather than have your skills considered frivolous.

I am concerned, however, that the training students receive – particularly in many UK schools – is seriously inadequate. Architectural education is expensive, but if it is not useful, it will be of questionable value to the profession and to society. If it is to have a future, the profession of architecture needs to consider very carefully its own value and usefulness.

I wish I could offer you brilliant insights and a vision for the future. I do know that I would not want to set up in practice again today.

The model of practice we use is a rather well known one. We undertake one-off projects. We do not have a large client base and most of our work in recent years has been won through one form of competition or another.

We have never done anything that we are not proud of, although some projects have more architectural potential than others. We are running an architectural studio, but it is also a business that employs between 15 and 20 people, and this is in itself a big responsibility. In time, we have learnt lessons and developed systems for running our business. If our first intention had been to make a lot of money, we would not be using this model, which is too limited and too risky.

To conclude, I would like to make a few points in relation or in addition to what I have been trying to address:

- Architectural practice is inextricably linked to a much, much bigger economic situation, one that we have an almost negligible capacity to affect.
- In our experience, the pressure to make savings on a project, while requiring more time to explore how such savings can be achieved and therefore affecting the profitability of our fees, has often resulted in a better project.
- Architectural practice is a business that offers a degree of choice in terms of the model that can be adopted but, with the changes occurring so widely in the building industry, it is necessary for architects to consider carefully their relevance and where they can meaningfully operate.
- Economy should always be considered: the design of buildings can and should be informed by the financial circumstances in which it is proposed.
- Consideration should be given to the way a contemporary building can respond to the brief and the client's requirements, but we should also be aware of the local conditions of the building industry, of locally available building materials and known forms of construction. While architects secretly yearn to be innovators, this always involves a greater level of risk and financial uncertainty than tried-and-tested models.

13

AN OPTIONAL EXTRA

Valuing architecture at the
Brompton Boilers

Mhairi McVicar

> The cost of the building as above specified, and shown in accompanying drawings would be about nine thousand eight hundred pounds (£9,800); if, with an architectural front of cast iron from £1,000 to £1,400 additional, according to design.[1]

The statement above is an excerpt from a written specification for the Iron Museum, a three-bay iron structure designed and constructed in 1856 in London by a firm specialising in prefabricated iron structures, Charles Denoon Young and Company. Constructed as the first, albeit temporary, addition to Brompton Park House as part of the newly created South Kensington Museum (later renamed the Victoria and Albert Museum, or V&A) the structure, originally clad in painted corrugated iron, was dismantled in 1867 following public derision and maintenance problems. Upon its relocation to Bethnal Green to form what would eventually become the Bethnal Green Museum of Childhood, Victorian architect J.W. Wild's proposals for an expansive entrance addition were rejected amidst cost concerns, and a much-reduced and comparatively utilitarian entrance constructed instead. In 2006, Caruso St John Architects were selected to finally provide the civic frontage the Museum had hitherto lacked in its previous iterations. Describing their proposals for a decorative CNC stone façade,[2] and acknowledging Wild's modelled brick façade beyond, Caruso St John wrote:

> In the 19th century such decoration was carried out by hand. With the rise of industrialised processes in the building crafts, so decoration became prohibitively expensive. However, with recent advances in computer controlled stone cutting it is again possible to achieve complex decorations at an affordable price.[3]

The relationship between economy and value highlighted here – the relationship between the cost concerns underpinning any architectural project and the desire to provide an appropriately civic architectural response – was uniquely emphasised in mid-nineteenth-century responses to the Iron Museum in its original form. Embodying both the promises and fears offered by the output of the Industrial Revolution, and following the recent precedent of Joseph Paxton's 1851 Crystal Palace, contemporary critiques of the 1856 Iron Museum highlighted the challenge of arguing the value of architecture in an economically minded context. This chapter examines the mid-nineteenth-century context of the design of the Iron Museum and its implications for an architectural profession attempting to quantify its own value.

'An architectural front'

Known more derisively as the 'Brompton Boilers'[4] following its initial construction, the Iron Museum was conceived following the varied acclaim and critique of Joseph Paxton's Crystal Palace of the 1851 Great Exhibition. Nicholas Pevsner has described the Crystal Palace as 'the mid-nineteenth century touchstone' for three reasons which the Iron Museum replicated.[5] As with the Crystal Palace, the Iron Museum was not designed by an architect; it was constructed using industrial materials and processes; and it was designed for industrial quantity production of its parts – factors that were reviewed as either offering an innovative way forward for the architectural profession, or alternatively as representing the end of craftsmanship, and of architecture itself. The written specification that accompanied its proposal embodies a particular concern identified by critics of the Iron Museum. In offering an 'architectural front of cast iron from £1,000 to £1,400 additional, according to design', this specification categorically reduced architecture to an optional extra: a luxury to omit if costs did not permit. This one line captures the precarious position of a developing architectural profession in the mid-nineteenth century as it debated the value of architecture within an economically minded context, a debate that has continued to shape the architectural profession in the 100 years spanning the original 1856 construction of the Iron Museum and Caruso St John's 2006 Bethnal Green addition.

The value of the Iron Museum

When the Royal Commission for the Exhibition of 1851 recommended the establishment of an institution 'to extend the influence of Science and Art upon productive Society',[6] the Commissioners, headed by HRH Prince Albert, initially approached the German architect Gottfried Semper to prepare plans for buildings on the Great Exhibition site of Brompton Park House. When the Commissioners rejected plans and a cardboard model submitted by Semper as 'financially impracticable',[7] Prince Albert instead proposed the erection of a temporary iron house. Four days later, the 1851 Commissioners received a written specification from Charles

Young and Company[8] concisely specifying the Iron Museum as 'in form, 266 feet long, and 126 feet broad, and about 30 feet high to the eaves'.[9] The remainder of the specification outlined the dimensions and quantity of stairs, ventilators, windows and doors and proposed a finish of 'three coats of oil paint', concluding with a cost of £9,800, not including the optional extra of the 'architectural front'. In a report by the Commissioners of the 1851 Exhibition, the efficiency and economy of the proposal was highlighted:

> Irrespective of its simplicity and cheapness and the remarkable facility with which it can be constructed, it enjoys the great advantage, in a pecuniary point of view, of being designed of a material which possesses a permanent pecuniary value, to which the cost of the labour employed in its construction bears only a small proportion. While, therefore, it could on the one hand be taken down and re-erected if necessary, on another site, or in another form, at a very trifling expense, it could, on the other hand, be resold, should circumstances render it hereafter desirable, at no great deterioration of value.[10]

The Commissioners here defined value strictly in economic terms – a fast, cheap and re-usable solution, using a material that had been claimed as embodying an original and innovative future for an architectural profession struggling to define, to an 'economy minded public',[11] its value amidst claims of retrogression and costliness (Figure 13.1).

FIGURE 13.1 Exterior view of the South Kensington Museum (the 'Brompton Boilers') under construction, looking south with the houses of Cromwell Road and Thurloe Square visible in the background, 1856

The promise of iron

'For three centuries', an 1843 article in the Victorian journal *The Builder* proposed, 'we have been flitting about, reviving old styles, but settling upon none, as indeed was certain to be the result, for nations do not make steps in retrogression'. Adapt your buildings, the article continued, to the specific need, the location and the materials available, and a contemporary and unique style would naturally emerge. 'To iron, then, we look, as the determining circumstance in our career as an original architectural people',[12] *The Builder* concluded. Iron, initially overlooked by architects since its first structural application at Coalbrookdale Bridge in 1777, had recently been brought forth as a significant architectural element at Henri Labrouste's 1843 Bibliothèque Ste-Geneviève in Paris. An 1846 series of lectures given at the Royal Arts by Professor of Architecture C.T. Cockerell now declared iron to be the 'osteology of building'. Our buildings, Cockerell proposed, 'would have bones, giving unity and strength which never before existed'.[13] In separating structure from skin, iron, *The Builder* reported, would, for the first time, allow architects to exhibit 'abundant originality',[14] freeing architects from a cyclical debate over which historical style they should adopt. Paxton's Crystal Palace was, in this light, hailed by some critics as embodying a revolutionary approach to architecture, satisfying unprecedented economic expectations by embodying the materials and efficiencies of the Industrial Revolution.

The production of the Crystal Palace

Described as 'the first clear architectural application of Adam Smith's division of labour',[15] the Crystal Palace, requiring 800,000 square feet – 'a space between three and four times as large as that occupied by any previous exhibition abroad'[16] – had required planning and execution on an industrial scale from its earliest inception. An invitation for architects to provide 'suggestions for the general arrangements' required for the Exhibition had received 233 designs and specifications, none of which were considered to satisfy either the 'principle or detail' of the brief.[17] 'Plans of an architectural character were generally too monumental, too much divided, and far too expensive',[18] the Commissioners concluded: none of the architectural proposals had resolved the unprecedented demands of an industrial scale, temporary nature and speed of construction. The solution instead emerged from landscaper Joseph Paxton's experience in the standardised industrial production of glass-houses, and engineer–contractors Fox and Henderson's experience of railway building.[19] A 1851 review of the Crystal Palace in *The Builder* praised, in addition to its grandeur and magnificence, its correctness, regularity and the simplification and repetitiveness of construction processes in a structure assembled by men 'working like ants'.[20] Although the architectural profession's involvement was limited to the margins of refinement and interior colour schemes,[21] for *The Builder* the application of industrial materials and processes embodied a new architecture freed from historical constraints.[22] For others, such as critic John Ruskin, the Crystal

Palace signalled the end of craftsmanship as the primary mode of cultural production, the end of the appreciation of aesthetic value and a significant challenge to the relevance of the architectural profession to an economy minded context.[23] Such criticisms would be central to the profession's overwhelming rejection, only five years later, of the Iron Museum at Brompton Park (Figure 13.2).

The production of the Iron Museum

'Its ugliness is unmitigated', *The Builder* concluded of the Iron Museum at Brompton Park House in South Kensington. 'Railway sheds and locomotive depots often have some little bit of art or taste about them, but here there is nothing: up one side and down the other, all is blank and offensive.'[24] Central to *The Builder*'s critique was the omission of a professional architect, *The Builder* charged, from a process focused on economy in lieu of design: 'On such a system, in place of a process of art, the production of this museum building was a matter of mere multiplication, and the employment of trade-capital.'[25]

The Builder's review was not a rejection of iron itself, but an accusation of the omission of architectural value. 'The fact that iron has great capabilities is

FIGURE 13.2 Exterior view of the south front entrance of the South Kensington Museum (the 'Brompton Boilers'), 1862

understood and acted upon', *The Builder* continued, 'but, both in structure and decoration, iron has been grievously misused, and by those who assumed to know better than others its advantages'.[26] At the core of *The Builder*'s complaints was the cladding of a civic museum in corrugated iron, which, they argued, was unacceptable given the civic value of this emerging national museum.[27] The Iron Museum, on the one hand adopting materials and processes that had so recently promised an innovative future for architecture, simultaneously manifested the fears of a newly self-defined architectural profession: that the architect, and architecture itself, could become superfluous in a building culture focused on the values of efficiency and economy.

The role of the architect in the nineteenth century

In the mid-nineteenth-century context, the rise of Master Builders[28] and the adoption of 'Contracts by Gross' had significantly changed design and construction processes. Superseding the trade guilds, Master Builders had emerged out of the prosperity of the early nineteenth century. In the space of half a century, E.W. Cooney observes, 'an industry which had been organised primarily on a craft basis had, without the stimulus of any technological advances, thrown up a group of large, complex and markedly capitalist businesses'.[29]

It was economy, not technological advances, suggests Cooney, that was the catalyst for the emergence of the Master Builder and the deterioration of the Guilds. The adoption of the 'Contract by Gross' – a contract in which a builder agreed a predetermined price for the construction of an entire building – exemplified a growing demand amongst an 'economy minded public' for cost certainty on large public works. During the first half of the nineteenth century, Cooney writes, 'the industry's customers, including public bodies, came to believe that competitive tendering with fixed costs could offer the best basis by which to undertake building works'.[30] Vigorous debates followed over the implications the Contract by Gross would have upon craft, quality in architecture and role of the architectural profession. A fact sorely and frequently lamented by architects throughout the nineteenth century, M.H. Port observes, was the steady decline in the standards of building craftsmanship.[31] In an 1812–1813 Parliamentary Select Committee Report, the architect of the British Museum, George Saunders, warned against inevitable erosion in quality and care if tradesmen were selected by a Master Builder intent on making a profit under a low tender. The architect, Saunders argued, in having no direct control over the Trades, would be powerless to control quality on site, and forced to redirect control through increased precision in the specifications given to the Master Builder. 'No specification for a contract in the gross, however long', Saunders testified, 'has ever yet been found sufficient to ensure a due execution of what is requisite; except in very small, plain or rough Works'.[32] Sufficiently precise specifications for sufficiently precise cost certainty would be possible, in these terms, only at a cost of architectural simplicity and plainness. This accusation not only places the hostile reviews of the 1856 Iron Museum and its corrugated iron cladding into context, but also laid the foundations for an ongoing debate in which the architectural profession would be compelled to argue its value beyond that of supplying, as an optional extra, a decorative façade.

The place of economy in architecture

The absence of an architect at both the Crystal Palace and the Iron Museum reflected, in each case, a schism between the values of the architects and the values of the client. In each case, the value offered by architects was resolutely rejected as failing to provide value in economic terms. Varying definitions of economy and value have always shaped the character of the architectural profession: from Vitruvius' proposal that architects should hold personal liability for cost-overruns as a means of ensuring care in calculating and stating the limits of expenses,[33] to Le Corbusier's declaration 'everything in architecture is expressed by order and economy'.[34] All works of architecture have always been shaped as much by economic parameters as by conceptual intentions. Yet the definition of value so clearly highlighted in the Iron Museum specification – value specifically defined by quantitative measures of economy in lieu of architectural quality – can perhaps be understood within a nineteenth-century cultural context as the culmination of 300 years of the disembodiment and abstraction of measure applied to concepts of value.

In a post-Galilean context, in which the certainty of quantitative measure had sought to replace the uncertainty of qualitative human senses, architectural measure had been redefined in the seventeenth century as an applied science devoid of its historical metaphysical implications,[35] embodied by Durand's *Précis des Leçons* curriculum at the École Polytechnique,[36] which had emphasised mathematic reasoning over the arts and humanities by promoting building technology and delegating the 'art' of architecture to ornament and decoration as a sub-discipline of civil engineering.[37] Durand emphatically rejected ornament as 'an accessory decoration',[38] proposing that beauty would emerge from the rationalisations and simplifications demanded by economy.[39] Viewed thus, architecture was faced with the challenge of defining its value as intrinsically embedded within rationalised systems, or facing delegation as either, as Alberto Perez Gomez and Louise Pelletier have argued, a 'prosaic technological process or mere decoration'.[40] The varied reactions of an emerging mid-nineteenth-century architectural profession to the economy-driven processes behind the Crystal Palace, and, subsequently, the Iron Museum and its optional architectural front, can be viewed, in this context, as a battle to define the value of architecture as substantially more than either a prosaic process or mere decoration.

The value of architecture

The question of value was at the heart of an architectural profession in the process of defining itself following the formation of the British Institute of Architects in

1834.[41] An 1891 opening address from RIBA president John Macvicar defining the architect as 'artist, constructor and man of affairs'[42] encapsulated concerns that proposed regulation of the profession to counteracting widespread title could examine only quantifiable factors – business and economics – and set aside the unquantifiable values of design. The Memorialists' opposition of regulation, published as the essays *Architecture: A Profession or an Art*,[43] set out the fear that architecture, subject to examinations and defined by formulae, would become 'a dull, lifeless thing of no value to any one'.[44] Art, the Memorialists held:

> Is not an ornamental something – a gilding or a varnish – which may be laid upon bare construction and so transform it into architecture. It is an influence, a motive, that must reign supreme from the very first moment, and guide the construction equally with considerations of strength and security.[45]

Here, the fears of some nineteenth-century architects were laid bare: that architecture would be defined by concerns of costs, predictability and certainty; that the ambiguous, indefinable values of art and craft would become subservient to the unambiguous accountability of economic values; that architecture might, if defined quantitatively, rather than qualitatively, be reduced to no more than an ornamental surfacing, an optional and luxurious extra; that the architect, in such a scenario, might no longer be required. In the context of the Iron Museum, the arguments set forth by Augustus Pugin's 1841 *True Principles*, Owen Jones' 1856 *Grammar of Ornament* and John Ruskin's *Seven Lamps* can be understood as arguing for the value of the aesthetic in architecture as integral within every aspect of an architectural work, for ornamentation as necessarily embedded throughout structure and form, for the need and value of the aesthetic as integral to beauty, quality of life and human wellbeing. 'Construction should be decorated', Owen Jones proposed, 'decoration should never be purposely constructed'.[46] Such arguments, emerging as the consequences of mechanised production and industrialisation were becoming apparent at the Crystal Palace and the Iron Museum, highlighted the precarious position of the architectural profession as structure and services became the territory of others, reducing the architect to provider of a cheap and optional decorative façade.

The qualitative value of architecture

The justification of architectural value has been the key defining problem for the architectural profession since the pivotal moment exemplified by the Crystal Palace, and reinforced by the reduction of architecture to no more than an optional decorative façade at the Iron Museum. One-and-a-half centuries later, the delegation of architecture to a decorative skin remains a challenge for the profession, as evidenced by the dropped ceiling and web of ducting of Rem Koolhaas' 2014 *Fundamentals* Venice Biennale. 'Architecture today is little more than cardboard', Koolhaas observed, 'our influence has been reduced to a territory that is just 2cm thick'.[47] That an economic argument was required to underpin Caruso St John's Design and Access statement for their 2006 entrance addition to the relocated Iron Museum; that an innovative, decorative façade referencing cultural, historical and contextual references for a major civic institution[48] had to make an argument in an economically minded context for 'complex decorations at an affordable price'[49] is an indication of how little has changed for the architectural profession as it continues to quantify the deeply qualitative value of its contribution.

Notes

1. Third report of the Commissioners of the Exhibition of 1851, presented to both Houses of Parliament by Command of Her Majesty, London, 1856, Appendix T, p.270. This specification is reprinted in John Frederick Physick, *The Victoria and Albert Museum: The History of its Building* (Oxford: Phaidon, 1982), p.281, Appendix 1.
2. See Mhairi McVicar, 'Specifying intent at the Museum of Childhood', *arq: Architectural Research Quarterly*, 16 (3) (2012), pp.218–228.
3. Caruso St John Architects, *Stage E Report Rev A* (unpublished report, 2004), p.12.
4. 'Like three huge Boilers placed side by side', *The Builder*, 19 April 1856, p.213.
5. Nikolaus Pevsner, *The Sources of Modern Architecture and Design* (London: Thames & Hudson, 1986), p.11.
6. Physick, pp.19–20.
7. Physick, p.23.
8. Physick, p.23.
9. Third report of the Commissioners, Appendix T, p.270.
10. Third report of the Commissioners, Appendix T, pp.265–266.
11. H. Port, 'The Office of Works and Building Contracts in Early Nineteenth-Century England', *The Economic History Review*, 20 (1967), pp.94–110, p.94.
12. *The Builder*, 25 March 1843, p.77.
13. *The Builder*, 12 January 1856, p.13.
14. *The Builder*, 12 January 1856, p.13.
15. John McKean, *Crystal Palace: Joseph Paxton and Charles Fox* (London: Phaidon, 1994), p.211.
16. First report of the Commissioners for the Exhibition of 1851, presented to both Houses of Parliament by Command of Her Majesty, London, 1852. p.xxiii.
17. First report of the Commissioners, p.xxiv.
18. First report of the Commissioners, p.xxv.
19. For a detailed account of the 1851 Exhibition architectural competition and the circumstances in which Paxton's design was brought forward, see John McKean, *Crystal Palace: Joseph Paxton and Charles Fox* (London: Phaidon, 1994).
20. *The Builder*, 4 January 1851, p.1.
21. Andrew Saint, *Architect and Engineer: A Study in Sibling Rivalry* (New Haven, CT; London: Yale University Press, 2007), p.6.
22. Andrew Saint has described it as 'the original raw engineering concept that stuck in the architectural imagination', Saint, p.6; Nicholas Pevsner has described the Crystal Palace as the touchstone between the nineteenth and twentieth centuries, p.11.
23. See John Ruskin, pamphlet, *The Opening of the Crystal Palace Considered in Some of its Relations to the Prospects of Art*, 1854, which dismisses the Crystal Palace as no more than a conservatory. On industry and craft, Ruskin wrote:

> What we have to admire is the grand power and heart of the man in the thing, not his technical or empirical way of holding the trowel or laying the mortar ... It matters not what the thing is as that the builder should really love it, and enjoy it, and say so plainly.

John Ruskin, edited and abridged by J.G. Links, *The Stones of Venice* (London: Pallas Athene in conjunction with Ostara Publishing, 2001), p.21.
24 *The Builder*, 19 April 1856, p.213.
25 *The Builder*, 24 January 1857, p.46.
26 *The Builder*, 24 January 1857, p.46.
27 *The Builder*, 24 January 1857, p.46.
28 In 'The Origins of the Victorian Master Builders', E.W. Cooney defined the 'Master Builder' of the nineteenth century as a builder who employed, more or less permanently, labourers and workmen in all principal building crafts to erect complete buildings. This was a system emphatically different from that of the varied and specialised trade guilds, whose organisational roots reached back to the twelfth century. The title of 'first' Master Builder is ascribed by Cooney to Thomas Cubitt (1788–1855), whose contracting business developed between 1815–1820 set up an organisational framework that would oversee the entirety of a building project, employing each of the major trades in a permanent workforce of over 1,000 men who were promised continuous employment. E.W. Cooney, 'The Origins of the Victorian Master Builders', *The Economic History Review*, 8 (1955), pp.167–176.
29 Cooney, p.173.
30 Cooney, p.174.
31 Port, p.101.
32 'Report from the Commissioners of Inquiry into the Conduct of Business in the Office of Works', House of Commons Parliamentary Papers Online, 1812–1813, p.194.
33 Vitruvius, *The Ten Books on Architecture*, trans. Morris Hicky Morgan (New York: Dover Publications, 1960), p.16.
34 K. Harries, *The Ethical Function of Architecture* (Cambridge, MA: MIT Press, 1997), p.230, quoting Corbusier.
35 Paul Emmons' study of architectural authority in early modern England highlights the distinction between the 'liberal' and 'mechanical' arts in the seventeenth century, in which the liberal arts were demarcated as those free of labour, and in pursuit of the 'contemplation of truth', while the mechanical arts were concerned with 'the occupations of this life', including architecture. Paul Emmons, 'Architecture before Art: Imagining Architectural Authority in Early Modern England', *arq: Architectural Research Quarterly*, 10 (2007), pp.275–283, p.276.
36 Robert Tavenor, *Smoot's Ear: The Measure of Humanity* (New Haven, CT; London: Yale University Press, 2007), p.111.
37 Tavenor, p.111.
38 Sergio Villari, *J.N.L. Durand (1760–1834): Art and Science of Architecture* (New York: Rizzoli, 1990), p.15.
39 Villari, p.67.
40 Alberto Perez-Gomez, *Architecture and the Crisis of Modern Science* (Cambridge, MA; London: MIT Press, 1983), p.11.
41 Frank Jenkins, *Architect and Patron: A Survey of Professional Relations and Practice in England from the Sixteenth Century to the Present Day* (London: Oxford University Press, 1961), p.211, footnote 1.
42 Jenkins, p.225.
43 R. Norman Shaw, and T.G. Jackson, eds, *Architecture: A Profession or an Art – Thirteen Short Essays on the Qualifications and Training of Architects* (London: John Murray, 1892).
44 Shaw 1892, p.viii.
45 Shaw 1892, p.xxi.
46 Owen Jones, *The Grammar of Ornament* (London: Day and Son, 1856), p.5.
47 Oliver Wainwright, 'Rem Koolhaas blows the ceiling off the Venice Architecture Biennale', *The Guardian*, 5 June 2014, www.theguardian.com/artanddesign/architecture-design-blog/2014/jun/05/rem-koolhaas-architecture-biennale-venice-fundamentals [accessed 8 January 2015] (paragraph 4 of 18).

48 See Mhairi McVicar, 'Reading details: Caruso St John and the poetic intent of construction documents', in Grace Lees-Maffei, ed. *Writing Design: Words and Objects* (London: Berg Publishers, 2012), pp.149–161.
49 Caruso St John, p.12.

14

THE ARCHITECT

A disappearing species in a financialized space?

Silke Ötsch

Work in financialized capitalism

The latest financial and economic crisis has caused professional associations and journalists to observe that an increasing financial pressure is being put on architects. This is true for architects working in diverse economies. The subheading of an article in *The Independent*, for example, reads: 'Unless you're a "star architect", chances are you end up creating mediocre glass-clad hangars.'[1] Since the economic crash of 2008, the article continues, 'there has been a 40 per cent slump in demand for architects' services. Many practices have not only dropped their fees, but are doing design-preparation work for nothing.' The journalist of this article expects that 'blingkrieg' (respectively extraordinary) architecture will soon be realized only in a few 'prime locations'. The question thus arises as to whether this situation should be seen as a short-term crisis or rather as a development related to financial capitalism that in the long run is leading to the decline of the profession, namely architect.

Research on financial capitalism and reciprocal effects between the financial sphere and the real economy has largely been carried out in regard to listed companies in the field of industrial sociology. There is fundamental debate on the question of whether capitalist systems converge in the long run due to capitalist logic. Listed corporations' indications of convergence include short-term profit maximization, hostile takeovers, various forms of dependency on financial backers (banks, investors and shareholders) and the market for corporate control exercised by transfer institutions.[2] Transfer mechanisms include an orientation towards maximum yield and limited employment, workers' flexibility, and the splitting up of companies into units that are expected to generate a certain return, otherwise they will be liquidated.[3] However, since financial market constraints are often put forward as a pretext in order to push through the interests of elites – executives, for example[4] – or can be understood as management or narrative rhetoric,[5] it is not easy to clearly identify which restructuring operations actually originate in financial constraints. And yet scholars do unanimously agree that financial criteria play an increasingly important role. Does this also apply then to architecture? And if so, what does it signify for the profession of the architect?

Since architects identify strongly with their profession, and less so with their activities as entrepreneurs, to do them justice in respect to research on financialization aspects of the sociology of professions must be considered, especially architects' specific professional ethics.[6] Sociologists Christian de Montlibert and Florent Champy, for instance, refer to special characteristics of the so-called free professions. Unlike entrepreneurs, members of free professions do not primarily focus on financial returns but exhibit their expertise in design and advising. Moreover, they are independent both of those involved in the construction (such as engineers) and of the clients, whom, in case of doubt, they should be able to contradict.[7] According to Champy, the strong focus on 'architectural qualities' is one of the reasons why the architectural profession, vis-à-vis comparable free professionals, has had difficulties in succeeding in the marketplace.[8] The architect's point of reference predates the tradition of the profession. Architects in former times were much more likely to work for a small number of noble or wealthy clients; they took little notice of the public's concerns or of social needs.[9] Indeed, as can be inferred from the contributions on the origins of the professional image of architects in Spiro Kostof's anthology *The Architect*, architects in Europe and in the United States strongly identify with the work of artists and orient themselves to the Renaissance ideal of the universal scholar. According to this viewpoint, architects are less concerned about the user (of the building), about technical issues and about usability.[10] Research so far on the professional image of architects explains the economic decline of the profession largely as a result of architects lacking the ability to adapt to new conditions due to professional ethics and traditions.[11] The reciprocal effects of financial capitalism are addressed only indirectly.

Judith Blau investigated the connection between professional ethics and the capitalist economy. In a study on American architectural firms, she showed that there appeared to be a Marxian dialectical move among offices, namely 'the economic forces that pull firms into the orbit of successful enterprise run counter to the forces of professionalism'.[12] As I have shown elsewhere, the professional ethics of architects is partially (but not completely) eroded: they depend, among other things, on the chosen business model.[13] When authors such as Montlibert and Champy do elaborate on the professional group's characteristic qualities, they hardly address the current transformation of the profession into smaller subunits, nor the fact that the situation differs a lot for different kinds of architects.

Should, however, the findings on the effects of financial capitalism hold true to architecture, then it may be assumed that there are tendencies in this profession that are comparable to financialization in the business sector (e.g. an orientation towards profitable spheres, financial pressures), which cannot be traced back to professional ethics. And yet, research done in the field of political economy often ignores 'soft factors' such as professional ethics. My research project – a case study on architects – aims to make a preliminary contribution that analyses both sides of the coin: financial capitalism and professional ethics. I intend to 1) present how architects in various contexts of financial capitalism perceive financial pressure; and 2) offer a critique (on the basis of my research) of the hypothesis that the profession of architects is about to disappear since architectural criteria do not correspond to the requirements of financialization.

Methods

In order to find out how architects perceive financial pressures and what sort of leeway they have to realize architecture in accordance with their professional ethics, I conducted over 40 qualitative, half-structured interviews with architects from four countries (Austria, France, UK and the US) and in four different contexts of financialization. Between June 2010 and June 2011, I interviewed ten architects from each country in chosen cities of so-called second rank. Once industrial cities, they later opted for the service industries. The various national frameworks are of interest first because the markets in countries such as Austria and France traditionally were more strongly incorporated institutionally than markets in the UK and the US; and second since these latter economies have a more developed financial sector compared to the real economy. My research included studying the local architectural scene and receiving feedback from the local chamber of architects. I also selected as broad and diverse a spectrum of interview partners as possible: male and female, including varied age groups, local business models and office sizes. Among other things, I inquired about the architects' financial situations, their experiences with crises, with banks, about their (office) business strategies and activities, the structure of their clientele, their general expectations, possible existing conflicts due to costs, their satisfaction regarding income and about their motivation. I aspired to understand which architects in which contexts are financially 'rewarded' – and who are not – and whether professional merits are also remunerated and acknowledged. The interviews were transcribed, and the textual elements were coded and assigned to categories, which were generated from the interviews, taking into account results of research on financialized capitalism in the business sector. I also compared information provided to me by the architects with data and reports on the situation of architects.

Architects in financialized spaces

The analysis of the interviews confirmed the supposition that most architects are exposed to increasing pressure regarding costs and are having difficulties in practising their profession according to their expectations. However, each architect did not experience the financial pressures with equal intensity. Whereas interviewed architects in the UK and the US often reported contract fluctuations due to business cycles or bankruptcies following busts, those in Austria and France pointed to an increasing medium-term financial pressure to perform. A majority of architects reported that actually prior to the crisis their clients had become more exacting and demanded that architects provide more results and greater services. Some of the interviewees told me that they could not support themselves on income solely based on their core business. The architects' other major sources of income were advising services (in municipal development plans, urbanism and environmentally oriented construction planning), university teaching, organizing cultural events or being active as entrepreneurs in the real estate sector. In each city it was the young or inexperienced architects who faced particular difficulties, such as often being compelled to become freelancers due to a shortage of employee positions. This is an option grasped particularly by young architects in Austria and France who could secure contracts via competitions. At the same time financially well-positioned architects, apart from their architectural activity, were also involved in business: for example, through shares in their building projects.

When asked whether they were content with their income, almost all of the architects reacted disapprovingly: the vocation, they said, was so fulfilling that they were not in this profession for the money. However, many later qualified their answers by saying they found it unjust to be paid worse than other professionals with comparable skills and work schedules. According to a French architect, the pay had become so bad that, as he said, 'the belt cannot be tightened any more' and they have no more leeway to reduce their fees. How strongly architects differentiated the valuation of their income depended as well on the position they held in a company.

Competitive situations, judging from the interviewees' statements, differed in each location. In the Austrian city, for example, it was especially young and ambitious architects who complained about established architects working as the house architects of banks and about building cooperatives. They also complained about proven star architects who prevented the younger architects access (indeed, the attitude towards star architects was ambivalent in other cities as well). By contrast, architects from France and the US referred to competition from engineers, whereas architects in the UK in particular complained about competition in design-build and about other architects who took advantage of their special relationships with the city council. Architects in each location, however, reported on competition by one-person companies: that is, architects who work 'at the kitchen table' and for a dumping price of a few euros or dollars an hour. And yet – according to interviewees in the UK and the US – there was also competition at the other end of the spectrum. After the 2008 crisis, big architectural offices expanded into the markets of medium- and small-sized offices and drove them out. Still, not all architects complained about financial pressure. Those architects who were better positioned in each location had uninterrupted commissions from businesses or else built for affluent private individuals. An advantage of large and more experienced offices appeared to be specialization. Smaller offices engaged more risk in such a strategy. Moreover, architects who acted as businessmen or women (by partially turning the client–expert relationship into one between business partners) seemed to earn remarkably well.

Various interviewees distinguished two types of clients: those who guaranteed good incomes and those who allowed architects to realize quality architecture. As clients with high-quality standards, public clients in particular were in demand in France – and, in part, also in Austria – even when the revenues were not above average. In the United States, however, such clients were less in demand. According to the interviewees there, the decision-making procedures could last an incredibly long time, due to the fact that public entities had to cover their bases in order not to be confronted with the reproach that they squandered taxpayer money.

In each location the most sought-after clients were affluent private individuals who intentionally selected architects based on recommendations. Although most of the architects disassociated themselves from networks or networking, some of their colleagues reported that a portion of the success of locally established architects could be traced to being well-connected to banks, businesses, private clients or to the municipality. Architects in the French and the American cities openly addressed this issue and also pointed out that there were various networking approaches, such as big specialized architectural offices demonstrating their know-how to large investors operating at international levels (e.g. universities) or the face-to-face cultivation of clients, such as at golf courses or celebrity events (US); this latter strategy, however, is for architects whose scope of activity reaches the local level. Interestingly, unofficial names for certain types of such architects have emerged, such as the 'local yokel' (US) or the 'Platzhirsch' (Austria), translated approximately as 'top dog', or literally the buck who defends his place.

What connection may then be drawn between architects' professional capacity – their 'architectural quality', in the language of architects – and their financial performance?

In each city, I interviewed two or more architects who – although not world-class stars – were recognized personalities by the profession, whose buildings had been featured in national and to some extent in international architectural journals. Some had won competitions and received awards. In the Austrian and the French cities, the interviewees who were particularly acknowledged by the architects, however, did not apparently count among those who were doing the best financially. Based on their earnings, they were rather at or below average. Curiously, the richest interviewee in Austria (according to newspaper reports) was hardly known among his peers. The American city appeared to have the most harmony between professional recognition and financial success, and star or name architecture plays a rather secondary role. Internationally known star architects, however, were considered an exception (see Figures 14.1–14.3).

Several European interviewees were of the opinion that because the designs of 'real stars' had to be innovative and provocative, and because they had to invest their earnings back into their architecture, they could not (possibly) be rich. Indeed, most of my interview partners viewed architecture as something that cannot be created in a way that would enable planning for profits. The 'Bilbao effect',[14] they said, was an exception. If an office was managing well financially,

FIGURE 14.1 Power Tower, Linz

Note: designed by Weber/Hofer architects, built by a locally established entrepreneurial architect.

FIGURE 14.2 Betham Tower, Manchester

Note: designed and built by a locally established entrepreneurial architect.

FIGURE 14.3 Centre Commercial Euralille, Lille

Note: designed by Jean Nouvel, built by a locally established architect.

they continued, then it was still not of a quality that was produced in the most rational way. Architects in each location compared themselves and their architecture with car models, specifically with cars built for the middle class: e.g. the Audi. Perhaps this was meant to suggest that they provide quality but are not high-priced status symbols, which in turn were equated to the architecture of star architects. Indeed, offices that are established financially are not headed by stars. Rather, they provide services that are technologically accomplished and contemporary and yet offer neither avant-garde nor experimental architecture.

Table 14.1 shows the various types of architects and their strategies in the four investigated local contexts, combined with their income and working conditions. The indications are based on the interviews with architects, on assessments by professional colleagues, on research on architects' business models and on additional available information, such as found on websites (e.g. lists of projects) and in specialized journals and daily presses.[15]

To sum up, the interviews illustrate that architects follow a variety of different strategies. The situation of most architects is increasingly strained, whereas some, however, earn well and do not complain about the tender or commission situation. Architecture that from a professional viewpoint is good to average, but not the best architecture (in the estimation of the interviewed architects and in terms of publications in architectural journals and professional rewards such as prizes), appears financially promising.

Architects: a subtle shift from professional to financial criteria

Three main conclusions may be drawn from my investigation. First the interviews demonstrate that assumptions on financialization in large companies cannot be applied on a one-to-one basis to architecture. However, many of the architects reported on increasing financial pressure and competition, rising expectations of the clients and a resulting time pressure. In addition, 'inside–outside dynamics'[16] emerged in offices, due to increasing differences between permanent staff and a flexible workforce on the one hand, and income differences between senior architects and others on the other.

Second, my study shows that financial capitalism affects the various types of architects differently. Insofar as payment to architects is concerned and with respect to quality standards, absolutely no general trend towards (price) dumping is visible. Rather, the significant factors that influence the financial situation are: a) the type of offers which, apart from the individual orientation of the architects, depend on office size; and b) the type and standards of the clients as well as the contacts architects have to certain client groups. As the comparison of the professional renown of the interview partners and their indications about their income demonstrates, there appears to be no direct correlation between professional accomplishment and income. Nor does financial success or failure appear happenstance. Architects in small- and medium-sized offices seem to be financially profitable when their

TABLE 14.1 Architects' strategies and earnings

Architects' strategy and financial situation	Strong service firms[1]	'Platzhirsche' (the buck who defends his place)	Star architects	Small- + medium-sized offices with affluent clients	Specialized architects or offices	Medium-sized offices without specific clientele	'Sustainer'
Occurrence	Esp. US, UK. A few offices in AT and F. Small number of offices, but a lot of employees	All locations of study	AT, F, UK. To a smaller extent also USA	All locations of study	All locations of study	All locations of study	AT, F. To a smaller extent also UK and US
Strategy	'Professional' services, experience, wide range of services, service oriented. At a certain scale: dominated by engineers	Medium size, local networks (clients, local decision makers, such as bankers or city council members, executives in charge)	Focus on professional discourse: journals, competitions international profile, avant-garde	Less known among peers, but more known among clients and their networks	Niche, experience	Broad building types, but not too specialized. Broad range of clients	Small offices. Much work for small fees. Accept every kind of work

Architects' strategy and financial situation	Strong service firms[1]	'Platzhirsche' (the buck who defends his place)	Star architects	Small- + medium-sized offices with affluent clients	Specialized architects or offices	Medium-sized offices without specific clientele	'Sustainer'
Financial pressure	Moderate	Little	A lot of work in the pre-star phase and few financial rewards. Star phase: less financial pressure, often financial freedom because of university job	Moderate	Either very high financial pressure or moderate (niche)	Tense. Put out of market by bigger more 'professional' firms and small firms (dumping prices)	Tense. Often architects cannot live from income of professional work and have additional occupations or earning wives/husbands
Motivation/ scope of action	Entrepreneurial prior to architectural mission	Entrepreneurial prior to architectural mission	Professional criteria, architectural mission	Focusing on the clients' wishes. Convincing clients of semi-professional criteria (used for distinction)	In some cases successful. Risky strategy for small offices	Differs	Differs. Usually: focus on professional criteria
Working conditions	Very good to moderate	Very good to moderate	Bad to very bad (except in some cases for the star)	Good	Moderate to bad. In some cases good (niche)	Moderate to bad	Bad

Note

1 Notion see: Robert Gutman, *Architectural practice: A critical view* (Princeton, NJ: Princeton Architectural Press, 1988).

contracts come from affluent private individuals or from businesses. The majority of businesses in this category appeared to be subject to financial pressure, however, and lucrative clients were rather infrequent. Once a specific scale for a building tender is reached, it seems that other qualities are demanded, which particularly large and experienced offices can supply, namely highly professionalized services, such as in the university and healthcare sectors. Moreover, competition here is less, since only established businesses can provide the appropriate services.

The third conclusion is that there is a subtle erosion of professional criteria due to the fact that professional criteria are less rewarded and that institutional backing is weakening. Based on my research, however, it can be determined that the weak financial situation of the majority of architects cannot be traced to their professional ethics alone and to adaptive difficulties as a result. Thus one finds that architects in a variety of positions, types of businesses and contexts of financial capitalism develop various gradations of professional ethics or have different ideas about quality.

Whereas interviewees in Austria and France were indignant regarding their clients' ignorance of architectural values and their service expectations, most of the American interviewees seemed proud of their distinctive services for their clientele, which had nothing to do with the traditional competence of architects. Unlike the American or UK architects, those in Austria and France had the opportunity to obtain tenders in which professional criteria played a greater role. In Austria and France in particular, architects took the position that architectural quality should be more convincingly conveyed and institutionally shored up. Methods for maintaining the professional qualities, however, are more and more frequently linked to the public sector. The quality standards of financially rewarded 'Platzhirsch' architectural offices are different from those of acknowledged architects. Having good contacts to clients and decision-makers or professionally arranging and accommodating clients' wishes, are not standards that are usually emphasized in professional journals (i.e., focus on concept, quality of achievement, details, innovative solutions). Rather, these qualities play much more to the expectations of financially strong clients. This is well illustrated by a UK office, which on its homepage goes out of its way to dissociate itself from star architecture:

> There is no 'house style' … We give a free rein to design talent but ensure our standards of excellence are maintained with rigorous internal procedures which safeguard quality. We discourage flights of fancy preferring to exceed our clients' expectations by seeking imaginative yet practicable solutions to their problems.[17]

Finally, because of the growing public (sector) austerity, architects are losing opportunities to assert their quality standards. This could theoretically be compensated by the private sector, but it is not institutionally guaranteed.

The links between the financial sphere and architecture are therefore to be seen less in the area of maximum yields and more both in a transformed client structure and in the expectations that clients have regarding architecture. That is, a gradual shift is coming to the fore, as professional groups break apart and client orientation increases.

This article is based on the research project 'The intermediary role of architects in financialization', which is funded by the Austrian Research Fund (FWF).

Notes

1 Jay Merrick, 'The death of architecture', *The Independent*, 4 April 2011.
2 Paul Windolf, 'Was ist Finanzmarkt-Kapitalismus?', in *Finanzmarkt-Kapitalismus*, ed. by Paul Windolf (Wiesbaden: VS Verlag, 2005), special issue 45/2000: *Kölner Zeitschrift für Soziologie und Sozialpsychologie*, pp. 20–57.
3 Klaus Dörre and Hajo Holst, 'Nach dem Shareholder Value? Kapitalmarktorientierte Unternehmenssteuerung in der Krise', *WSI Mitteilungen*, 12 (2009), pp. 667–74.
4 Peter Folkman, Julie Froud, Sukhdev Johal and Karel Williams, 'Financial Intermediaries: Working for themselves?', in *Financialization at Work*, eds Ismail Erturk, Julie Froud, Sukhdev Johal, Adam Leaver, Karel Williams (London: Routledge, 2008), pp. 150–62.
5 Julie Froud, Sukhdev Johal, Adam Leaver and Karel Williams, *Financialization and strategy: Narrative and numbers* (London: Routledge, 2006).
6 On professional ethics of professionals from creative industries (including architects) see: Cornelia Koppetsch, *Das Ethos der Kreativen* (Konstanz: UVK, 2006). See also: Judith Blau, *Architects and firms: A sociological perspective on architectural practice* (Cambridge, MA: MIT Press, 1988), p. 145; Florent Champy, 'La culture professionnelle des architectes', *Sociologie des groupes professionnels*, ed. by Didier Demazière and Charles Gadéa (Paris: La Découverte, 2010), pp. 152–62; and Silke Ötsch, 'ArchitektInnen zwischen Paternalismus und Kundenorientierung', *Momentum Quarterly*, 2.4 (2013), pp. 183–95.
7 Christian de Montlibert, *L'impossible autonomie de l'architecte: sociologie de la production architecturale* (Strasburg: Presses universitaires de Strasbourg, 1995), p. 43.
8 Florent Champy, 'Professional discourses under the pressure of economic values', *Current Sociology*, 54 (2006), pp. 649–61. For a more descriptive, overview of changed framework conditions for architects maintaining largely the traditional professional profile, see: Guy Tapie, *Les architectes: mutations d'une profession* (Paris: L'Harmattan, 2000).
9 Champy, *Current Sociology*, p. 654.
10 James Wilton-Ely, 'The rise of the professional architect in England', *The architect: Chapters in the history of the profession*, ed. by Spiro Kostof (Berkeley: University of California Press, 1977; repr. 2000), p. 191. See also: John Draper, 'The Ecole des Beaux-Arts and the architectural profession in the United States', *The architect: Chapters in the history of the profession*, ed. by Spiro Kostof (Berkeley: University of California Press, 2000), pp. 209–37.
11 Champy, *Current Sociology*. See also: Florent Champy, 'La culture professionnelle des architectes', *Sociologie des groupes professionnels*, pp. 152–62. See also recommendations of professional associations: American Institute of Architects, *2014 AIA Firm Survey* (2014); The Royal Institute of British Architects, *RIBA Business Benchmarking, 2013/14* (London: 2014); François Rouanet, *Observatoire de la profession: Les architectes et l'évolution du métier à l'horizon 2030*, ed. by Ordre des architectes (Paris: 2013). For a critique of Rem Koolhaas' adaptive strategies, see: Silke Ötsch, 'The Emperor's new firm: Inside the global ¥€$ … and how to get out', *Graz Architecture Magazine* 4 (2007), pp. 108–33.
12 Judith Blau, *Architects and firms: A sociological perspective on architectural practice*, p. 145.
13 Silke Ötsch, 'ArchitektInnen zwischen Paternalismus und Kundenorientierung', *Momentum Quarterly*, 2.4 (2013), pp. 183–95.

14 The notion 'Bilbao effect' depicts the stimulating effect of a building perceived as outstanding for a city or a region. It goes back to the Guggenheim museum, finished in 1997 and designed by Frank Gehry, that attracted a big number of wealthy and middle-class tourists. For more examples see: Bruno Frey, 'Superstar museums: An economic analysis', *Journal of Cultural Economics*, 22 (2–3) (1998), pp. 113–25.

15 This list makes no claim of being complete; it contains strategies that were either presented in the four investigated localities or else addressed by the interviewees. Additional categories could be included, such as 'the participating architect' or 'the architect as researcher'.

16 Klaus Dörre, 'Die neue Landnahme', *Soziologie – Kapitalismus – Kritik: Eine Debatte*, eds Klaus Dörre, Stephan Lessenich and Hartmut Rosa (Frankfurt am Main: Suhrkamp, 2012), pp. 21–86.

17 Homepage of the office Buttress Fuller Alsop Williams, www.bfaw.co.uk [accessed 12 October 2010].

15

THE PAN-AMERICAN HIGHWAY

Informal urbanism in Latin-American border cities

Cristian Suau

Introduction

Border conditions are linked with the establishment of socio-economic forces that rule the production and occupancy of every-day spaces in cities. This phenomenon represents a *new geography of centrality and marginality*,[1] which is characterised by motion, contestation, internal asymmetries and discontinuous transgressions[2] between territories in friction, mainly in borderlands and border towns. Contemporary economists and geographers have pointed out that urban forms have often been driven by neo-liberal trends[3] with a stark augment in urban and regional dissimilarities; growth of environmental problems; displacement of rural communities; expansion of slums;[4] informal trade and employment; and the dismantling of societal protections and well-being.

Infrastructural and informal settlements in border towns play a crucial role in aligning the unplanned forces of urbanisations. Being formalised systems, infrastructural urbanism offers the support to stimulate alternative temporary, intermittent and mutable urban forms. This phenomenon of border environments can be analysed through interurban (within the same city), transurban (between various cities) and transregional (between more regions, states or countries) levels. Border conditions along transnational highways are manifested by visible versus invisible; hard versus soft; formal versus informal; and isotopic versus heterotopic environments. Urban corridors, mega-urban regions and border towns are predominant spatial organisations across political borders where border cities operate like strategic economic gateways.

Whilst natural boundaries are defined by the internal structure of enclosed territories, mostly man-made borders delineate a diffuse urban territory. As a result, these borderlands are depopulated peripheral zones, highly controlled and militarised. These buffer zones are allotted between frictional political, ethnic and economic disparities. They are vulnerable to processes of demographic shrinkage, political or economic abandonment or ecological dereliction.

This chapter investigates the border conditions of Pan-American cities such as Santiago and the border towns of Arica–Tacna and El Paso–Ciudad Juárez – predominantly ruled by informal trade and illegal migratory flows – alongside the largest land-transport infrastructure on Earth called the *Pan-American Highway*.[5] However, the result of border pressure and land proximity has reshaped urban economies along the Americas towards asymmetric models of production, consumption and exchange. Is this type of urbanity a key factor in the development of emerging border cities in developing economies? How do informal settlements mutate, resist or perish in different border regions?

This chapter reflects on the North–South border dilemma of two paradigmatic border towns ruled by specific formal vs. informal economies, which expand or constrain alongside a common land-transport infrastructure organised by differentiated control systems, passageways, gateways, checkpoints and trade zones. It puts special emphasis on the dynamic transformation of *differential spaces*[6] through spatial configurations of informality in distinctive housing and commerce spaces.

The methodology analyses the spatial configuration of informal border urbanisation situated in key nodes along the Pan-American Highway through satellite photography and fieldworks made by the author. Mapping[7] is employed as the principal research cartographic technique. The mapping method is supported by geographic and urban maps, transect zones, urban drift techniques[8] and photography.

Transgressive informality in Pan-American cities

The notion of informal economy is often associated with developing countries where up to half of the labour force works alternatively. With the rapid transformation of post-Fordist modes of production in emerging economies, many workers are displaced from formal into informal employment. Due to the rapid externalisation of production and services and the flows of capital and new transport networks, informal economies are transforming the border condition of cities and regions towards dynamic systems of trade and migration. The resultant *informalism* generates a type of *instant urbanity* that constructs transitory, elusive or spontaneous geometrical patterns. They change frequently: seasonally, daily or even hourly.[9]

Cities are primarily shaped by infrastructures, which rapidly transform the occupied territory in productive spaces where formal and informal economies overlap. They are the vascular system of any urban economy. Nowadays Latin America is experiencing a new phase of modernisation towards a more urban-based economy where informal built environments are characterised by a unique repertoire of border conditions, which define the identity of any Pan-American city. The corridor is not only defined as the main continental trade artery but as a transformative infrastructure, which is grouped in four main trade blocs: North American Free Trade Agreement (NAFTA), MERCOSUR, ALBA and recently the *Alianza del*

Pacífico (Pacific Alliance). Accessibility is the key factor of regional integration. It is driven by the principles of *metapolisation*[10] and the transformability of borderlands – territories of urban frictions or porosities – along the corridor. They provide an exceptional inventory of urban configurations and types, consisting of diffuse lands, militarised borders, illicit urbanism, and devastated or untouched ecologies (Figure 15.1).

Whilst natural boundaries are defined by the internal structure of geographies, artificial borders delineate hybrid territories. Man-made borderlands appear as peripheral voids. They are mostly vacant lands or *terra incognita*, which are vulnerable to severe ecological dereliction and demographic abandonment. However, what are the common informal urban dynamics of Pan-American cities?

Urban form follows economics. According to Manuel Castells, the phenomenon of informal economy constitutes

> a major structural feature of society both in industrialised and less developed countries. And yet, the ideological controversy and political debate surrounding its development have obscured comprehension of its character, challenging the capacity of the social science to provide a reliable analysis.[11]

There are still not enough consistent urban studies that examine the dynamics of informality along infrastructural urban networks and its physical adaptation.

Generally, urban informal economies are characterised by small scales, evasion of formal regulations, flexible sites and family businesses, but they differ in meaning and functions depending on the economical oscillations. In Latin America, the largest informal economy is composed of Bolivia, followed by Panama and Peru.[12] These interconnections are intermittent or permanent, central or peripheral depending on the distribution of low-income social groups in cities. However, Michel Laguerre affirms that

> informality is seen in the interstice of the formal economy, either as an enclave or as an extension of the formal economy. The interstitial niche occupied by the informal within the boundaries of the formal economy help smooth the functioning of the formal economy. That informal function is produced by the formal for formal ends.[13]

Santiago de Chile: the Pan-American Highway as instant linear city

The Pan-American cities are characterised by a strong tension between formal and informal socio-spatial productions. It exceeds the structures of order, control and homogeneity found in consolidated urban tissues. According to Michel Laguerre, the manifestation of unregulated spaces 'may not be under direct control of city government. It can either precede the establishment of formal space or be produced by formal space or the formal use of spaces.' Laguerre states that

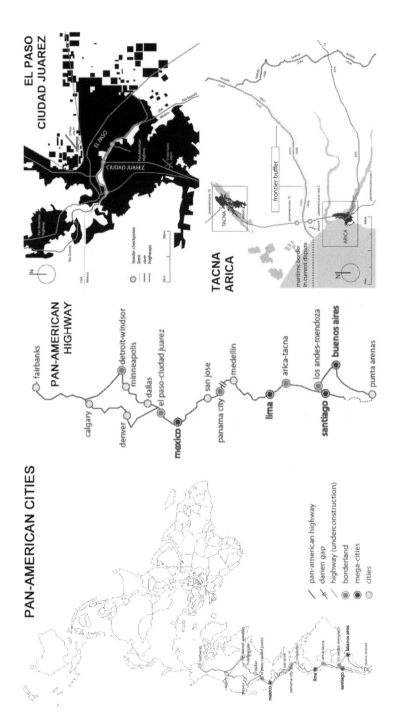

FIGURE 15.1 Comparative maps of borderlands, edge cities and mega-cities along the Pan-American Highway and the border cities of Tacna (Peru) and Arica (Chile) and the conurbation El Paso (USA) and Ciudad Juárez (Mexico)

informal space is also a product of the formal use of the urban space. Because the formal space is unable to meet the expectations of every member of the city community, individuals feel it necessary to transform formal space into informal space to conduct their informal activities. Informal space develops in this instance within the formal spatial system. It is an outgrowth of that system.[14]

This can also be seen in terms of supply and demand.

Everyday informal commerce and dwellings, which lie outside public control and depend upon non-monetary transactions, are perhaps most representative of emerging urban economies in Latin America. These exhibit the bartering of goods and services, mutual self-building, unclassified jobs, street and highway vending, servitude and other similar expressions.

Regarding the geography of informal spaces, the sociologist Erving Gottman frames out the theatrical setting of *vis-à-vis* interactions in cities.[15] The front area is generally a formalised place, the locus of the cultural hegemonic. The rear area represents the informalised and transformative space. How do front and back regions mutate? The Pan-American frontage is characterised by a soft frontline, an ambiguous and residual archipelago.

In Santiago de Chile, the informalisation of the immediate public realm is less abrupt than in most of the Latin-American cities. The Pan-American Highway crosses and cuts the urban core. This infrastructural strip creates new forms of front and back regions and accentuates the urban asymmetries. Is this corridor a *space of flows* from core to suburbia? Informality is expressed from a low degree of visibility in the centre and a rapid degradation of the formal frontage towards the periphery, whilst marketplaces such as fairs, scrapyards and sweatshops take over its margins. This subaltern urbanism constructs transitory, elusive or spontaneous urban patterns and architectural types, which flee from any conventional spatial scheme.

Latin-American commerce is mainly categorised by informalised fairs and street trading activities in both urban and suburban areas. By mapping socio-economic groups we can track low-income families that live and trade along the *back zones* of the main land-transport infrastructure with a considerable expansion towards the northern and southern periphery of Santiago. Due to the recent privatisation of public highways, so-called *vías concesionadas*, the metropolitan authorities are increasingly *branding* a formal urban image of progress but they are still neglecting the reality of urban poverty along the spine of the public Pan-American Highway (Figure 15.2).

As a result the public frontage has been transformed as a catalogue of billboards, business parks or spots of gentrified housing condominiums. However, informal trade is displaced to the rear region with distinctive types of macro and micro retail spaces. They are concentrated in the low-rise and low-income periphery. Three key types of trade systems can be identified in this region: *Ferias Libres*, *Vendedores Ambulantes* and *Carretoneros*.

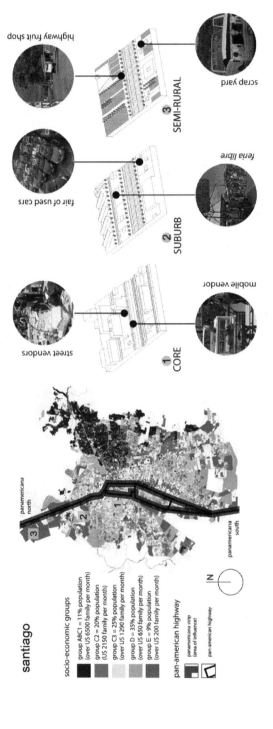

FIGURE 15.2 Distribution of household income in Santiago (left) and sequence of informal commerce along the *Panamericana* in Santiago (right), 2014

Ferias Libres *as informal* barrio *shopping*

The concentration of informal macro commerce is expanding towards the poorest suburban areas in the North and South of Santiago. There are four predominant informal retail types: food fairs, flea markets, fairs of used cars and scrap yards. *Ferias Libres*[16] (or open-air food fairs) are culturally conceived as a temporary public place for weekly trade and public encounters. They contain a polyvalent usage of sporadic street events allowing different manifestations of agro-commercial activities at local scale. The phenomenon of informal domestic food trade resembles the externalisation of rural immigration legacy.

Architecturally *Ferias Libres* are linear fairs with a central passageway supported by lighweight and mobile tent-like structures or marquees alongside. They are the principal marketplaces that activate the public and civic life of many neighbourhoods or *barrios*. Each trader has a sector marked on the street designated by the municipality. Vendors employ collapsible awnings for climatic protection. In suburbs the *Ferias Libres* do not just provide food markets, but can also act like flea markets, so-called *Mercados Persas*. In the periphery some second-hand car marketplaces are connected to open food markets or shopping malls. Informal trade in marginalised areas enhances the sense of every-day appropriation of public spaces by revealing the concealed rural idiosyncrasy of the Chilean society.

The programmatic adaptability of the street life deals with the resilient capacity to host both formal and informal economic activities and social interactions beyond mono-functional planning regulations. Therefore the *Ferias Libres* are a transgressive space against the hegemony of supermarket chains. These informal spaces are also the catalysts of the local political arena and a variety of empowered social interactions.

Vendedores Ambulantes *as informal micro-vending*

Informal small commerce is a sole trader's activity that mostly occurs in main pedestrian streets, principal avenues and inside public transport vehicles in Santiago. This business takes place in street junctions during rush hours and traffic jams; massive sport events or political celebrations; or inside buses or subways. Street vendors normally sell food, electronics items, clothes, etc. Alternatively they can also be street entertainers or acrobats.

Carretoneros *push-carts*

Carretoneros are informal sole traders on wheels, and are truly urban junk recyclers. The suburban streetscape is also occupied by these mobile sole traders who sell agricultural products or carry paper cards, bottles or metal goods, but who also offer short-distant moving or building services. They normally park beside streets or highways, junctions, or near petrol stations or traffic lights.

Border towns and informality along the Pan-American Highway: Arica and Tacna, El Paso and Cuidad Juárez

Informal commerce and shantytowns are common practices of urban transgression in Pan-American border towns. This chapter identifies distinctive commercial and housing spaces within the borderland of Tacna (Peru) and Arica (Chile) and the conurbations of El Paso (US) and Ciudad Juárez (Mexico). For instance, informality between Arica and Tacna is defined by a soft border condition, mainly associated to precarious housing and sporadic trade outside each urban limit. It is commonly allocated in gateways and adjacent to the main industries along the transport corridor. Future urban expansion towards the frontier should be driven by the consolidation of inter-regional markets and the porosity of the demarcation zone. On the contrary, informality between the borderland of El Paso and Ciudad Juárez represents a hard border condition. The borderline of Rio Grande is one of the most militarised and controlled migration zones on Earth. It is also characterised by illicit retail, which is trafficked immediately after the checkpoints of each border.

Southern border towns: Arica, Tacna and the borderland of the 'Linea de la Concordia'

Arica (Chile) is a port city with a population of 185,269 inhabitants in an area of 41.89 km^2. Arica spreads outward into the desert and the Peru–Chile border (situated only 18 km away). Economically, it is also the hub of railway communication with La Paz (Bolivia) and Tacna (Peru) by separate railroad lines. According to the last census (2012), Arica province spans an area of 4,799.4 km^2 and has 213,595 inhabitants. Of the whole population 95.7 per cent lives in urban areas and 4.3 per cent in rural areas. The population *Ariqueños* still have a kinship with the cultures of Peru and remotely Bolivia. Many residents commute partly because many goods and services cost less on the Peruvian side.

Tacna is an inland city situated in southern Peru. It is located between the Pacific Ocean and in the valley of the Caplina River, only 35 km North of the border with Chile. It has a population of 242,451 people. Commercially Tacna is a high-active city, based on mercantile activities with the North of Chile (Arica and Iquique). Since it is a duty free zone, Tacna competes with its rival Arequipa as southern Peru's main business area. Commerce between border cities is gradually increasing as they are fuelled by free trade accords, duty free zones and well-equipped infrastructure (two airports, one railway and ports).

Informal housing beyond 'Zona Urbana' in Arica

This informal settlement was established just outside the urban limit of Arica (East side), in a zone between the Azapa Valley and the Pan-American Highway. Mostly Peruvian immigrants live in *casas de carton* (cardboard houses). Situated outside the urban limit, this shantytown has been legally marginalised of the socio-spatial articulation with the formalised urban fabric. This unauthorised urbanisation is made by reclaimed cardboard and shipping boards, materials supplied by fairs. Since 2009 dwellers have self-constructed a group of one-storey housing units in a squatted land. Many of the people living here are not officially registered in the municipality. This precarious situation raises issues on the *right to the city* and land co-ownership. This slum also lacks basic services such as medical and sanitary services, and fire regulations. Local NGOs and humanitarian groups provide consultancy and empower dwellers to gain access to public housing schemes, through the purchase and land management of affordable subdivided land, densification of the existing settlement by progressive enlargements, management of an acceptable level of public services (water, sanitation and electricity), and education, environmental, health and civic amenities.

Northern border towns: El Paso–Ciudad Juárez as militarised cross border

The Chihuahuan Desert surrounds El Paso (US). It lies at the intersection of three states (Texas, New Mexico and Chihuahua) and two countries (US and Mexico). El Paso is the nineteenth most populated city in the United States of America and the sixth most crowded city in the state of Texas. In Texas, cross-border commerce is highly categorised by illicit urban practices. The illicit activities increase when residents perceive the state's intervention in the impoverished *colonias* as illegitimate, whether in the form of fees, taxes or regulation.[17] The metropolitan area covers all of El Paso County, whose population (census 2010) is 800,647 inhabitants. The El Paso metropolitan area has over 736,310 people; 80 per cent of El Paso is predominantly Hispanic (75 per cent are Mexican). The density is 874 inhabitants per km².

El Paso and Ciudad Juárez represent an asymmetric urban development made of generic American suburbia and Mexican slums (Figures 15.3 and 15.4). The Rio Grande River defines the geographical and political border of the conurbation

FIGURE 15.3 Informal settlement: immigrants dwelling outside the urban limit of Arica, Chile, 2014

FIGURE 15.4 Informal commerce: the Fox Flea Market is an illicit marquee in El Paso, USA, 2014

El Paso–Juárez. They have a combined population of two million, two-thirds of which reside in Juárez. El Paso and Ciudad Juárez comprise the second largest border metropolitan area on the US–Mexico demarcation after San Diego–Tijuana with a combined population of 2.1 million inhabitants.

Ciudad Juárez, formerly known as *Paso del Norte*, is a large city in the Mexican state of Chihuahua. The city lies on the South riverside of the Rio Grande. *El Paso–Juárez* is one of the 14 cross-border towns along the US–Mexico border. It has grown substantially in recent decades due to a large influx of people moving into the city in search of jobs with more than 300 *maquiladoras* (assembly plants) located in and around the city. This rapid economic growth has originated slum-housing communities called *colonias*. Ciudad Juárez has 1,321,000 inhabitants (2010 census). The average annual growth in population over a period (1990–2000) was 5.3 per cent. Ciudad Juárez has experienced much higher population growth than all the state of Chihuahua. It is one of the fastest growing cities in the world despite being called 'the murder capital of the world'.[18] Local sources estimate that over 116,000 houses have been abandoned and more than ten thousand formal businesses – 40 per cent of the total – have shut.

Informal retail at the Fox Flea Market in El Paso

In El Paso (US) street trade activities run differently to the rest of Latin-American border cities. Informal retail is banned in the city core whilst it remains active in the impoverished suburban areas of Tejas, Chamizal and Segundo Barrio. As result, the informal Fox Flea Market has shrunk and displaced in less visible spaces backwards.

The Fox's every-day life creates a vivid expression of domestic economies that are marginalised from the formal sector. Regarding the informal commercial spaces, large and small manifestations are situated in the city core as gateways and immigrant quarters of El Paso. The Fox Flea Market is well known as a marketplace for local and domestic trade situated in a disused large car park lot. Informal trade in marginalised areas of El Paso enhances the sense of every-day appropriation of vacant public and private lots. The adaptability of the street life has to deal with the ability to overlap formal and informal activities and interactions.

Conclusion: beyond transgressive border urbanism

Border urbanism offers opportunities to dwell in new edges, frontiers and boundaries between consolidated urban fabrics or infrastructural systems.[19] It uncovers alternative ways of mapping and grouping complex and multiple spatial interrelationships between the disciplines of urbanism, geography and landscape. Border urbanism generates accidental spaces along the main land-transport road, a kind of *instant city* that emerges from the edges along main corridors with junk-spaces in motion free from conventional spatial definitions. Its *unlabelled* border condition offers opportunities to deal with edges, frontiers and boundaries between consolidated urban fabrics or infrastructural systems, which engenders new spaces of centrality and subsequently spaces that have alternative attributes. Geographically the informalisation represents paradoxical space characterised by contestation, internal differentiation and continuous transgression, in which the social interaction of work, recreation and education become increasingly diffuse. Informal economies in border towns are neither residual nor marginal but rather the most dynamic sector of any fast growing economy.

The urban forms in Pan-American mega and border cities are driven by informalised spatial manifestations along the main regional transport system of *Panamericana*, which offers a unique toolbox of *subaltern urbanism*[20] in border environments. The northern case reveals a hard porosity whilst the southern case offers permeability towards their boundaries.

The lesson of Pan-American border urbanism transgresses the conventional notion of urban planning and architecture. Regarding the *right to the city*, it demands agile urban game plans and the activation of marginalised commercial or housing areas that arise from motorways, checkpoints, tolls, junctions, exits, train tracks, elevated highways or derelict lands. The selected informal spaces are elastic, transformative and subversive. They are not anomalous interferences within the urban fabric but rather *loose spaces*, which are connected with spaces of insurgency, resistance and *quiet encroachment*.[21] Hence transgressive border urbanism is a state of spatial contradictions, exceptions and ambiguities where temporary structures can be proven to be highly resilient.

Notes

1 Brenner, N., Peck, J. and Theodore, N., *Afterlives of Neoliberalism* (London: Bedford Press, 2012), pp. 56–62.
2 Transgression (etymology): late fourteenth century, from Old French *transgression* (12c.), from late Latin *transgressionem*. In classical Latin, *a going over*, from *transgressus*, past participle of *transgredi* (*go beyond*), from *trans-* (*across*) (see *trans-*) + *gradi* (past participle *gressus*) *to walk, go*. Transgression (definition): *An act that goes beyond generally accepted boundaries*. *Webster's Universal College Dictionary* (New York: Gramercy Books, 1997), p. 836.
3 Bayat, A., 'From Dangerous Classes to Quiet Rebels: Politics of the Urban Subaltern in the Global South', *International Sociology* 15 (3) (2000), pp. 555–557. Online at http://iss.sagepub.com/content/15/3/533.abstract, accessed 26/03/2015.

4 Roy, A., 'Strangely Familiar: Planning and the Worlds of Insurgence and Informality', *Planning Theory* 8 (7) (2009), p. 9. Online at http://plt.sagepub.com/content/8/1/7, accessed 26/03/2015.
5 This titanic route, so-called *Panamericana* in Spanish (more than 32,700 km), represents a systematic attempt of linking and organising cities and regions in the Americas, through formal and informal dynamics of transportation, economic development and urbanisation's processes.
6 Lefebvre, H., *The Production of Space*, Chapter 5 'Contradictory Space' (Malden: Blackwell Publishing, 1974), pp. 329–340.
7 Alfred Korzybski stated *'a map is not the territory it represents, but if correct, it has a similar structure to the territory, which accounts for its usefulness'*. Korzybski, A., *Science and Sanity: An Introduction to Non-Aristotelian Systems and General Semantics* (New Jersey: Institute of General Semantics, 1994), p. 58.
8 Debord, G., *Introduction à une Critique de la Géographie Urbaine* (Brussels: Les Lèvres Nues, 1955), p. 6.
9 Suau, C., 'Transgressive Urbanism, Creativity Game', *Theory and Practice of Spatial Planning Journal*, University of Ljubljana (2013), pp. 71, 74.
10 The *Metapolis* is constituted as a polarised system of interconnected global metropolises thanks to the proliferation of high-speed means of transport. '*Metapolisation* is double process of metropolisation and formation of new types of urban territories called metapolis.' Ascher, F., *New Principles of Urbanism* (Madrid: Alianza Editorial, 2004), p. 56.
11 Castells, M., Portes, A. and Benton, L., *The Informal Economy* (London: The John Hopkins University Press, 1989), pp. 1, 24–27.
12 Schneider, F., *Size and Measurement of the Informal Economy in 110 Countries Around the World* (World Bank Rapid Response Unit, 2002). Online at https://openknowledge.worldbank.org, accessed 26/03/2015.
13 Laguerre, M., *The Informal City* (London: Macmillan Press, 1994), p. 3.
14 Ibid., p. 26.
15 Gottman, E., *Behaviour in Public Spaces* (New York: Free Press, 1963), pp. 3–12.
16 According to the report of the National Chamber of Commerce (CNC) *Ferias Libres* sell about 173,000 million CLP (350 million USD) per year. Online at www.ccs.cl, accessed 26/03/2015.
17 Richardson, C. and Pisani, M., *The Informal and Underground Economy of the South Texas Border* (Austin: University of Texas Press, 2012), pp. 139–167. The chapter *Informal Cross Border Trade* explores exemplary cases of undocumented economies in the South Texas border area as a whole. It shows unique insights into the origin and ramifications of subaltern economic channels.
18 Allen, N., 'Mexican City is Murder Capital of the World', *The Telegraph* (2009). Online at www.telegraph.co.uk/news/worldnews/centralamericaandthecaribbean/mexico/6409484/Mexican-city-is-murder-capital-of-the-world.html, accessed 19/10/2014.
19 Hauck, T., Keller, R. and Kleinekort, V. (eds) *Infrastructural Urbanism: Addressing the In-Between* (Berlin: DOM Publishers, 2011), pp. 9–17.
20 Roy, A., 'Slumdog Cities: Rethinking Subaltern Urbanism', in Angelil, M. and Hehl, R. (eds) *Informalize!* (Berlin: Ruby Press, 2012), pp. 109, 114–121.
21 Bayat, A., 'From Dangerous Classes to Quiet Rebels: Politics of the Urban Subaltern in the Global South', *International Sociology* 15 (3) (2000), pp. 533–545.

PART 4
Politics and economy

The indivisibility of politics, economy and architecture is shown by the chapters in this final section of the book. For Marx, studying political economies meant studying the means of production of the capitalist system – understanding the mechanisms by which a small elite produces profit from habits socialized into working people, in systems of control, exploitation and alienation. Lefèbvre, among others, proposed that consumption, distribution and branding produce the spaces of capitalism, and are produced by it. Turning to building production and its 'uses' the architectural profession can find itself employed merely as a political tool within economic stimulus packages crudely designed to counteract each monetary crisis. The essays presented here consider the global consequences of the interplay between politics, economy and architecture at a local and national level; from top-down approaches that deploy 'starchitecture' as a major instrument of national importance aimed at establishing the global presence of a city, to bottom-up strategies in which architects and/or communities define new ways of practice as independent, entrepreneurial enablers. The book concludes with an argument for the value of social capital in articulating spaces of freedom and craftsmanship in modern economies, and questions what benefits accrue from the architectural 'goods' produced.

In the UK – as in many other modern economies – complex public–private instruments have been devised to foster regeneration, often with mediocre urban outcomes, and limited democratic controls or oversight. The leading commentator and polemicist **Owen Hatherley** opens this section with an evaluation of the links between the state, developers and architecture during the 'New Labour' era and its overtures to neoliberal capitalism – as defined by Tony Blair and Gordon Brown in 1994. Usually realized through Design and Build procurement methods that limit architects' control, the effect of these policies was the pretentious and poorly built urban scene Hatherley calls 'Pseudomodernism' – a 'style' lacking the ethical or aesthetic ambitions of Modernism itself. Continuing his argument up to the present he finds local government still largely powerless – it can affect little but the cladding. In London the busy 'New Labour' 'bar-code' facades have been overtaken by more sober languages of brick which – despite their better construction and detail – still serve to cloak and humanize the underlying realities of developer-led over-development, and mounting extremes between wealth and poverty.

As above, politicians often use architecture rather blindly as an instrument of regeneration and economic stimulus but with scant attention to architectural quality or the real needs of users. On the other side of the globe – as **Hannah Lewi and Cameron Logan** examine – the Australian Federal Government strove to mitigate the effects of the global credit crisis through massive investment in building new educational and community facilities. In a different scenario to the UK example – but with similar effects – one of the results of these sudden demands on the industry was to damage the rich economies of exchange between architect and client in which worthwhile results can be calmly evaluated. In a superficial way 'template' projects were encouraged to minimize 'costly' architect–client dialogue and tailored solutions, but no substantive attempt was made, for example, to interrogate the potentials of prefabrication.

Though marketed as a 'stunning work of art' the Burj Khalifa in Dubai – tallest building in the world at the time of writing – is still little more than an object of exchange, and a mighty political instrument, to achieve brand-recognition for this effervescent city in global markets. The physicality of the Burj Khalifa is undeniable but often – as **Kevin Mitchell** argues in his study of the role of architecture in making Dubai – its earlier representations, and even those of unbuilt projects never to be realized, were sufficient objects of exchange to fuel a speculative frenzy. These are also examples of the increasingly seductive power of architectural simulations over the cultural spaces for reflection that more traditional forms of representation once allowed.

Rather more modest strategies of procurement can also richly inform city-making, successfully marrying the ambitions of major public institutions, diverse residential groups and smaller businesses. In a spatial and ethnographic analysis of the Bankside Urban Forest project in south London, **Suzanne Hall** explores city design as smaller-scale spatial 'searching', involving both private and public actors. In contrast to the major top-down political acts described in the previous chapters, this paper explores somewhat subversive practices of architectural production where communities imaginatively pursue the possible with limited means.

Much of the above seems pessimistic in identifying the massive political forces that instrumentalize architecture through the most monetary definitions of value, which divide users from designers, and makers from building. At the same time there are latencies of a different kind of bottom-up politics in the worlds of digital design and assembly, CNC (Computer Numerical Control), parametrics and so on, prompting a revisiting of what craft and making mean now, as seen in the thinking of, for example, Richard Sennett and Lars Spuybroek. These scholars have addressed a new-found relevance in the works of John Ruskin, who in texts such as *Unto this Last* (1860) was early in leading the attack on the reductivist 'science' of Political Economy, in humanizing the notion of value in his dictum 'There is no Wealth but Life', while championing the freedom of craftspeople in the making of architecture. These are matters explored in **Stephen Kite**'s investigation of the place of material and craft in the Victorian's still pertinent ideas, thereby ending this section on 'Politics and Economy' with a note of optimistic potential.

16

THE DEATH AND LIFE OF PFI URBANISM

Vagaries of style and politics in British cities, 2009–present

Owen Hatherley

Between 2009 and 2012, I worked on a series of columns for the by now nearly-defunct architecture paper *Building Design* called 'Urban Trawl', which were later published as two books.[1] The articles were commissioned after I had written on my personal blog a series of extended diatribes about the contemporary architecture of my hometown, one of which caught the eye of the editor of the aforementioned paper, who asked me to do the same to a series of other towns and cities. However, if I look at some of those posts – Southampton being the city in question – I can see that some of the projects that were upsetting me have not, nor are ever likely to, come to pass. This port city of 230,000 people was, around 2007, promising to embellish its skyline with a series of towers of 'luxury flats'. One was going to be designed by Richard Rogers, placed on a riverside site that formerly housed the Vosper Thorneycroft shipyard. Several others were by journeymen commercial firms and were for student housing and miscellaneous 'stunning developments', all on sites close to the parks that mark the northern edge of the city centre. All of them were quite terrifyingly bland, all of them private and all of them 'iconic', but none of them will ever actually exist. The tallest buildings in the city remain a riverside tower block on the 1960s estate of Weston Shore, and the 1930s clock tower of the Civic Centre. Nobody will ever mourn these buildings, or see them as a road not taken in the city; they will not be exhibited or thought about. They have just disappeared, casualties of the 2008 financial crisis, which stopped this sort of overdeveloped, steroidal, empty-headed urbanism – at least outside of London.

The change we could see: New Labour urbanism

The articles bookended a political moment: the end of New Labour, as a political project defined by Tony Blair and Gordon Brown in 1994 as the embrace and partial redistribution of neoliberal capitalism by the hitherto still social democratic

Labour Party – and the beginning of something else. Looking back at them now, it is important to remember just how important the outgoing government's building projects were to their self-image. In 2009, the dying Labour government came up with one of the more amusing of its political gambits. As urban regeneration, and the new building programmes of the Private Finance Initiative (PFI) were so prominent and so popular, how about a campaign focusing on them, presenting the buildings that resulted as proof positive that New Labour had not broken its promises, that it was the party of change, that it was rebuilding Britain and that social programmes were at its heart? The campaign was christened 'The Change We Can See'. When you went to the website – it asked when you clicked on it 'always trust labour.org.uk?' but you had to humour it – you find the explanation:

> Since 1997, we've changed this country – rebuilding the lives of children, older people and families. Make no mistake this could not have happened without supporters like you. Now we face an opposition who wants to deny our successes and cut the public services we rescued. We must stand together and show how proud we are of these historic achievements.

So, it asked the public to submit photographs of PFI Hospitals, City Academies, Sure Start early-learning centres and the like to a Flickr group.

Sadly, it instantly met with a torrent of ridicule and subversion, on a spectrum from political opponents to the editor of the *Architects' Journal*. 'The Change We Can See' entailed Sure Start centres that looked like Asda supermarkets, a surgery that looked like a close of volume-house-builder Barratt Homes, a court (sorry, 'Justice Centre') in the most lumpily jolly 1986 postmodernism that was, astonishingly, completed in 2005, a primary school that resembles Belmarsh Prison, and much that is less immediately shockingly appalling, but all in the chillingly blank PFI idiom of clean lines, bright colours, red bricks and wipe-clean surfaces, as if furnishing a children's ward. Soon, the Flickr group was being subverted – new 'luxury' tower blocks that looked like Soviet barracks, CCTV cameras, lamp-posts capped with spikes to deter vandals, 'stop-and-search cards', images of poisoned brownfield land soon to be developed into housing, all of them contributed by mischievous Flickr users with the subheading 'Vote Labour'. This was not merely some architectural criticism of a real political advance that aesthetes and snobs just did not appreciate. The functions are as awful as the forms – the omnipresent PFI schemes, the bizarre notion that gentrification, as represented by the penthouses of Manchester's Beetham Tower, 'rebuilt the lives of children, older people and families', other than the children, elderly and families of the decidedly affluent. 'The Change We Could See' was horribly depressing – more depressing, even, than the reality. My own contribution, of the first PFI hospital, Darent Valley in Dartford, was happily accepted by the Flickr group (Figure 16.1).

Why is it, then, that actual British architecture, 'The Change We Can See', is so very bad? The answers to this question are usually tied up with the particularly baroque procurement methods of New Labour and an ingrained preference for

FIGURE 16.1 Exurbanism and PFI: Darent Valley Hospital, Dartford

the cheap and unpretentious, causing a whole accidental school of PFI architecture to emerge – often constructed via 'design and build' contracts that removed any control over the result from the architects, with niceties such as detailing and fidelity to any original idea usually abandoned. The forms this took were only partly dictated by cost, however, but also by amateurish parodies of exactly the kinds of high art architecture mentioned above, creating something that Rory Olcayto of the *Architects' Journal* suggested calling 'CABEism',[2] after the Commission for Architecture and the Built Environment, the design quango whose desperate attempts to salvage some possibility of aesthetic pleasure from PFI architects and their developers led to a set of stock recommendations, whose results can be seen everywhere – wavy roofs to give variety, mixed materials so as not to be drab, windswept 'public realm' as a concession to civic valour – but here I will call it Pseudomodernism, a style I regard as being every bit as appropriate to Blairism as postmodernism was to Thatcherism and technocratic, well-meaning modernism was to the post-war compromise.

The most impressive of neoliberal sleights of hand, and one pioneered in Britain before being eagerly picked up everywhere else, has been the creation of what Jonathan Meades neatly calls 'social Thatcherism'.[3] It has existed ever since the mid-1990s, and was not begun by the Labour Party – from John Major's avowed intent to create a 'classless society' to New Labour's dedication to fight 'social exclusion', the dominant rhetoric has been neoliberalism with a human face. The misinterpretation of this among liberals has long been that this proves the existence of some kind of 'progressive consensus', some kind of continuation of social democracy, albeit in a more realistic, less 'utopian' manner. In the built environment, the thesis of a social democratic continuum that connects, say, the Labour of Clement Attlee to New Labour has appeared to be supported by the resurgence, after an eclectic postmodernist interregnum, of modernist architecture, and an apparent focus on the city rather than the suburbs, something proclaimed as the 'Urban Renaissance' by Lord Richard Rogers, in a series of books and white papers with titles that now sound deeply melancholic, and not merely because of the dyslexic architect's verbal infelicities – *A New London, Architecture: A Modern View, Cities for a Small Planet, Cities for a Small Country, Towards an Urban Renaissance, Towards a Strong Urban Renaissance*…

This was enforced by bodies such as the Architecture and Urbanism department of the Greater London Authority locally, and the Urban Task Force and CABE nationally, with mixed success. It enshrined in policy things that leftish architects such as Rogers had been demanding throughout the Thatcher years – building was to be dense, in flats if need be, on 'brownfield' i.e. ex-industrial land, to be 'mixed tenure', and to be informed by 'good design', whatever exactly that might be. The result – five-or-six storey blocks of flats, with let or unlet retail units at ground floor level, concrete frames clad in wood, aluminium and render – can be seen in every urban centre. Similarly, new public spaces and new technologies were intended to create the possibility of a new public modernism. However, what may have looked like an extension of social democracy was actually its inversion.

Instruments brought in after 1945 in order to legally bypass the interests of slum landlords and landowners – Compulsory Purchase Orders, Development Companies – were now used to the opposite end. In this New Labour were not the pioneers. The first to use the instruments of social democracy against its social content was Westminster Council under Shirley Porter, in the 1980s. Finding that the Council was at constant risk of falling to Labour, the local Conservative leadership found that Council tenants, spread liberally across the area by earlier reformers, were more likely to vote Labour. The Council had the legal capabilities to get them out, rehousing them in inferior accommodation out of the borough and offering their – often very fine – flats for sale to upwardly mobile buyers. This programme was called, with an impressive prefiguring of New Labour nu-language, Building Stable Communities. Of course, this was gerrymandering, and Porter herself is still essentially on the lam from justice because of it[4] – but New Labour would do something very similar, only without even the rational excuse of ensuring electoral success. Under the banner of making Communities more 'mixed', council estates such as the huge Heygate Estate in the Elephant and Castle or Holly Street in Hackney were sold off and demolished, their tenants transferred elsewhere or heaped onto the waiting list, in the name of what Deputy Prime Minister John Prescott would call Building Sustainable Communities.

The main semi-governmental organ of 'regeneration', English Partnerships, was designed to bring together business and state, with the latter often sponsoring the former to an extent where it would have been cheaper just to build on its own. It formed part of a weird grey area of almost entirely state funded private companies

– the Arm's Length Management Organisations to which much council housing was transferred, PFI and outsourcing specialists such as Capita and QinetiQ, both of which were formed out of government departments – embodiments of the phase of neoliberalism described by (the writer rather than Labour politician) Mark Fisher among others as 'market Stalinism', where state *dirigisme* continues and grows, only this time working in the service of property and land. By 2009 English Partnerships had transmogrified into the Homes and Communities Agency, where its immediate task was to respond to the 2008 property crash with a house-building programme. Early on, there was some hope that this would lead to a new wave of council building, particularly given that waiting lists had spiralled after the crash, but instead private enterprise continued to be subsidised by the state, in the form of the Kickstart stimulus programme. This offered £1 billion of direct state funding to private developers and builders for 'high quality mixed tenure housing developments', which would be assessed for said 'quality' by the aforementioned aesthetics quango CABE. After its first schemes were unveiled at the start of 2010, it was heavily criticised by CABE for extremely low scores on all their measurements – in terms of energy-efficiency, design quality, public space, access to facilities and public transport and much else. Both bodies refused to name the schemes that had been assessed, despite a Freedom of Information request by *Building Design*, its head Bob Kerslake claiming it would damage the house-builders' 'commercial confidentiality'. At the very end of the New Labour project was a massive programme of public funding for substandard private housing. This was the change we could not see, as we were not allowed to know where the schemes actually were.

The 'Urban Renaissance' was key to all this, and irrespective of its courting of suburbia, New Labour was very much an urban party. Its bases remained in ex-industrial cities, and its hierarchy was drawn from North London, Greater Manchester and Edinburgh. The Tories, irrespective of their capture of the Greater London Authority, are essentially an outer-suburban and rural party, so it will be instructive to find out what they plan to do with this major Blairite shibboleth. Coined in the late 1990s by Ricky Burdett, Anne Power or Richard Rogers, under the auspices of John Prescott and the Urban Task Force, this has become the optimistic term for a middle-class return to the cities, and an attendant redevelopment of previously demonised urban spaces. This is inextricably associated with the urban paraphernalia I have attempted to define as Pseudomodern, as in terms of architectural artefacts, the urban renaissance has meant lottery-funded 'centres', entertainment venues and shopping/eating complexes, clustered around disused riverfronts (Salford Quays, Cardiff Bay, the Tyneside ensemble of Baltic, Sage and Millennium Bridge); in housing, the aforementioned 'mixed' blocks of flats on brownfield sites, the privatisation of council estates, the reuse of old mills or factories; extensive public art, whether cheerful or enigmatically Gormleyesque, usually symbolising an area's phoenix-like re-emergence; districts become branded 'quarters'; and, perhaps most curiously, piazzas (or, in the incongruously grandiose planning parlance, 'public realm') appear, with attendant coffee concessions, promising to bring European sophistication to Derby or Portsmouth.

The process is partial and unevenly scattered, but reaches its most spectacular extent in the miles of luxury flats in the former London Docks, the new high-rise skyline of Leeds, the privatised retail district of Liverpool One or the repopulation of central Manchester (Figure 16.2).

Irrespective of the virtues or otherwise of these new spaces, this urban renaissance is widely considered to have ended in aforementioned city-centre flats sitting empty, as if the exodus from the suburbs to the cities was a confidence trick, and with half-finished, empty or cheaply let towers in Glasgow, Stratford or Sheffield standing both as symbols of the euphemistic 'credit crunch' or the failure, as suburban boosterism might have it, of an attempt to cajole people into a form of living alien to British predilections – although the linked sub-prime crash in the USA was a suburban rather than inner-city phenomenon. However, at least during the boom the cities could argue they were receiving investment, at least they could imagine they were at the heart of some kind of national 'strategy'. This would end under the coalition government.

Exporting the poor: Tory disurbanism, after the urban renaissance

There have been a few striking moments where the sheer scale of the housing crisis and the coming exodus from London suddenly became obvious, and one was when the London Borough of Camden announced early in 2015 that it was planning to rehouse 761 families who would no longer be able to afford to pay the local rents after the various benefit caps, taxes and cuts, somewhere outside of London.[5]

FIGURE 16.2 Regeneration, pre-crash: Manchester skyline

What made it particularly shocking was not so much that this was a London Labour council acting in this fashion. Indeed, Newham Council's strikingly cynical proposals for 'decanting' its tenants to Stoke-on-Trent had already got a few headlines. But Newham is Newham and Camden is Camden. While Newham has never had a great reputation as either a borough or a provider of council housing, Camden, as Ken Livingstone pointed out in his recent autobiography, has long been a minor London showcase for the possibilities of municipal socialism, with 'the best run social services, libraries and council housing in London'.[6] Even after its shift to New Labour policies, Camden, unlike Hackney, Southwark or Tower Hamlets, did not offload its more potentially lucrative stock to developers or Housing Associations,[7] and still maintains a large social infrastructure. It can still residually resemble the nearest thing London has to a not entirely dysfunctionally run local government. If Camden, too, is reduced to throwing up its hands and expelling its less wealthy inhabitants, then we are in a crisis that sweeps across political and municipal boundaries, that is seemingly beyond the abilities of even relatively conscientious local government to do anything about, an unprecedented onslaught on the remnants of council housing and Britain's relatively socially mixed cities that leaves councils unprepared, even in the event that they are willing to defend their tenants and residents. At the time of writing, estimates of the amount likely to be made homeless begin at 100,000 and go upward.

The litany of policies that are exacerbating this crisis are by now familiar. The 'bedroom tax', where those with 'too large' flats are deliberately coerced into moving by punitive housing benefit cuts; the ending of lifelong tenure in council flats; the various caps on benefits, targeting especially those who have been breeding at a rate that evidently unnerves the coalition government; the collapse of even the tiny trickle of Housing Association 'social' housing that was being built under New Labour; the final criminalisation of squatting; the continuing rises in rents and house prices, thus far freakishly unaffected in the south-east by a double-dip recession; the redefinition of 'affordable housing' as a preposterous 80 per cent of market rent; the abolition of the obligation upon councils to quickly house the homeless in local areas; new incentives for tenants to exercise their 'right-to-buy' in order to take out even more council housing stock – all of them quickly announced and quickly passed, in the coalition's now-familiar, blizzard-like approach. They are then accompanied by even more psychotic proposals from strategic outliers such as the thinktank Policy Exchange, who can frequently be found in the mass media advocating demolishing all tower blocks or selling off all council housing in 'rich areas' so 'affordable' housing can be built somewhere cheaper.

However, this destructive programme was not heaped upon a 'healthy' housing stock, but one that is already deeply dysfunctional. The imperative to offload, sell or raze council estates (whether 'eyesores' or 'icons', either can be spun the right way), the baleful 'Housing Market Renewal' programme in the north, the legacy of right-to-buy and decades with an effective prohibition on new council housing, the favouring of landlords and the nonexistence of rent control, the use of housing speculation to propel an entire economy – all these already existed under New

Labour. The new situation is seemingly designed to create what New Labour's urban policies appeared to aim at all along – a 'Parisian' form of city where a wealthy urban core is surrounded with a proletarian banlieue, a situation that exists in only a handful of British cities, such as Oxford or Edinburgh. Accordingly, it is hardly well placed to try and hold back this torrent.

Camden, when formed as a borough in the mid-1960s, embarked on the most impressive of London's various municipal housing programmes. Under the direction of architect Sydney Cook, its housing department favoured individually designed, low-rise, neo-modernist estates that were frequently very expensively built. Many of them – Alexandra Road, Dunboyne Road, Branch Hill, Highgate New Town, Mansfield Road, Maiden Lane – have become architecturally famous, while unassumingly carrying on as well-used and (usually) well-maintained council housing stock.[8] Camden was able to do this not because it was unusually noble or well-intentioned, but because it could afford it. Given that the borough contained some of the wealthiest areas of North London alongside various ex-industrial areas, it could raise enough in tax to fund much more ambitious and careful schemes than its neighbours. Newham, an amalgamated borough formed at the same time, had no such luck; its most famous effort in late-1960s housing was Ronan Point, a jerrybuilt prefab tower, part of a package deal with Taylor Woodrow, that notoriously collapsed in May 1968.

Not wholly coincidentally, in the late 1960s and early 1970s, when most of these schemes were being built, Camden was one of the first London areas to really experience 'gentrification' as we now know it – the middle classes moving into working class areas, not in Burdett-Coutts fashion in order to bring light to darkest London, but in order to snap up down-at-heel early nineteenth-century housing in a location convenient for central London and various picturesque, bygone-age-evoking local amenities, such as the junk market and the canal.[9] These media professionals and proto-hipsters, the 'knockers-through' as one of their number, Alan Bennett, dubbed them, were the first of a now very familiar sub-class, bringing chic restaurants, antiques shops and rent rises in their wake. That this did not create a situation of total working class exodus is largely to do with the massive housing programme that was unfolding at the same time. Not only that, but when the council shifted at the end of the 1970s away from large-scale modernist undertakings, it started buying up and letting to council tenants exactly the early Victorian housing stock that had become so desirable to the knockers-through. The fact that Camden did not wholly become Chelsea, a haute bourgeois ghetto, is surely due to this legacy. Without having quite the same spectacular architectural success, a lot of other areas in larger British cities can tell similar stories.

The difference between gentrification 1970s-style and the present day is, of course, that no such attempt at alleviation (even if it was here fairly inadvertent) exists. In fact, these processes are encouraged by Labour councils, and have been since the mid-1990s. This cannot be put down entirely to mere venality, but the confused groping around for a purpose that overtook local governments in the aftermath of rate-capping, the Greater London Council (GLC) and Metropolitan

County Council abolitions, the crushing of Liverpool and Sheffield. Despite the scattered examples of Camden, Notting Hill or Islington, or the 'Merchant City' in Glasgow, few urban local governments in 1992 could have seriously considered their main problem to be an influx of the wealthy into working class or low-rent districts. After 1997 especially, an apparatus of quangos and propaganda was gradually pieced together by local authorities and central government, heralded as early as Richard Rogers and then Labour culture secretary Mark Fisher's *A New London*. The components of this, now quite familiar, entailed an uncritical embrace of the 'continental' city, for various reasons. Barcelona, Bilbao, Amsterdam, Rotterdam, Berlin, Paris, were all cited extensively in the mid-1990s, usually for the same reasons. Social democratic local authorities holding both power and the trust of business; concerted, planned (as opposed to 'enterprise zone'-driven) building on former industrial sites; a culture of apartments, rather than single-family houses; a situation where the middle classes often live in the centre of cities; investment in public space, parks and riverside promenades; and a willingness to employ young and untried architects to design finely, expensively wrought architecture.

In several respects, what they saw in Barcelona was a sort of super-Camden, with the crucial difference that council housing and the mix of classes (and, for that matter, races) was largely absent in their European examples; as Fisher and Rogers noted with regret in 1992, the Barcelona Olympic Village never became the 'mixed class' development that local government intended.[10] Neither, obviously, would the Olympic Village in London twenty years later. By that point, the process had taken on a momentum of its own. No longer was it sufficient to house the new urban middle classes, the 'urban safarians' as one tactless developer called them,[11] in post-industrial conversions or high-density newbuilds. *Home Sweet Home*, Enrica Colusso's film on the Heygate Estate,[12] includes a leader of Southwark Council declaring that in the early 1990s the borough woke up and realised that rather than being a poor area, it was in fact a central London borough, a potentially *rich area*. It is a short step from that to Policy Exchange's proposals that council tenants and housing benefit claimants be moved out of *rich areas*. What were they doing there in the first place?

The earliest demolitions of council estates and their replacement with the requisite 'urban renaissance' newbuild were relatively uncontroversial, entailing some degree of genuine 'consultation' and direct rehousing of those who were to be cleared; the demolition of the 1970s estates in Hulme, Manchester, even gave rise to a mildly radical housing co-operative on part of its former fabric, in amongst the usual developers' 'townhouses'. Again, however, the process rapidly shed its social democratic covering, and became increasingly ruthless. In Keeling House or Balfron Tower in London or Park Hill in Sheffield, clearance was justified architectural fame (all three are listed buildings, and hence need expensive levels of care) and a convoluted socio-historical argument whereby the clearance of 'communities' in the first instance when these places were built justified the clearance of the 'communities' that lived there by the 2000s. Other estates were demolished not as icons awaiting a better class of clientèle, but as a way of 'saving' residents from the unbearable burden of secure, low-rent housing in large city centre apartments: the Three Towers and the Cardroom estate in Manchester, the Ferrier and Holly Street estates in London and, currently, large estates in the Elephant and Castle, Earls Court and Stratford, to name but a few. Alongside them, came the much larger-scale Pathfinder programme in the north of England, where areas of 'low market demand' and sluggish levels of property speculation were given a fillip by massive demolition programmes of publicly owned housing, with tenants and owner-occupiers alike being offered new houses far from the city centre, in order to create a 'better social mix' in the inner city. What Boris Johnson calls 'Kosovo-style cleansing' was, it must be admitted, hardly the sole product of his party.

What the coalition have done is abandon the 'positive' aspect of New Labour's housing policy, the optimistic elements, the 'vision thing'. The jolly rhetoric of high-density-city-living-is-good-for-you has disappeared, replaced with the grim hectoring of austerity. The notion that cities would need the 'good design' considered so important by the Barcelonists was an early casualty. CABE had its public funding withdrawn, as more recently has Design for London; Michael Gove – when Secretary of State for Education – took a particularly hard line on the suspicious notion of 'architecture', preferring supermarket-like prefab kits or adaptive re-use for his meagre 'free schools'. The Regional Development Agencies, hardly particularly admirable organisations, taking on the functions previously performed by the Metropolitan County Councils without any aspect of democratic accountability, were abolished across the North and Midlands, and with them the quasi-state funding of the new city skylines. The focus on the inner city (especially the northern inner city) was itself threatened by the reforms of the National Planning Policy Framework, which attempts, with an unusually incremental approach due to the influential lobbying of those in the shires, to encourage new development in that small part of south-east England where the increasingly desperate house-building industry can still collect a decent profit on their speculation – something that is no longer true of, say, condos in Leeds. The government's early rhetoric around mythical 'garden grabbing' was aimed at attempting to break with the notion of dense, tall housing in inner cities. It gives some indication of the curiously retro nature of coalition urban policies. They have even resurrected the 'enterprise zone' – a policy that was initially aimed at taking post-industrial spaces ripe for development in inner cities out of the hands of 'loony left' local authorities. Now that the local authorities are cowed and quiescent, it appears as a kind of zombie Thatcherism – if it worked in 1986, maybe it will work now.

The change we can see, now: cladding the problem

On the face of it, apart from the renewed intensity of development in London and the increasing parlousness of its working class population, not much has changed. In architectural terms, however, London took a turn for the sober. The journeys I regularly take from south-east to central London, by train, by Docklands Light

Railway (DLR) or by bus, have always been a good place to watch 'regeneration' at work. Entire districts that did not exist previously – 'Greenwich Central' on Creek Road in Deptford and other such geographical improbabilities – arise without fanfare. Creeks, canals and streets previously defined by strung-out light industry or GLC estates would be replaced with first, concrete frames, then massive (but 'broken-up' and demonstratively irregular) blocks of flats, covered in all manner of generalised stuff – trespa panels, aluminium balconies, swooping roofs, slatted wood. Anyone who has been to any British city in the last decade is familiar with the genre. Lately, the same frames have gone up, in much the same ex-industrial places, and with more or less the same cram-as-many-units-as-possible approach to massing. But that chaos of jollily clashing materials is gone and, instead, is a new coating of traditional London stock brick. London has a new typology – the austere yuppie flat, the tasteful 1950s-style modernist non-dom investment.

You could see it first in architects Maccreanor Lavington's redevelopment of King's Cross, where the quality of materials is extremely high. To anyone used to the way that contemporary London architecture feels intangible, tinny, tacky, afraid of physicality or permanence, it is bracing to visit their cluster of towers on the Regent's Canal. Suddenly, various qualities long missing from the city's housing – rhythm, moulding, a sense of weight and depth – are deployed on a grand scale. At first, the result is intense and impressive (Figure 16.3).

What is perhaps more impressive, though, is the fact that the reason for this concern with physical surface may be much the same as that motivating the previous use of wood-effect trespa and multicoloured panels – that is, the breaking up by the architect of the mass dictated by the needs of the developer. Maccreanor Lavington's towers are as ultra-dense as any scheme by MAKE or their ilk, and similarly attempt to mask that through various kinds of display and contortion, pulling themselves into craggy shapes and skylines so as to humanise the dogged filling of every inch of the site. This is more obvious at the lesser scheme in the Royal Docks, where the budget has not stretched to the expressionistic modelling used so interestingly at King's Cross, and you have instead just unusually well-clad yuppie flats.

The new London brick is ultimately the result of Design for London guidelines, that is, coming from one of the offices set up by the Mayor of London to influence London's town planning and architecture. It shows that while local government seems to have no ability or interest in influencing *what* developers build, it is able to influence how they clad it; and in a city with so captive a market as this, buyers and investors are presumably not too put off by the replacement of the barcode facade with the brick panel. However it is taking critics some time to notice that the aesthetic of London today, at the nadir of its housing crisis, at the moment where the gap between rich and poor is wider than at any time since the 1930s, is no longer the screaming plutocratic cacophony of St George's Wharf or Stratford High Street. It is sober, well mannered, increasingly well made. It is as if the response to the housing crisis was to make housing less conspicuous, less of an aggressive imposition on the eyes of the unfavoured. It says 'look, we live in normal brick houses, just like you'.

FIGURE 16.3 Regeneration, post-crash: Kings Cross

Notes

1. *A Guide to the New Ruins of Great Britain* (London: Verso, 2010) and *A New Kind of Bleak: Journeys Through Urban Britain* (London: Verso, 2012).
2. Rory Olcayto, 'The Mill, Ipswich, by John Lyall Architects', *Architects' Journal*, 6 October 2009.
3. In *On the Brandwagon* (BBC, 15 June 2007).
4. Andrew Hosken's *Nothing Like a Dame: The Scandals of Shirley Porter* (London: Granta, 2006) brilliantly profiles the use of housing as an instrument in class war, but it should be remembered that the policy *worked* – Westminster has been a safe Tory council for some time.

5 Randeep Ramesh, 'Camden council plans to move 761 poor families from London', *The Guardian*, 13 February 2012. Suggestions for rehousing on the part of the many London councils planning outward movements of their tenants include, as well as south Essex and north Kent, towns such as Stoke and Merthyr Tydfil – i.e. areas with the highest rates of unemployment in the UK.
6 Ken Livingstone, *You Can't Say That* (London: Faber & Faber, 2011), p. 139.
7 Not for want of trying, however – tenants voted against attempts to make them give up their council status.
8 There is as yet no book on the subject, but there was an exhibition at London's Building Centre, 'Cook's Camden': see Michal Boncza, 'Cook's Camden: London's Great Experiment in Social Housing', *Morning Star*, 3 December 2010; note also the film *Rowley Way Speaks for Itself*, on the most famous of the Camden estates.
9 See the frequent notes on the 'knockers-through' in Alan Bennett, *Writing Home* (London: Faber & Faber, 1994); and see also the recurrent references to Camden in Raphael Samuel's *Theatres of Memory: Past and Present in Contemporary Culture* (London: Verso, 2012).
10 Mark Fisher and Richard Rogers' *A New London* (London: Penguin, 1992) prophetically notes, in amongst the praise, 'the almost total elimination of social housing at affordable rents in the new Olympic Village apartments' (p. 67). If it was obvious that early on…
11 The guilty party is the developers Igloo, speaking of their Bermondsey Square development. Dan Stewart, 'Operation Hip', *Building*, 29 May 2009.
12 Enrica Colusso, *Home Sweet Home* (film, 2012).

17

A STIMULUS FOR EDUCATION

Global economic events and the design of Australian schools

Hannah Lewi and Cameron Logan

On 3 February 2009, the Australian Government announced a 14.7 billion (AUD$) dollar plan to upgrade and build new facilities for the nation's schools. It was by far the biggest single component of a 42 billion dollar fiscal stimulus package, which the government hoped would help avert a recession in Australia in the midst of the global credit crisis. The main part of the so-called Building the Education Revolution (BER) was a programme aimed at providing every primary school (Preparatory or Kindergarten to Grade 6) in the country with a new building that included – and in some cases combined – a library, multi-purpose hall and/or classrooms. By August 2010 more than 18,000 projects had been approved, creating a huge wave of demand for educational design, documentation and project management.[1] In this chapter, we argue that this recent wave of building under the BER programme – unprecedented in its national size and scope – has magnified long-standing tensions between the pursuit of individualized design innovation and ad-hoc provision of schools on the one hand, and the adoption of standardized design and delivery on the other. Moreover, the programme highlighted an apparent incompatibility between the goal of short-term economic stimulus and innovations that might lead to longer lasting economies in construction process. While the government encouraged, even mandated, 'template' design solutions it did not consider the rationalization of construction through prefabrication. In other words, architects were to respond to the emergency by streamlining the design process, but the building industry was to continue on in its conventional fashion. So while the economic stimulus of the recent economic crisis had a visible impact on architecture, the design and motivations of the emergency package strictly delimited the kind of innovations that it might produce.

The multiplier effect

The volume of work involved in the BER programme was proportionally comparable to the British Government's 'Building Schools for the Future' scheme announced in 2004, which was generally acknowledged in the United Kingdom as the biggest school building programme since Victorian times. Even compared to the New Deal infrastructure programmes in the United States enacted between 1933 and 1943, the recent Australian school building programme, measured either by project or per capita investment, was substantial.[2] Yet more than the sheer size of the project, it was the rapidity of delivery that defined this scheme. The Australian federal government's belief was that if the economic stimulus package was to succeed they must, in the words of then Treasury Secretary Ken Henry, 'go early' and 'go hard'. This conviction was based on the well-established efficacy of the multiplier effect, first elucidated by John Maynard Keynes. The theory suggests that government expenditure made early in a downturn has a greater impact on the overall economy by underpinning consumption and improving the prospects for employment. There was, therefore, a premium placed on rapid delivery of all the ensuing stimulus measures, including the school building projects, and this resulted in the imposition of very short timelines for design, documentation, procurement and construction.

Conservative opposition parties and sections of the media decried the school building programme at the time as excessive and wasteful.[3] But economists generally hailed its success. In August 2010, 51 academic economists signed an open letter stating that the package had indeed prevented a 'deep recession' and 'a massive rise in unemployment' in Australia. They noted that the school building programme 'boosted the construction industry and created thousands of new jobs' and 'also provided a much needed increase in the stock of public capital'.[4] The same month, visiting Nobel laureate Joseph Stiglitz was likewise sanguine about the effect of the Australian government's stimulus measures. He described the package as 'the best designed stimulus package of any of the … advanced industrial countries, both in size and in design, timing and how it was spent'.[5] The success of the school building programme, therefore, as a macro-economic measure is widely acknowledged. But what of its impact on architecture and on the school buildings that resulted from the programme?

While architecture firms were amongst the seemingly obvious beneficiaries of the government largesse, the response to the BER policy by the architecture profession in Australia was equivocal, if not disappointed. As in the wider community, some architects almost certainly did not understand or agree with the central assumptions of the stimulus package, especially the focus on rapidity of expenditure demanded by the multiplier effect, that led to irrationalities, market distortions and poorly conceived projects. No doubt others were simply miffed that they did not benefit from the boom in school design work. But the somewhat suspicious reaction of architects is also based on some inbuilt assumptions in the scheme's aims that arguably put a low value on architectural design. The BER programme emphasized three main objectives: i) the macro-economics of stimulus; ii) improvement in the quality of school facilities; and iii) value for money. Without any direct reference to architectural strategies, the near impossibility of achieving all three of these objectives – given their inherent tensions – was obvious. For, while terms such as 'shovel-ready projects', 'future-proofing' and 'sustainability' were daily themes of politicians' press releases and public service briefings, there was little specific reference to any discussion of architectural quality. The programme depended fundamentally on architectural expertise in school design but provided no direction about how to either draw upon, or foster, that expertise.

One intention that was quite clear from the way in which the Australian government delivered the money was that, despite the scope of the intervention, this policy was never intended as a means of returning to an expanded public sector, or of developing the kind of research-based, institutional knowledge and specialized expertise for which the best public-sector architectural offices were known in earlier decades. For most of the period in which Australian governments have taken primary responsibility for the provision of school infrastructure – from roughly 1870 to the present – the bulk of the design was undertaken by public works departments and state government architects' offices. But after a generation of market-oriented reform, which saw governments divest themselves of assets and responsibilities, such departments are now almost entirely gone. This stimulus package was not, therefore, going to be used as a Trojan horse for the public sector. It was clearly an exercise in 'priming the pump' – a strategic, large-scale but short-term intervention not intended to promote any lasting government legacy aside from the buildings themselves. But, even given the apparent lack of targeted interest in architectural production, the programme had significant implications for public architecture and practice in Australia (Figure 17.1).

The template solution

Despite general – if at times grudging – agreement by governments about the desirability of improving school environments through innovative architectural design, robust buildings and servicing, and pedagogically driven spatial reforms, progress in Australia has continually been hampered by insufficient public funding and unpredictable demand for facilities due to changing demographics. Architectural experiments, solutions and new standard-setting have, however, somehow managed to emerge within tight economic contingencies in Australian school building during key periods of the twentieth century.

For example, in the early 1950s, in the context of postwar austerity and exponential rates of population growth, Victoria developed the Light Timber Construction (LTC) system. Devised by Percy Everett, the Chief Architect of the state Public Works Department, and based on an easily extendable linear plan, the LTC system was a rational and highly economical method for rapid delivery of school buildings. It marked a decisive move away from recognized modes of

A stimulus for education   **207**

FIGURE 17.1 Cartoon showing economic stimulus building in the likeness of former Prime Minister Kevin Rudd with chimney styled as Deputy Prime Minister and Education Minister at the time, Julia Gillard

Source: Cartoon by Nicholson, *The Australian*, first published 28 August 2009.

institutional decorum towards a simple, well-lit and unpretentious utilitarianism. In the following decade, in New South Wales the Government Architect's Branch developed a template plan for a new generation of high schools. While not setting out a completely rigid formula, it was based on grouping a series of square, doughnut-shaped classroom, laboratory and administration buildings in a pinwheel configuration around a large outdoor gathering area. This wave of schools was built according to a roof construction process that represented a significant efficiency at the time. In South Australia, the Public Buildings Department developed the South Australian Modular Construction system (SAMCON) in the late 1960s in an attempt to streamline and systematize the procurement and construction process. In each case, the educational authorities professed the dual ambition of improving the educational setting, while rationalizing the process of design, servicing and maintenance.

These innovations in Australian schools design paralleled international developments. In the UK for example, as a major study commissioned by English Heritage has noted 'post-war demand for places encouraged local authorities to think in terms of programmes of schools rather than one-offs'.[6] Consequently system building for new schools was extensive in this period, and various consortia were formed by local authorities as a means of achieving high levels of prefabrication.[7] In the United States Ezra Ehrenkratz's School Construction Systems Development (SCSD) model led to the construction of dozens of schools in Northern California in the late 1960s, with classrooms based around a fully serviced, factory-produced roof module.[8]

In Australia, in the 1970s and 1980s, such systematic approaches largely fell from favour. Rates of population growth in school-age children eased and new trends in teaching and learning undermined the impetus toward producing well-tempered, repeatable units of space with increasing levels of prefabrication. Moreover, pluralistic trends in architectural thought saw a move away from the expression of technologically driven solutions towards other concerns, such as the social and contextual situation of the school. At times, also evident, was a more experimental move away from the traditional classroom towards a greater focus on openness and adaptability.

Those in government who framed the policies for the BER school building programme in early 2009 therefore had a number of interesting precedents and possibilities to consider. As it turned out they prioritized predictability and repeatability of plan as the best means for achieving their policy aims. The federal scheme stipulated core constraints and strategies as follows:

> To further enhance efficiency and early take-up, design templates will be used … wherever possible. These templates must be used by each project unless a school or system has a pre-approved design available, or can demonstrate that the non-use of a template is reasonable, appropriate and that the building process can still be expedited and achieved within the prescribed timeframes.[9]

While the federal government designed the stimulus package and created the policy settings for the school building programme, it was state governments in their role as providers of public education who played the greatest part in implementing it. The Victorian Department of Education invited Hayball and Gray Puksand Architects – practices with a strong portfolio of educational sector work – to produce a limited set of template solutions in just three weeks (Figure 17.2). As one Hayball practice director remarked in hindsight, 'at the time no one really understood what the brief and project really was'.[10] The template concepts and combinations that they developed were based on the prioritized types of library, classroom modules, multi-purpose centres/halls including spaces for performing arts and science/language centres.

So how then should we understand this idea of the template in terms of an architectural strategy? Historically the concept has been wide-reaching, and at times has been used interchangeably with the more pervasive term 'type'. Yet the template does not only prescribe a set of functional types, nor does it simply evoke repetitive morphological elements and configurations embedded within the historical language of architecture or drawn from contexts.[11] In its more specific usage the term template denotes a pattern or gauge for fabrication. This

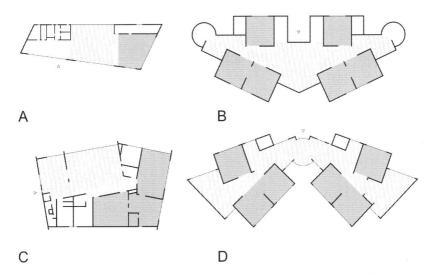

FIGURE 17.2 Example template designs by Hayball and Gray Puksand Architects for the Victorian Education Department, showing four configurations for primary schools in Victoria, identified as A – Multipurpose Centre; B – 21C Library and Learning Neighbourhood; C – 21C Science and Language; D – External Learning Settings

Source: image redrawn by A. Murray for reproduction, September 2014.

carries with it an obvious economic implication and it was this sense perhaps, of providing ready-made solutions and streamlined modes of delivery, that appealed to the BER policymakers in Canberra. Considered in this way it is closer in meaning (although certainly not in political motivation) to the concept of type as equating to 'standardization' or 'typification' (translated from *Typisierung*) as proffered by Hermann Muthesius via the *Deutsche Werkbund*.[12] And like typification, template here implies the seeking of a normative solution.

Aside from assisting in meeting economic imperatives, the templates were promoted as a means to introduce flexible and multi-purpose space and functional solutions regarded as more appropriate to twenty-first-century educational models. Flexibility here indicates both a practical approach to moveable infrastructure – i.e doors, windows, room layouts – as well as an organization and functional ideal reflective of multi-tasking and multi-purpose, collaborative teaching. Multi-purpose functionality catering for varied users also fulfilled another federal government brief objective that any new buildings should allow for, and indeed encourage, wider use outside of core educational functions to 'help … bring communities together'.[13] Neither the pursuit of flexibility, nor the ideal of community accessibility, was a novel aim. They had both been central to progressive ideals that exercised growing influence in education in the twentieth century. Walter Gropius and Maxwell

Fry's Impington Village College (1939) was, for instance, an influential model in this respect. And school architecture of the postwar decades in Australia, as in Britain, almost always included some gesture towards flexibility and community accessibility.

An interim review of the initial template schemes conducted by the Victorian Government Architect's Office suggested that the template design solutions should be 'calmed down' and made more anonymous and generic, so they could be better tailored to individual schools according to both context and functional requirements.[14] This advice reflected wider anxieties that this massive intervention – across some 750 schools in Victoria and built in a very short time period – would construct an overtly identifiable strata of work tying every school to this economic imperative: architecture as political branding and symbolic of 'big government' that would endure well beyond the controversial billboards prominently erected at every school receiving funding (Figure 17.3). In response, more attention was also paid to the changeability of appearance, especially materials and colour, with the creation of design packages analogous to an 'operation manual' accompanying the template designs to cater for varied contexts, environmental conditions and local construction techniques across urban and regional areas.

Concurring with the dominance of mixed public–private partnerships in the delivery of public facilities, the state governments managed the roll-out of design templates for individual schools through small, regional-based teams of private architects and consultants, and construction through a market-led tendering process by private building contractors. The whole programme was thus crafted around a set of compromises between the federal macro-economic agenda of stimulus, the private industry-focused, competitive procurement processes and the architectural product. It is hardly surprising then that the template solution has produced hybridized results. Architects involved were well aware of the pitfalls and challenges presented by the template strategy. As one remarked: 'The templates were meant to do everything for everybody everywhere – so whether you were in Mallacoota or Mildura you had access to the same templates.'[15]

The driving political ambition to keep building contractors at work in the traditional trades during the downturn implied shying away from wholesale standardized or innovative prefabricated approaches that have been explored for school building in the past. While dramatically streamlining the design process through the adoption of templates minimized the number of professional consultants, especially architects, involved. This agenda was reinforced through interview commentary:

> Really that was the pure intent of the Department … instead of getting several hundred teams documenting several hundred jobs – we have one base team document one set of alternatives – we hand the information over to the roll-out team to make it site specific.[16]

Again, reminiscent of the modernist aims of standardization through type, there was certainly hope that through a concentration of effort, standards would be ensured and predictability in production and performance would be maintained.

FIGURE 17.3 Building the Education Revolution billboard outside the newly completed multi-purpose hall for Fairfield Primary School, Victoria

This aspiration for standardization, albeit dressed in the palatable clothing of flexibility and variation, reflected the more general aims towards more centralization and universalization. The adoption of templates can therefore be regarded as a penetration into the built environment of recent political and economic aspirations towards the wholesale lifting and monitoring of educational standards.

While the template approach was the basis of the BER programme in all of the Australian state education systems, the non-government education sector also makes up a considerable part of primary education provision. Additionally, around 25 per cent of funded projects in the Victorian state schools were realized as non-template solutions undertaken where it could be demonstrated that template configurations did not fit functional or site conditions. Overall more positive publicity in the architecture media was devoted to non-government and non-template work under the BER. For example, an 'Unbuilt Architecture commendation' in 2011 was awarded to Phooey Architects for their performing arts centre design for Parkhill Primary (the Sydney Opera House translated to suburban Melbourne – shelved mid-way through the design process).[17] While in Queensland, the 'building-of-the-year', 2011, was awarded to Parkhurst Primary by Arkhefield,[18] and a number of other notable smaller design practices were commissioned by Catholic schools. Although, as seen in Britain where winning architecture awards for schools did not win favour with the previous Education Secretary Michael Gove,[19] architectural recognition was not one of the stated BER programme objectives.

Conclusions and compromises

What then were the most significant implications of the BER stimulus package and of the ensuing template solution? Despite its recentness and conflicting agendas, it is possible to capture some of the reactions to the programme and built outcomes from interviews, the media and the findings of an Auditor-General's report conducted into the BER. There is no doubt that the programme addressed a pressing need for bricks and mortar capital spending in the government education system. So, overall, those directly involved in the education sector, and parents and children using schools, welcomed the new school additions. The statistics around the sheer number of new buildings built remains impressive and was aired surprisingly little in media debates. There are many stories of educators' satisfaction with the Victorian template results some of them presented, as one might expect, on the Department of Education's own website.

However the tensions between design customization, quality and appropriateness, and the demands of time and perceived value-for-money, were clearly evident throughout. The national Auditor-General's findings reported mixed reactions to the template designs themselves, with around 20 per cent of school principals reporting that they did not understand the template process, or that the buildings were inappropriate to school's individual needs, and 40 per cent not satisfied with the opportunity for any design input (compared with less than 7 per cent in the non-government sector). These figures bear out the challenges surrounding centralized standardization. There were also strong levels of disagreement about the degree of flexibility and customization that the templates really offered.[20] This perhaps says more about the vexed notion of flexibility itself than the inflexibilities of this particular building programme.[21]

As mentioned at the outset, economic reports supported the effectiveness of the BER as a key part of Australian stimulus programmes, in underpinning employment and levels of spending. The political imperatives were first and foremost macro-economic, as was strikingly evident at one opening of a BER building in suburban Melbourne, where the message delivered by the member of parliament was all about the generation of 'jobs, jobs, jobs', and far less about education reform and community infrastructure. The adoption of designated templates was assumed to increase the speed of building delivery within the political cycle, as well as speeding the delivery of government money into the wider economy.

It is also clear that the flow-on effects of the BER were directed at construction employment and the short-term maintenance of the status quo in the industry – which had been operating in a boom-time mode prior to the global financial crisis. The massive government intervention, in terms of spending, led to minimal government intervention in terms of regulation of building contracts (a stark contrast to the desired levels of control of the design professions). This resulted in uneven distribution of work through market-driven competitive tendering, with other unforeseen repercussions in terms of labour and material supplies and inflated prices.[22]

Reactions from the architecture profession were mixed, obviously dependent partly on self-interest, but also based on substantive criticisms of the perceived lost opportunities for real innovation. The Victorian template buildings represented solid, un-monumental, low risk and tailorable architectural solutions that, in their quest for multi-purpose anonymity, were in tune with the government's message of practical, un-extravagant buildings; not quite utilitarian but often ordinary.

The Australian experience is also highly relevant to other international situations. For example the previous British Labour Government's 'Building Schools for the Future' programme was abandoned by the incoming Conservative Government's Secretary of State for Education Michael Gove in 2010. The programme was radically reconfigured through the adoption of a 'handful' of template designs, critiqued in one media report as 'overly-standardized identifit' or 'flatpack' solutions that are 'fit-for-purpose' but certainly not architecturally distinguished.[23]

For some architecture practices the economic downturn was dramatic and the increased work from government programmes kept them afloat. But the number of practices and consultants in Australia who directly received commissions under the BER was small in comparison to the volume of work. With the template strategy now established as a mode of streamlining design work for public buildings, concerns have been raised about the longer-term effects on the open commissioning of architects – with the possibility of extending the template solution to totally new-build schools symptomatic of this cutting out of individual design commissions. The BER programme also cemented the perception of an exclusive niche market of education-sector specialists. Other substantive criticism from the Australian Institute of Architects revolved around the need for long-term testing of claims of improved sustainability performance,[24] and on the general haste of the design process, that, in the main, bypassed the checks and balances of planning review and thorough heritage studies that might have mitigated detrimental change to existing campuses with architectural significance. The template design process was frankly summarized to us as 'brutal ... but it guaranteed value and a result'.[25]

How to measure or recognize the value of school architecture, as with any architecture, is a vexed issue. But in the context of a programme driven by the exigencies of macro-economic stimulus, it is not even clear that conventional economic value – more for less – is even applicable. Economy, under such circumstances, is perhaps best summarized as 'the quicker you spend it the more you get'. According to such macro-economic logic the nominal product of the spending, the schools, is not in fact the product at all. Economic growth was the product and school architecture merely the means of achieving it.

Acknowledgements

This research was funded by an Australian Research Council Discovery Grant and The University of Melbourne.

Notes

1. www.parliament.vic.gov.au/images/stories/committees/etc/BER_Submissions/Interim_Report/BER_Interim_Repo rt_FINAL.pdf [accessed 13 May 2011].
2. On the legacy of these programmes see Robert D. Leighninger Jr, 'Cultural Infrastructure: The Legacy of New Deal Public Space', *Journal of Architectural Education*, Vol. 49, No. 4 (May 1996), pp. 226–236 and Phoebe Cutler, *The Public Landscape of the New Deal* (New Haven, CT: Yale University Press, 1985).
3. *The Australian*, part of Rupert Murdoch's News Limited stable of newspapers, ran a forthright campaign to discredit the stimulus package and the school building programme in particular. See, for example, Lenore Taylor, 'Vital Details Left in Limbo', *The Australian*, 30 May 2009 and Justin Ferrari, 'Regulations Wreck Cleve Area School Build Plans', *The Australian*, 6 June 2009.
4. 'An Open Letter' signed by 51 Australian economists and sent to major Australian media outlets on 16 August 2010. http://images.brisbanetimes.com.au/file/2010/08/16/1781211/Labor%27s%20Stimulus%20Package%2C%202010.pdf [accessed 3 June 3 2011].
5. Kerry O'Brien, 'Troubles Ahead for World Economy', interview with Joseph Stiglitz, *The 7:30 Report*, aired 27 July 2010 (Sydney: ABC TV, 2010).
6. Geraint Franklin, with Elain Harwood, Simon Taylor and Matthew Whitfield, 'England's Schools, 1962–1988: A Thematic Study', *English Heritage, Research Report Series*, No. 33-2012 (2012), p. 1.
7. On prefabrication see Andrew Saint, *Towards a Social Architecture: The Role of School-Building in Post-War England* (New Haven, CT; London: Yale University Press, 1987).
8. Ehrenkratz's 'School Construction Systems Development' was discussed in Reyner Banham's *Architecture of the Well Tempered Environment* (London: The Architecture Press, 1969); more recently Theo Prudon has examined its survival and legacy. Theo Prudon, 'SCSD Forty Years Later' presented at Association for Preservation Technology 2009, *Preservation in the City Without Limits*, Los Angeles, 2–6 November 2009.
9. Australian Government, Nation Building, Economic Stimulus Plan – Building the Education Revolution Guidelines, Version 3, 21 September 2009, p. 3, www.adelaidedatacabling.com.au/docs/ber.pdf [accessed 3 June 2011].
10. Interview conducted by authors with a director of Hayball Architects, May 2011.
11. Georges Teyssot, 'Norm and Type: Variations on a Theme', *Architecture and the Sciences: Exchanging Metaphors*, ed. by Antoine Picon and Alessandra Ponte (Princeton, NJ: Princeton Papers on Architecture, 2003), pp. 141–164 and Adrian Forty, *Words and Buildings: A Vocabulary of Modern Architecture* (London: Thames & Hudson, 2000), pp. 304–311.
12. See Forty, p. 307, and see Tim Benton, Charlotte Benton and Dennis Sharp (eds), *Form and Function: A Source Book for the History of Architecture and Design, 1890–1939* (London: Crosby Lockwood Staples, 1975).

13 As quoted from BER guidelines:

> The objectives of the BER programme are first, to provide economic stimulus through the rapid construction and refurbishment of school infrastructure and, second, to build learning environments to help children, families and communities participate in activities that will support achievement, develop learning potential and bring communities together.

14 Interview conducted by authors with a director of Hayball Architects, May 2011.
15 Interview conducted by authors with a director of Hayball Architects, May 2011
16 Interview conducted by authors with a director of Hayball Architects, May 2011.
17 'Un-built Prize 2009', *Architecture Australia*, January/February 2010.
18 Australian Institute of Architects, media release, 'BER Project wins Central Qld Regional Architecture Award', Friday 11 March 2011, http://dynamic.architecture.com.au/i-cms?page=15281 [accessed May 2011].
19 'And we won't be getting Richard Rogers to design your school, we won't be getting any award-winning architects to design it, because no-one in this room is here to make architects richer.' Michael Gove, Education Secretary, Merlin Fulcher, 'Gove: Richard Rogers won't design your school', *The Architects' Journal*, 2 February 2011.
20 The Auditor-General Audit Report No. 33 2009–10, Performance Audit, Building the Education Revolution—Primary Schools for the 21st Century. Attorney-General's Department, Canberra.
21 Alan Colquhoun has addressed the difficulties associated with the idea. See Alan Colquhoun, *Essays in Architectural Criticism* (Cambridge, MA: MIT Press, 1977), pp. 110–119.
22 Examples abounded in the media of, for instance, roofing contractors with 80 schools on the go at once.
23 Jessica Shepherd, 'Schools Should be Built from Template Designs', *The Guardian*, 8 April 2011.
24 Robert Puksand for the Australian Institute of Architects to Karen Elingford, re: Parliamentary Inquiry into the administration of the Federal Government BER program in Victoria, 28 July 2010, www.parliament.vic.gov.au/images/stories/committees/etc/BER_Submissions/56_Australian_Institute_of_Architects_280710.pdf [accessed 10 March 2015].
25 Interview conducted by authors with a director of Hayball Architects, May 2011.

18
RESTRICTED BY SCARCITY, STRIVING FOR GREATER BOUNTY

The role of architecture in making Dubai

Kevin Mitchell

In an essay titled "The Future Promise of Architecture in Dubai," which was written during the frenzied period of the city's growth prior to the global financial crisis in 2008, I discussed how architecture had become an object of consumption as defined by Hannah Arendt in "The Crisis of Culture: Its Social and Cultural Significance."[1] Although Arendt's essay was useful, the time that has elapsed between completion of the essay and its appearance in print allowed further reflection and reconsideration of the use of Arendt's categorization, which was articulated in a postscript:

> Ultimately contemporary architecture in Dubai has been treated as an object of exchange, whether in the form of speculative buildings for the purpose of rent or re-sale or prestige projects constructed to house cultural institutions brought from abroad. Worth is determined by the potential for profit or the possibility of enhancing status via iconic expressions or "brand recognition," not by the particular architectural qualities of buildings or contributions to creating urban spaces.[2]

Architecture played a central role in supporting speculative real estate development and attracting substantial foreign direct investment (FDI) that, in turn, seemed to indicate that demand far exceeded supply. This cycle could be maintained as long as investors were enticed by the potential for profit and continued to enter the market, but problems surfaced when those who purchased promises in the form of renderings and sales brochures realized that there were significant issues resulting from construction quality and the structure of ownership agreements. Challenges were compounded by an oversupply of residential units and office space that remained vacant following completion. Following the crisis in 2008, Dubai exercised much greater control over the real estate market through measures such as establishing the Real Estate Regulatory Agency (RERA). This agency is responsible for regulating all aspects of the sector, including the management of a rent index based on the obligatory registration of all rental contracts.

It is not surprising that works of architecture have been privileged for their exchange value in Dubai, which has established itself as global trade center and tourist destination by taking concrete steps in terms of improving infrastructure, establishing of free trade zones, and continually increasing capacity by expanding its ports. This chapter considers the role of architectural production and describes how works of architecture in Dubai have functioned as objects of exchange. I begin by examining the Greek term *oikonomia* in order to demonstrate the significance of scarcity, which is essential for understanding the role that architecture has played in the city's rapid rise at the beginning of the twenty-first century. After a brief overview of the foundations for Dubai's contemporary economy, I will discuss two projects that illustrate the relation between economy and architecture in the city: International City, a large-scale, mixed-use development that includes residential areas with themed apartment blocks, and the Burj Khalifa, a high-rise that remains the world's tallest building as of 2014.

The origins of *oikonomia*

The Greek term *oikonomia* originally referred to the administration of persons and goods belonging to the *oikos* (household). During the Classical period the term was applied to "the ordering of a household estate of an Athenian family, under the monarchal rule of a citizen, the master of the house."[3] *Oikomomia* derived from *oikeó* which originally meant to inhabit, to settle in or to dwell, and *nomos*. With regard to the earlier meaning of *oikeó*, Kurt Singer states:

> Spatial relation is thus stressed, but not as strong as in *chora* which at the outset denotes free space, range, place, position, region, land but also acquires the meaning real estate, field, father-land, while *oikeó* extends its meaning to managing, directing, administering, governing.[4]

Oikeó extended its meaning beyond managing, directing, administering, and governing. All of these activities were aimed at "preserving" the *oikos*, as well as the *polis*, by ensuring self-sufficiency. Aristotle summarized this in the *Politics*:

> Every *polis* exists by nature, inasmuch as the first partnerships exist; for the *polis* is the end of the other partnerships, and nature is an end, since that which each thing is when its growth is completed, we speak of as being the nature of each thing, for instance a man, a horse, a household. Again the chief object for which a thing exists, its end, its chief good; and self-sufficiency is an end, and a chief good.[5]

The root of the latter part of the term *oikonomia*, *nomos*, derives from *nemein*, which means to distribute, to possess (what has been distributed) and to dwell. Throughout the epic works attributed to Homer, one finds the verb form of *nemó* (to deal out, to dispense) and the terms *nemésis* (to distribute, to allocate) and *nemesis* (retribution, or the distribution of what is due).⁶ *Nemó* also possesses a second meaning with relation to the life of herdsmen: to pasture, to graze the flocks or feed them, to drive them out to pasture. Distribution, or allocation, implies the existence of a limitation whereas the meaning associated with putting flocks out to pasture implies expansion or extension.⁷ As Kurt Singer notes:

> Like many other ancient words *nemó* has thus two opposite meanings and may be called amphibolic (or rather amphitypical, from *amphitypos* which means in epic language two-edged), one meaning pointing to limitations imposed by acts of appropriation and apportioning, the other to expansion – a polarity in which, by some stretch of imagination, a modern economist may divine a dim anticipation of the dual aspects of an economy: restricted by scarcity, striving for greater bounty.⁸

The origins of Dubai's contemporary economy

Dubai has certainly been restricted by scarcity, and its extraordinary rise at the beginning of the twenty-first century was due to strategic decisions and bold steps to maintain financial independence that have since proven prescient. With limited natural resources until the discovery of oil and natural gas, Dubai and other Gulf cities turned outward toward the sea or inward to date palm oases for sustenance. Until the collapse of the pearling industry that was precipitated by the introduction of cultured pearls into the market in the 1930s, Dubai and neighboring cities depended heavily on this source of income. However, unlike other cities in the Gulf, even at the beginning of the twentieth century Dubai had established itself as an entrepôt in a vibrant trade network that extended across the Gulf and throughout the Indian Ocean. Recognizing opportunity in the increasing customs duties at ports along the Persian coast in 1902, the ruler of Dubai enticed merchant families to emigrate from across the Gulf and settle in Dubai with promises of greater economic freedom.⁹

Merchants continued to benefit from Dubai's efforts to transform the natural environment to facilitate trade. There is a history of substantially altering the coastline that goes back to the dredging of Dubai Creek at the end of the 1950s. This measure facilitated access for larger vessels and Dubai moved ahead of its neighbors in terms of competitive advantage. With the opening of Port Rashid in 1972, followed by the establishment of a significantly larger port at Jebel Ali and the Jebel Ali Free Trade Zone, Dubai has now secured its position as a major global trade hub. According to World Shipping Council data from 2012, Jebel Ali is the ninth largest container port in the world and is the only port in Asia to be in the top ten.[10] While contemporary projects such as the Palm Islands have been summarily dismissed as folly, this may preclude more nuanced interpretations that seek to explain how Dubai has sought to overcome scarcity through manipulation of the boundary separating land and sea to maximize available resources for financial benefit in spite of ecological costs.

Economic diversification has been a necessity for Dubai, which lacked the oil reserves of neighboring Abu Dhabi. The United Arab Emirates government reports that an estimated 92.2 billion barrels (94 percent) of the country's oil reserves are within Abu Dhabi, as compared to approximately 4 billion barrels in Dubai.[11] The United Arab Emirates also has natural gas reserves, but these are concentrated in Abu Dhabi. Although Dubai has limited reserves, it must import gas to fuel the power plants that provide electricity for the city.

Just as Dubai exploited its strategic location within a regional trade network during the early part of the twentieth century, there was a strategic effort to benefit from the flow of money back into the region from the United States and Europe at the beginning of the twenty-first century. By establishing free trade zones and enacting legislation that allowed freehold ownership, Dubai provided a destination for capital to settle in a place with liberal banking and investment regulations and a stable environment. Allocating space for free trade and freehold ownership transcended both the physical boundaries of the city by increasing the flow of goods and people and the existing legal structures through exemptions from local legislation. The use of space, both at the scale of individual buildings and at the urban scale, has contributed to overcoming scarcity by exploiting the potential for profit. To borrow a phrase from Kurt Singer, "acts of appropriation and apportioning" of space extended Dubai's economic interest in areas ranging from trade to tourism.

A tale of two projects

International City and the Burj Khalifa represent two tendencies that characterized architecture and urbanism in Dubai during the period of rapid growth that preceded the sudden cessation of construction in 2008. International City is one of many enclaves initiated by Dubai's competing state-sponsored real estate developers. The project is one of numerous "cities" within the city that are connected by a vast road network that both reflects and reinforces automobile dependence. International City is part of an expansion outward from previously existing centers around the creek and along the coast. In contrast, the Burj Khalifa is the ultimate example of the growth of the city upward through high-rises that are designed to establish an iconic presence. As discussed below, International City and the Burj Khalifa illustrate the relation between economy and architecture and can be interpreted as objects of exchange within a system in which the value of buildings is determined by the possibility for profit or status-enhancing potential rather than by the quality of the built work.

International City

Like most projects proposed during the height of the real estate boom, International City was launched in January 2004 and sold off-plan prior to construction; by mid-July of the same year it was reported that 90 percent of the units had been purchased. Like other off-plan developments, apartments were sold and re-sold (or "flipped") multiple times prior to completion. Construction delays, proximity to a major sewage treatment plant, and traffic issues continue to impact buyers and residents but, as discussed below, economic conditions have resulted in the use of buildings in ways that were unanticipated.

International City was originally proposed as an affordable alternative to high-end freehold developments near the coast such as Jumeirah Lakes Towers and the exclusive Palm Jumeirah. The developers described the project as follows:

> International City offers affordable living in a flourishing residential district. With over 22,000 residences, including spacious studios and one-bedroom apartments, spread throughout ten distinctly themed precincts, residents can enjoy a range of sports facilities, lush communal green spaces and the tranquil environment of the lake, together with efficient community infrastructure. The development also houses over 5,000 retail units on the ground floors of the 387 buildings, offering a range of essential community services and stores, from cosy cafés and restaurants to conveniently located supermarkets, laundries and offices.[12]

The project shared many of the characteristics of other large-scale residential developments in Dubai: themed buildings referencing another time period or other places and promises of communal facilities and "community." Also, in terms of planning, International City was similar to projects that privileged two-dimensional figural representations rather than patterns of urban form that resulted in humanely scaled spaces. Whereas the Palm Islands reproduced the date palm, the planners of International City organized apartment blocks according to an ordering system said to be inspired by patterns found in carpets throughout the region. Of course the patterns that appear when viewed from a satellite photograph cannot be perceived from within and what appears to be a fine-grained fabric from high above the earth's surface is actually experienced as a loose agglomeration of low-rise buildings separated by comparatively large expanses of paved surfaces for parking.

Whereas developments such as the "1 city–9 towns" project initiated by the Shanghai Planning Commission in 2001 sought to stage elaborately themed "towns" based on European models, International City was much less ambitious in terms of design intent and the connection to the original inspirations could be described as a faint resemblance rather than reproduction. A survey of completed buildings reveals that the use of theming was perhaps less about constructing distinctive environments and more about creating brand distinction in a highly competitive market (Figure 18.1).

The promises of sports facilities, lush communal green spaces, tranquil lakeside environments, and community services remain unfulfilled due to stalled construction and the lack of investment in amenities. As the supply of residential units increased and the expatriate population decreased following the economic downturn, rental rates for apartments in International City fell dramatically. In

Restricted by scarcity, striving for greater bounty   221

FIGURE 18.1. Apartment blocks in the China cluster in International City, Dubai

2011, it was reported that studio units were available for as low as AED 14,000 (USD 3,811) per year, which was less than 50 percent of the AED 30,000–35,000 (USD 8,167–9,528) per year recommended in the RERA rental index in 2009.[13]

By the second quarter of 2014, Dubai experienced a recovery and average rental rates for studio units had reached AED 35,000, which represented a 66% increase over those during the second quarter of 2013.[14] While rental costs for units in the development increased considerably, the growth rate in International City was only 3 percent during the second quarter of 2014 and the rise in rent seemed to be driven by a more competitive property market rather than by demand by potential tenants.[15] Assumed growth rates may not reveal the actual number of residents as many apartments are sublet and subdivided to substantially increase occupancy, with a number of people renting multiple "bed spaces" in a single unit.[16] In the case of International City, apartment blocks were designed with the intention of accommodating individuals and families. While the architecture has remained unchanged in terms of the apportioning of space, buildings have been appropriated in unforeseen ways due to economic circumstances.

Burj Khalifa

From the perspective of engineering and construction, the Burj Khalifa is an extraordinary achievement (Figure 18.2). As of 2014, the building remained the tallest in the world at 828 metres (2,716.5 feet). Claiming the title of the "world's tallest" has always been the basis of marketing efforts aimed at distinguishing the city and

FIGURE 18.2 Model of the Burj Khalifa on display in Dubai Mall

this is certainly the case in Dubai. Interestingly, even the promotional literature on the website dedicated to the building refers to the scarcity of natural resources and celebrates the fact that oil did not contribute to the city's transformation:

> World's tallest building. A living wonder. Stunning work of art. Incomparable feat of engineering. Burj Khalifa is all that. In concept and execution, Burj Khalifa has no peer. More than just the world's tallest building, Burj Khalifa is an unprecedented example of international cooperation, symbolic beacon of progress, and an emblem of the new, dynamic and prosperous Middle East. It is also tangible proof of Dubai's growing role in a changing world. In fewer than 30 years, this city has transformed itself from a regional centre to a global one. This success was not based on oil reserves, but on reserves of human talent, ingenuity and initiative. Burj Khalifa embodies that vision.[17]

When considering the relationship between architecture and economy, the physical attributes and architectural aspects of the Burj Khalifa are less important than the way in which the building was part of a larger strategy aimed at establishing Dubai as a major city capable of competing on a global scale. The extent of media attention garnered by the Burj Khalifa and the appearance of the building in films from Bollywood to Hollywood have contributed to promoting Dubai across the world. Unlike the exchange value of International City, which is established by the resale through "flipping" apartment units and rental returns, the Burj Khalifa has enhanced Dubai's status in the region and beyond.

Perhaps the most interesting aspect of the relation between Burj Khalifa and the economy of Dubai is the naming, or rather the re-naming, of the building. The building was known as the Burj Dubai throughout the design, sales and construction phases, but during the opening celebrations on January 4, 2010 it was announced that the building would be known as the Burj Khalifa in honor of Sheikh Khalifa bin Zayed Al Nahyan, the President of the United Arab Emirates and Ruler of Abu Dhabi (Figure 18.3). The change of the name of a building that played such an important role in Dubai's aspirations to attain global brand recognition was significant, and the timing raised questions. A few weeks prior to the opening, it was reported that Abu Dhabi had provided the Dubai government USD 10 billion to settle a portion of the substantial debt accumulated during the years characterized by excess.[18]

Concluding remarks

Although the consequences of unbridled growth were severe prior to the global economic crisis, a July 2014 International Monetary Fund (IMF) report on the United Arab Emirates noted a strong recovery in the real estate market. However, the report warned that

> speculation in the residential segment of the [sic] Dubai's residential market may still return at a significant scale. A number of measures that are expected to reduce flipping activity have already been introduced. More measures from the macroprudential and fiscal toolkit for containing real estate booms may be needed, particularly if signs of flipping activity emerge strongly.[19]

FIGURE 18.3 The Burj Khalifa shown in the context of Dubai's skyline

Architecture played a key role in the speculative frenzy that resulted in extraordinary economic gain for some and significant losses for others. As "flipping" activity drove real estate prices to extraordinary levels, architects were increasingly expected to ensure differentiation and distinction through projects that were marketed using rendered representations and sold off-plan prior to construction. Works of architecture and, in many cases, the mere representation of planned projects, functioned as objects of exchange that were intimately connected to the rise and fall of Dubai's fortunes. Curiously, the absence of physical buildings supported economic growth and the presence of completed projects has come to represent the problems of excess, which include sustainability related concerns, labor protections in the construction industry, and the challenges associated with building hastily in a harsh environment. Proposed works of architecture, rather than the actual buildings, attracted significant FDI and supported a speculative off-plan market in which sale price far exceeded the actual value of the "product."

Landor – the branding consultant commissioned to market the Burj Khalifa – provides a succinct summary of how the absence of an actual building was of little importance:

> Even before the foundation was poured, an auction was scheduled for apartments that would one day fill the tower. With nothing tangible to show bidders, the auction became a test of one of Walter Landor's guiding principles: "Products are made in the factory, but brands are made in the mind." At this point, the "product" didn't exist. So we invited prospective bidders to experience the brand.[20]

The consultants measured their success by the fact that every apartment was sold within 24 hours, "netting more than half a billion dollars."[21] Clearly in the case of the Burj Khalifa, brand recognition was more important than the existence of the "product."

As noted in the introduction, the term *oikonomia* originally referred to the administration of the household in a manner that ensured self-sufficiency. In spite of the fact that the scarcity of natural resources and a harsh arid environment prohibit attaining true self-sufficiency, Dubai has appropriated and apportioned the space of the city into free zones and freehold developments in order to maximize economic potential. International City and the Burj Khalifa differ significantly in scope, scale, and architectural expression, but both have played a role in supporting Dubai's growth and they serve to illustrate the effervescent nature of the city and its economy. In the case of International City, architectural intentions and the promise inherent in pre-construction renderings were subverted almost immediately after the project was complete due to changing economic circumstances. The promotion of the Burj Khalifa provides an example of the substantial effort invested in attaining "brand recognition" in a global market and the re-naming of the building is indicative of the complex relationship between architecture and economy.

The transformation of Dubai's built environment has been extraordinary and the attendant consequences have been significant. As the city seeks to overcome the challenges associated with scarcity in the future, time will tell whether the search for greater bounty will transcend tangible economic measures in order to allow for architectural and urban projects that respond more sensitively to their environment and their inhabitants.

Notes

1. Hannah Arendt, "The Crisis of Culture: Its Social and Cultural Significance" *Between Past and Future* (New York: Penguin Books, 1993), pp. 197–226.
2. Kevin Mitchell, "The Future Promise of Architecture in Dubai," *The Superlative City: Dubai and the Urban Condition in the Early Twenty-First Century*, ed. by Ahmed Kanna (Cambridge, MA: Graduate School of Design Aga Khan Program/Harvard University Press, 2013), p. 165.
3. Kurt Singer, "*Oikonomia*: An Inquiry into Beginnings," *Aristotle (384–322 BC)*, ed. by Mark Blaug (Brookfield, VT: Edward Elgar Publishing Company, 1991) p. 75.
4. Ibid., p. 79.
5. Aristotle, *Politics*, tr. H. Rackham (London: William Heinemann, 1972), 1252b.
6. The concept of *nemesis* is connected to the religious realm via the goddess *Nemesis*. A marble relief found in Piraeus represents the goddess as a winged figure standing upon the back of a naked man, and in her right hand is a measuring rod. According to A.B. Cook, "As *Láchesis* was a goddess of the lot (*lachein*, "to get by lot," *láchos*, "lot"), so *Nemesis* was a goddess of the greenwood (*némo*, "I pasture," *némos*, "glade") – a patroness of animal and vegetable life" (A.B. Cook, *Zeus: A Study in Ancient Religion* (New York: Bilbo and Tannen, 1964), Volume I, p. 273.
7. Plato, in the following passage from the *Critias*, illustrates the way in which putting flocks out to pasture was associated with limitless space: "And besides, there were many lofty trees of cultivated species; and it produced boundless pasturage for flocks" (Plato, *Critias*, tr. Rev. R.G. Bury (London: William Heinemann, 1981), 111C.
8. Singer, pp. 82–3.
9. For an account of Dubai's early development, see Frauke Heard-Bey, *From Trucial States to United Arab Emirates* (Dubai: Motivate Publishing, 2004).
10. www.worldshipping.org/about-the-industry/global-trade/top-50-world-container-ports [Accessed August 23, 2014].
11. "Energy in the UAE," www.uae-embassy.org/uae/energy [Accessed August 21, 2014].
12. www.nakheel.com/en/leasing/international-city [Accessed August 25, 2014].
13. www.arabianbusiness.com/international-city-rents-slip-below-aed15-000--411155.html [Accessed August 1, 2014].
14. Asteco, *Dubai Report-Q2 2014* (Dubai: Asteco Property Management, 2014).
15. Ibid.
16. Jay B. Hilotin, "International City: Squalor Township," *Gulf News*, February 24, 2011.
17. www.burjkhalifa.ae/en/TheTower/Vision.aspx [Accessed August 1, 2014].
18. "Abu Dhabi Gives Dubai $10bn to Help Pay Debts," http://news.bbc.co.uk/2/hi/business/8411215.stm [Accessed August 1, 2014].
19. International Monetary Fund, *IMF Country Report No. 14/188, United Arab Emirates*, July 2014, p. 14.
20. http://landor.com/#!/work/case-studies/burj-khalifa-(formerly-burj-dubai) [Accessed August 1, 2014].
21. Ibid.

19

DESIGNING PUBLIC SPACE IN AUSTERITY BRITAIN

Suzanne Hall

Introduction: urban austerity and design dispositions

Austerity is more than the limited availability of public resources. Austerity, as we have come to know it over recent years, is a severe restriction on public resources as a matter of political action pursued in a context of economic fragility. Since the global financial crisis of 2008, 'austerity' has been used to preface national ideologies of fiscal restriction, with distinctive effects in the limitation of public resources, thereby fundamentally altering the composition of the urban landscape.[1] Here, I bring together the state commitment to 'Austerity Britain', with the ongoing evolution of a public space project in Bankside, south London. The aim of this chapter is to explore the role of design in an economic context of state cut backs paralleled with burgeoning urban regeneration. By following the early stages of the 'Bankside Urban Forest' project, an initiative framed by its incremental and potentially 'economical' approach, I explore what imaginations and participations are possible within a modest design process. The questions that emerge are whether an incremental design process is sufficiently agile and adaptive to circumvent the strictures of austerity, or whether design-by-accretion inadvertently pays lip service to public inclusion through constrained forms of public delivery.

In the course of the chapter the fieldwork material suggests that 'austerity urbanism' is not simply a condition of aggressive market logics (although 'accumulation by dispossession'[2] is a feature of recent redevelopment in the broader south London area in which the Bankside Urban Forest is located). Austerity urbanism is also a context of limitations in which creative forms of public activism and alternative design processes challenge dominant design and regeneration logics invested in the 'world-class city' motif.[3] Public resistance to the current mode of austerity governance has voiced pressing public concerns: Who gets? Who pays? Who is rewarded? And perhaps most crucially: Who is penalized? These questions are raised across a public spectrum, often in creative re-interpretations of public action and redress.[4] Such concerns have also entered into architectural practice, with consequences for how public projects are conceived of and delivered during a frugal and conservative dispensation.[5] In considering how to recognize and envision the social dimensions of public space, design potentially engages with the formalized shapes and textures of place and with how local capacities are actively incorporated in the making and maintenance of public space.[6] This chapter addresses a design economy that allows for less formalized consultation and more vivid public involvement, and less programme in the interest of more interpretation. In outlining, at the early stages of the Bankside Urban Forest, the emergence of two of its initial projects – Redcross Way and the Urban Orchard – the tactile dimensions of space are analysed, alongside interviews with architects, policy and delivery agencies and individuals who live and work in Bankside.

The Bankside Urban Forest project emerged in 2007 on the cusp of an era of economic prosperity and New Left optimism for the role of design in the transformation of public urban space. The 'Mayor's 100 Public Spaces Programme' launched in 2002 by mayor Ken Livingstone provided a key reference point, while public organizations such as CABE (Commission for Architecture and the Built Environment) and the Architecture Foundation developed an infrastructure of ideas, intelligentsia and programmes to promote and support design capacities in the shaping of urban environments. By 2008 the mayor's Public Spaces Programme had been cut, and by 2011 CABE had been dismantled and substantially reduced to merge with the Design Council. However, pre-2008 regeneration ebullience established the launch of an invited design competition with the remit of recomposing the urban realm broadly between the River Thames and the Elephant and Castle, and Blackfriars Road and Borough High Street. The competition and subsequent project was overseen by 'Better Bankside', an independent, business-owned and led BID (Business Improvement District) company, with partners including the London Borough of Southwark, Tate Modern, Design For London, the Architecture Foundation and well-established community organizations such as the Bankside Residents' Forum and Bankside Open Spaces Trust.

In 2007, Witherford Watson Mann Architects (WWM) were appointed as lead consultants for the public space regeneration process in the Bankside area. Their report *Bankside Urban Forest* (May 2007),[7] commissioned through an invited competition, contained procedural and spatial ideas about regeneration that were explicitly embedded in local texture. In their detailed report, WWM's urban framework included mappings of existing interior landscapes, patterns of activity and networks of local civic groups, and visual and interview material from individuals and groups who lived in the area. The project is equally embedded in a complex urban landscape, actively developed over the last decade by both public and private programmes, and is associated with an urban land market that can be described as nothing less than buoyant. While the Bankside area is marketed as a highly desirable area in which to live, work and invest, remnants of an industrial river landscape endure. A less prestigious but entirely significant network of spaces and practices support a range of established residents who are confronted by escalations in land value, a rise in public and speculative interests, and a dramatic increase in tourism. If a core issue for the Bankside Urban Forest is to recognize and meet local needs, then this challenge cannot be separated from the challenge of attending to varied, and at times conflicting, needs. How do architects think about the different and competing values of public space? By referring to aspects of an emerging, imperfect and exploratory project, this chapter expands on the economy of city-making in the context of austerity: as the imaginative pursuit of what is possible, within the necessary adage of using less to build more.

An incremental approach

The *Bankside Urban Forest* report expressed a number of ideas for thinking about local regeneration as a collection of small-scale initiatives alongside a slower-paced delivery process, through which local expertise is fostered. The design intent is encapsulated in three core ideas, the first of which emphasizes the role of small interventions that support an existing network of spaces central to the everyday life of residents in the area, including schools, parks, churchyards and a public library. From this spatial perspective follows the second idea of working with the expertise of large and small organizations in the area, ranging from community groups to businesses. Finally, a reflective approach to delivery and project reviews is proposed, where lessons learnt from the early projects refine further strategies and projects. The proposed incremental approach is 'do-able': small budgets can be readily accessed through less bureaucratically incumbent procedures; and the order of the projects can shift with necessarily changing priorities. Moreover, public projects delivered in partnerships with local interest groups accord with planning policy in the UK (see for example Planning Policy Statement 1 2005; Local Development Frameworks 2004).[8] In an endorsement of the essence of the project, Peter Bishop, former head of the London Development Agency states:

> The Urban Forest has a robust approach. It is robust because this is a time when you are constantly shifting; shifting because of changes in funding and changes in opportunity; shifting because of big politics and small politics; and shifting as you learn, as you implement, as indeed you should do. One of the attractive points of the Bankside Urban Forest project is that it is incremental; it fits with the pressures we have with our budgets. We know where we are trying to end up, and we can get the sequences different. We can take the opportunities as they come and we can amend and change our plans according to any of the external factors. And that makes this almost an exemplar.[9]

In reality, however, an incremental approach relies on coordinating diverse and competing interests, and retaining the integrity of key ideas over what is often a lengthy and distorting timeframe. Similarly, a key challenge for Bankside Urban Forest project lies in the co-ordination of a diverse client body and the collaboration of interest groups, all of whom are differently funded, and some of whom are required to give of their labour, local capital and expertise. Further, the complexity of including diverse user groups, through a process of public place-making, is compounded by the disparate physical and social urban fabric of Bankside. This is nowhere made more apparent than in taking a walk along the east–west stretch of Southwark Street, with its northern edge fronted by large blocks of new, corporate development rendered in plate glass and granite, synonymous with the formation of prestigious global cityscapes.[10] An historic array of brick buildings form the southern background to Southwark Street, including small shops, social housing estates and schools.

In reflecting on development trends, an elderly resident who has lived and worked in Borough since the late 1970s comments:

> A little too much Tate, and the mania for bars and cafes ... If you go to Bankside 3 and look around there, there's all these corners identical, they all look exactly the same ... What about people with children, what about pensioners? What about families? They don't go to those sort of places ... But, you know, we desperately need ordinary shops and ordinary cafes, somewhere where you can take children and families ... most people here are not on £30,000 a year.[11]

Local residents of SE1 described their mixed and changing neighbourhood as a transient place, and talked about the benefits and frustrations of living in an area in which so many people pass through. These short-term occupations include the large student population who reside in the area in close proximity to education institutions such as South Bank University and the London College of Communication, and who are housed in an increasingly profitable and privatized form of housing provision for students in London. Even shorter-term occupations are evidenced in the increasing stream of tourists who venture between London Bridge and Westminster Bridge, along the River Thames. The idea of a 'mixed community' was therefore expressed by the residents neither in terms of class nor ethnicity, but in temporal terms as those who have a long-term investment in the local area, versus those who use the area fleetingly and whose needs and affiliations are more short term.

The sense of a public world sought after by longer-term residents was encapsulated by a comparatively informal, commonplace public, as described as 'in-off-the-street' and 'don't-book-in-advance' spaces. These included elements as perfunctory as sitting spaces, with one resident insisting: 'You shouldn't have to buy a cup of coffee to sit down.'[12] Residents raised both the loss of established spaces associated with day-to-day life in the local area and also the emergence of new kinds of public space and activities more inclined towards tourists and office workers. Through the notion of an 'urban forest' the architects' conception of public space resonates with an 'everyday urbanism',[13] and is spatialized as a web-like series of places within local enclaves as well as more overt 'places of exchange'.

The underlying essence of these public worlds, is that the architecture should support a 'less prescriptive sociality':

> There are a number of existing places in Bankside and Borough which in differing ways have the capacity to bring people who do not know each other into contact, places which 'suggest' social engagement between different racial, ethnic and class communities, where people can flourish – 'Places of Exchange'.[14]

However, these are precisely the public worlds that are often publicly sponsored, places in which since 2008, programmes or actual spaces have been operationally reduced or simply closed as part of the austerity rationale.

From the outset, WWM's observations and site analysis included fine-grained records of spaces and activities across the day and night. This early process of analysis engaged local expertise including the involvement of local young people in mapping their area. Their participation subsequently became formalized, and the 'Bankside Urban Pioneers' initiative was steered by the Architecture Foundation, an independent non-profit agency, with their remit 'to engage teams of 16 to 19 year olds in areas of London undergoing dramatic transformation'.[15] Learning from the base of the Urban Forest project, the initiative expanded under the leadership of the Architecture Foundation, to regeneration areas including South Bank, King's Cross, Deptford, Battersea, Upper Lea Valley, Barking, Canada Water, Willesden Green and Heathrow, and the Architecture Foundation also established an 'Urban Sages' programme to incorporate the expertise of elderly residents. Together with the energy of other organizations such as the Bankside Open Spaces Trust, the notion of a spatial web of public worlds readily expanded to include existing and imminent webs of social worlds. The spatial web is an interpretation of public space as that which emerges, not simply through official design, procurement and authorization, but through the engagement of informal memberships and local 'know-how'. While this involvement represents a public process of participation and making, it is also a fragile and asymmetrical process, dependent on a loose cohesion of resources and expertise, many of which are publicly funded, and whose efficacy in times of austerity is therefore reduced or immobilized. In contrast, Better Bankside, the appointed Business Improvement District company, whose income is in part drawn from an annual levy of some 480 companies in the BID area, retains an income stream and a motivation 'to improve the area for commercial activity'[16] – notwithstanding its significant community outreach programme.

The incremental process proposed in the Urban Forest project, which inherently supports an urbanism of accretion as opposed to completion, is developed in the architects' language as 'seeds' within a framework (Figure 19.1). A member of the design team stated: 'Basically the idea of the Urban Forest is that public space is made by people; it doesn't exist without people'; small interventions in the physical landscape or 'seeds' are explored as catalysts to engage and release further

FIGURE 19.1 Seeds of the Urban Forest

projects and initiatives. The 'seeds' of Bankside Urban Forest are both spatial and organizational, where inclusion through place-making takes a variety of organizational forms. Initiatives are potentially spearheaded by different organizations, under the umbrella of Better Bankside. The early teething pains that were identified in a variety of interviews relate to institutional overlaps and limited funding. Many of the well-established, community-based organizations have little funding and largely operate off the input of volunteers. But this is input, as stressed by local organizations, which is already stretched to capacity. For these organizations to be further involved, and for their local expertise to be recognized and valued, not only notionally but in organizational and financial terms, a far more detailed consideration of their participation in local development initiatives is required. However, local expertise and in particular the capacity to self-organize is, according to residents, a long-established response to the large-scale regeneration of the area, a response in which individuals and groups are increasingly competent:

> So there is now a tradition around here of people who are consulted, and people working dynamically, usually in small groups ... So these projects have grown people within. There are already, if you like, places for people to go to with their ideas.[17]

The framework for the Bankside Urban Forest project is conceived of and drawn as a stage-by-stage process (Figure 19.2). The architects' evocative drawings reflect the network of local spaces associated with schools, churches and housing estates, as well as prominent destinations such as Tate Modern and Borough Market. This is an economy of place-making rooted in the gradual processes of observation and participation over time, an overarching design ethos immersed in the spatial and social presence of place. The modest framework serves to establish a particular sensibility to influence large and small contributions and investments. The spatial and social mechanisms for maintaining exemplary project standards were not yet fully established during my six-month period of analysis in 2010 to 2011; how design principles translate into the procurement, briefing, management and evaluation processes were evolving – not without teething pains – alongside the delivery of the first projects. In seeking to establish inclusive design processes, however, the quality of the design framework, and how it translates into a publicly attuned, appropriately sensuous and optimistic 'first layer', cannot be underestimated. At this point, I turn to two of the early projects in the Urban Forest to explore their limitations and achievements as public spaces: places that attend to everyday needs, and that also have a sense of optimism.

Two projects

Development partners spoke frequently of the strategic value of small projects, where projects aggregate into larger social and spatial initiatives. The potential of a small intervention was shown in the first implemented project at 'Redcross

FIGURE 19.2 Maturing the Forest

Way', a space that links a local school and community garden. The contract value was a comparatively modest £279,700 and funding was pooled from Transport for London, the Forestry Commission, Section 106 agreements[18] and other smaller funds. The lustrous suggestions of space in the WWM drawings in the initial report, however, were somewhat diminished in the translation built in 2010. But public space is not simply what can be seen on site: there are social spinoffs accrued by the Redcross Way process. Local residents supported an application to Southwark's 'Cleaner, Greener, Safer' programme, and secured £60,000 to support initiatives to link surrounding housing estates and streets, incorporating a planting scheme for the Babington and Pattison social housing estates. Although the tactile components of the public space remain somewhat demure, here is a modest project that is a starting point for building on everyday networks and capacities.

In contrast to the Redcross Way project, a hoarded-off piece of land next to one of the railway bridges in Union Street was converted for two weeks over the summer of 2010 into a sensuous and social wonderland. The use of the land was granted by a benevolent landowner, and the energies of the Architecture Foundation, The Wayward Plant Registry, Better Bankside and the Bankside Resident's Forum combined to realise an 'interim use' project. As part of the aspirant exploration afforded by 'interim use' projects, the four-month transformation of the derelict site into 'The Union Street Urban Orchard' produced a profuse collage of trees, plants, seeds, vegetables and recycled materials.[19] The project literally grew, and in fourteen days over the summer, it became a public space that encouraged the imaginations of young and old and local and outsider. Heather Ring of The Wayward Plant Registry commented: 'Embedded in the design was a process that facilitated collaboration and experimentation.'[20] This seemingly temporary initiative has grown into more permanent projects where residents worked directly with The Wayward Plant Registry in local landscape and agriculture projects.

Conclusions: the incongruity of incrementalism and austerity

The strategic design framework and the socio-spatial public projects evoked by the Bankside Urban Forest suggest an incremental process of making public space with the potential to generate additional spaces, activities and investments over time. The incremental aspect accommodates exploration, flexibility and affordability, but such processes are only possible with the sustained investment of creativity, expertise and social capital developed by a network of organizations. The network often operates in an asymmetrical consortium, with disparate availabilities of income and resources, an imbalance compounded by cutbacks in public funding. While the fiscal capacities of local authorities, public organizations outside of the state and community-based groups are diminished under the austerity regime, the commercial funding stream for BIDs such as Better Bankside remain comparatively intact, potentially placing important public space experiments effectively in the hands of the private sector.

The Bankside Urban Forest project nonetheless reflects emerging modes of architectural practice that offer poetic, participatory and pragmatic possibilities for embedded processes of city-making in a context of limited resources. As conceived, the Bankside Urban Forest remains an appropriately modest – but never less than aspirational – project that probes, in both spatial and procedural dimensions, what it means *to grow* public spaces rather than to *complete* them. For architects to engage in the economics of an urbanism of accretion requires organizational and imaginative capacity, where the creative potentials of making reside as much in the sensualities of form as they do in the processes that animate space. They also require of architects endurance; a commitment to sticking with extended design and delivery processes often without significant financial remuneration. Such a design commitment is made all the more difficult in a climate of recession, where comparatively small but innovative design practices – that are significantly invested in public projects pushing the boundaries of what clients and users comprehend of as public space – are themselves pushed into the stringent realities of financially maintaining their practices. Since 2008, numerous design practices, with abundant reserves of social and spatial imagination, have fallen to the ruthless effects of recession. Incremental projects are crucial processes of spatial exploration, but for the architects involved, they are not necessarily sustainable ventures in financial terms.

In the larger context, the ideology of 'Austerity Britain' – despite the accompanying rhetoric of decentralized control and regard for local initiatives[21] – has inculcated an economic centralization that has effectively undermined local authorities,[22] and local capacities, through the severity of fiscal restraints. But 'the local', as suggested by the Bankside Urban Forest context, is a highly varied and complex terrain that consists of actors with differing access to power and resources, differing needs and varied commitments to fleeting or long-term investment. 'The local' is anything but a static, homogenous and small grouping. Rather, it is an aggregation of diverse and at times competitive groupings that requires structures and systems of representation and accountability. Whether in a context of prosperity or austerity, local public space projects therefore require more rather than less public financial support, more rather than less leadership and more rather than less co-ordination between variegated groups. The current neo-liberal proposition, for a decentralization of power, without a decentralization of resources, is therefore more than an unfortunate paradox skewed in the interests of the private sector. Both financial and political reform is required if the design of public space is to have any potential to genuinely engage with participatory transformations of the urban landscape.

Notes

1 Jamie Peck, 'Austerity Urbanism', *City* 16.6 (2012), 626–655.
2 David Harvey, 'The "New" Imperialism: Accumulation by dispossession', *Socialist Register* 40.40 (2009), 63–87.
3 Jon Beaverstock, Richard Smith and Peter Taylor, 'A Roster of World Cities', *Cities* 16.6 (1999), 445–458.

4 Margit Meyer, 'First World Urban Activism: Beyond austerity urbanism and creative city politics', *City* 17.1 (2013), 5–19.
5 Fran Tonkiss, 'Austerity Urbanism and the Makeshift City', *City* 17.3 (2013), 312–324.
6 Magda Anglès, *In Favour of Public Space: Ten years of the European Prize for Urban Public Space* (Barcelona: Centre de Cultura Contemporània de Barcelona and ACTAR, 2011).
7 Witherford Watson Mann, *Bankside Urban Forest* (an unpublished report generated for Better Bankside, 2007).
8 Planning Policy Statement 1 (PPS1) sets out the Government's overarching planning policies on the delivery of sustainable development through the planning system, and is given specificity and detail in Local Development Frameworks.
9 Interview conducted in 2010.
10 Leslie Sklair, 'Iconic Architecture and Capitalist Globalisation', *City* 10.1 (2006), 21–24, as well as Aspa Gospodini, 'European Cities in Competition and the New "Uses" of Urban Design', *Journal of Urban Design* 7 (2002), 59–73.
11 Interview conducted in 2009.
12 Ibid.
13 John Chase, Margaret Crawford and John Kaliski (eds) *Everyday Urbanism* (New York: The Monacelli Press, 1999), as well as Suzanne Hall, *City, Street and Citizen: The measure of the ordinary* (London and New York: Routledge, 2012).
14 Witherford Watson Mann, *Bankside Urban Forest*, p. 27.
15 Architecture Foundation Urban Pioneers, www.architecturefoundation.org.uk/programme/2010/urban-pioneers [accessed 8 August 2014].
16 Better Bankside, www.betterbankside.co.uk [accessed 2 September 2014].
17 Interview conducted in 2010.
18 Section 106, www.legislation.gov.uk/ukpga/1990/8/section/106 [accessed 8 August 2014].
19 Architecture Foundation, *The Union Street Urban Orchard: A case study of interim use* (London: Architecture Foundation, 2011).
20 Architecture Foundation, *The Union Street Urban Orchard*, p. 33.
21 Building the Big Society 2010, https://www.gov.uk/government/publications/building-the-big-society [accessed 8 August 2014], as well as the Localism Act 2011, www.legislation.gov.uk/ukpga/2011/20/contents/enacted [accessed 8 August 2014].
22 Nick Clarke and Allan Cochrane, 'Geographies and Politics of Localism: The localism of the United Kingdom's Coalition Government', *Political Geography* 34 (2013), 10–23.

20

THE BRICKS OF VENICE

Material and craft in John Ruskin's political economy

Stephen Kite

Introduction

This chapter engages with the question: 'What is the place of material and craft in John Ruskin's view of architecture and political economy?' In basic narratives Ruskin was an art and architecture writer up to the completion of *The Stones of Venice* (1851–3) and *Modern Painters* in 1860 at the mid-point of his life. With the publication of *Unto this Last* (1860) he then became a fierce social critic, attacking the 'science' of political economy, and humanizing the notion of value in his dictum: 'There is no Wealth but Life'. But this is too simple: Ruskin's works make a vibrant whole, and the *Stones of Venice* adumbrates his socio-economic thinking, as in the emphasis in his celebrated 'The Nature of Gothic' chapter on the dignity and quality of work in architecture. Here I have chosen to examine the 'bricks', not the 'stones' of Venice, using field and archive work into the notebooks and drawings from which Ruskin constructed the *Stones of Venice*. If Venetian building represents the apogee of Ruskin's 'school of incrusted architecture' of marble and stone, at the same time he recognizes that 'the body and availing strength of the edifice are … brick'.[1] And when Ruskin saw any hope of realizing the New Jerusalem in Great Britain – as when he lectured the mill-owners of Bradford on 'Modern Manufacture and Design' in 1859 – he recognized it would as likely be built in brick as marble. Ruskin's aesthetic and social ideas materialize out of a deep grasp of the stuff of architecture; watched closely, architecture indexes the economic and political structures of its making. So here a single arch will serve to disclose Ruskin's exegesis on the 'real use of brick', and his ideas of political economy.

Defining Ruskin's economy

In response to the deficit arising from the global economic collapse of 2008, libraries have been closed in parts of the United Kingdom, teaching funding to the arts and humanities at university level has been slashed and a number of commentators have recorded further increases in social inequality. Thomas Piketty's *Capital in the Twenty-First Century* records the enthusiasm shared by many in Europe in the period 1945–75 when it appeared that the defects of 'capitalism had been overcome and that inequality and class society had been relegated to the past', and how those same Europeans now have 'a hard time accepting that this seemingly ineluctable social progress ground to a halt after 1980'.[2] What do John Ruskin's views on political economy mean in these contexts? Those who shared the optimism of that 1945–75 period might have read his earliest systematic statements on political economy as part of history – namely his lectures to the mill-owners of Manchester on 'The Political Economy of Art' (July 1857). These were targeted against the, hateful to him, *laissez-faire* 'Manchester School' of economics then strongly in the ascendant; the '"Let-alone" principle is, in all things which man has to do with, the principle of death', Ruskin pronounced[3] (these Manchester talks were collected in his *A Joy for Ever* of 1857). But those social ends for which Ruskin argued in the second half of the nineteenth century, and which became part of a later twentieth-century liberal consensus in the United Kingdom – free libraries, free education, a reasonable wage, a national health service, green-belts, conservation and so forth – are no longer necessarily seen to be communally desirable.

Ruskin begins *Unto this Last* attacking any idea of political economy that disregards the moral function of the 'influence of social affection'. This culture of feeling, with its Wordsworthian overtones, is 'in its deepest origin, grounded in the social affections of home'.[4] For Ruskin, 'all economy, whether of states, households or individuals, may be defined to be the art of managing labour'.[5] Refuting the loose definition of 'economy' as the saving of money or time, as both bad English and 'bad Greek', he links it to the *oikonomia* of 'the administration of a house [and] its stewardship'.[6] Given the evangelical Protestant Biblical tradition of his background, his *oikonomia*, or 'House-Law', of good domestic management takes a picture from the book of *Proverbs* comparing the body politic to a household or farm based on co-operation, not competition, whose capable mistress

> riseth while it is yet night, and giveth meat to her household, and a portion to her maidens. She maketh herself coverings of tapestry, her clothing is silk and purple. Strength and honour are in her clothing, and she shall rejoice in time to come.[7]

Moving from the domestic, to the level of the polis Ruskin ends the first Manchester lecture with the fourteenth-century fresco of 'Good Government' from the town-hall of Siena where he uses Ambrogio Lorenzetti's portraits of Faith, Hope and Charity to link the domestic virtues of the mistress of *Proverbs* to the larger picture of the city-state.[8] But, it has to be admitted that Ruskin's society is primarily patriarchal; although his ethics inspired many socialists he did not call himself one. In the opening lines of his autobiography *Praeterita* he describes himself, and his father before him, as 'a violent Tory of the old school'.[9] Nonetheless, his *is* a communitarian vision, based on individual freedoms, as summed up in the celebrated (capitalized) motto of *Unto this Last*: 'THERE IS NO WEALTH BUT LIFE ... That country is richest which nourishes the greatest number of noble and happy human beings.'[10] For Ruskin the real wealth of the polis has nothing to do with 'the science of getting rich' and, though not an egalitarian, he argues fiercely against extremes of inequality, and for a just economic return for free labour. He distinguishes between a real *political* economy, and what he calls a *mercantile* economy that establishes maximum inequality for a few, as here in *Unto this Last*:

> The art of becoming 'rich', in the common sense, is not absolutely nor fully the art of accumulating much money for ourselves, but also of contriving that our neighbours shall have less. In accurate terms, it is 'the art of establishing the maximum inequality in our own favour'.[11]

In his paternal mien Ruskin accepts a measure of 'just' inequality, but unjust inequality he denounces as harmful;[12] as noted above, there used to be a communitarian sense that this was so in notions of a 'fair society' that are now far more contested. Moreover, Wilkinson and Pickett's much discussed *The Spirit Level* offers the compelling research of epidemiologists as to the damage of extreme inequalities to the body of nations, through a spectrum of indicators such as health, education, crime and social mobility.[13]

Material and craft

Within this outline of Ruskin's political economy we now turn to the questions of material and craft. Having seen that her household is justly fed, the good wife of the Bible's *Proverbs*, Chapter 31, is habitually busy with making: 'she seeks wool and flax, and works with willing hands' (verse 13); 'she plants a vineyard' (verse 16); 'she makes herself clothing of fine linen' and 'she makes linen garments and sells them' (verse 24). Richard Sennett's *The Craftsman* references Ruskin, as it re-debates the idea of craft, arguing against pointless competition and championing quality. Sennett points out how Ruskin wanted buildings made by, and for, men and women, not machines. What was radical in Ruskin was his desire to

> instill in craftsmen of all sorts the desire, indeed the demand, for a lost space of freedom; it would be a free space in which people can experiment, a supportive space in which they could at least temporarily lose control. This is a condition for which people will have to fight in modern society.[14]

En route to Manchester for his lectures, Ruskin had visited the construction of the experiment he supported for this 'space of freedom' – the Oxford Museum (opened 1860). He attacked the impact upon the soul of the deadening work of carving 20 Classical capitals to an identical design, arguing for the Gothic spirit where 'if you allow [workmen] to vary their designs, and thus interest their heads and hearts in what they are doing, you will find them become eager ... to get their ideas expressed'.[15] As he relates,

> Thomas Deane, the architect of the new Museum at Oxford, told me, as I passed through Oxford on my way here, that he found that owing to this cause alone, capitals of various design could be executed cheaper than capitals of similar design ... by about 30 per cent.[16]

Apart from Queen Victoria, Ruskin gave the largest subscription to this museum towards some of the carving of the west front, one of whose windows was carved to Ruskin's own design.[17] Ruskin supported the employment of the unconventional O'Shea brothers; as patron Henry Wentworth Acland wrote of their free spirit in *The Oxford Museum* of 1859:

> The temper of the architect has reached the men. In their work they have pleasure. The capitals are partly designed by the men themselves, and especially by the family O'Shea, who bring wit and alacrity from the Emerald Isle to their cheerful task. The carving of the capitals and the decoration of the windows ... have ever-living interest.[18]

The Tana window

Given Ruskin's vast and interwoven oeuvre, a full understanding of material and craft in his political economy might require readings of the 39 volumes of the *Complete Works*. Yet Ruskin's method allows something more manageable in these few pages – as Stephen Bann has written:

> Throughout his intense communion with the spirits of past Italy, he was attempting to recover an image of historical wholeness from the disorder, fragmentation and sheer anomaly of the contemporary Italian environment. How was this image to be secured? ... It had to be through the strategy of synecdoche – through the precise description of the detailed drawing that gave imaginative access to a whole greater than its parts.[19]

Using this strategy of the synecdoche let us examine just one window admired by Ruskin – from an alley beside Venice's Arsenal – for insights into the questions raised by this chapter and to foreground the humbler brick over the stones of Venice (Figure 20.1). Certainly Ruskin considered brick inferior to stone, preferring stone to be used solid or as a veneer 'incrusted' over a supporting brick carcass. Yet his discussion of the banded wall-veil also definitely encouraged the High Victorian aesthetic interest in vigorous displays of banded polychromy.[20] Here, he was anticipated by the work of James Wild, whose Christ Church, Streatham (1845) is praised in *Stones of Venice* for affording 'some idea of the variety of effects which are possible with no other material than brick'.[21] *Stones of*

FIGURE 20.1 Window 'at the Tana', Corte Contarina

Venice contains many close analyses of brick architecture, notably that of the apses of San Donato, Murano. On Plate 38 of *Stones of Venice* Ruskin gives examples of the 'more delicate and finished examples of Gothic work of this period'[22] demonstrating the floriated Gothic that arose in the late fourteenth and early fifteenth centuries: the first two examples from his plate that concern us still survive where Ruskin describes – in 'a narrow alley in a part of Venice now exclusively inhabited by the lower orders, close to the Arsenal' – Venice's former vast ship-building complex in the north-eastern part of the city.[23] To engage the readers of *Stones* with the fragments of Venice and its makers, Ruskin embodies the reader in the experience of his journeys: there are the powerfully evocative accounts of the approach to Venice itself across the lagoon, the walk to the Piazza of St. Mark's or the boat journey to Murano. To seek out these windows of the Arsenal district Ruskin urges us to a much simpler progress:

If the traveller desire to find them (and they are worth seeking), let him row from the Fondamenta San Biagio … and look, on his right, for a low house… Let him go in at the door of the portico in the middle of this house, and he will find himself in a small alley, with the windows in question on each side of him.[24]

Here in the Corte Contarina, off the Rio de la Tana canal, in this formerly poor district, was the *Canevo*, or hemp workshop, serving the needs of the Venetian fleet. As presented in the *Stones* plate, the two small line engravings of these openings, with barely visible detail, belie the level of scrutiny to which Ruskin subjected them.

The worksheets Ruskin made of these windows (his numbers 205, 206, and 207) are the very final ones of the exhaustive winter campaigns of 1849–50 and 1851–2 to record the city. Unusually, even the cross-related notes are found in a general diary, outside the major diaries – numbered M1 and M2 by Ruskin – that document most of this research.[25] Further notes confirm the valedictory context of these sheets; thus the same diary records, 'December 30th, 1851. Turner buried'.[26] While on worksheet 205 itself, Ruskin wrote: 'Sketched February 9th, 1852 in the afternoon the day of Mr Prout's death.' So, almost within a month, Ruskin records here the passing of two of the great artist mentors of his 'watching' of architecture, foremost J. M. W. Turner and the loved, but more conventionally picturesque artist, Samuel Prout (Figure 20.2).

Worksheet 205 (Ruskin Museum, Coniston, Cumbria) is a tenderly drawn record of the floriated moulded brick detail of the arch that Ruskin enthusiastically notes in the 1851–2 diary: 'Nothing can be more exquisitely sharp than the ornament on 205 … and all evidently moulded not cast.' Always, he is alert to that vital quality of 'changefulness' that, in his view, was slain by the mechanical architecture of the Renaissance: 'Note *leaf* for flower in third brick counting down on the right. Small flowers all of different sizes.'[27] As is typical in Gothic work there is much lively variety within the repeats of a rinceau motif as here – at this point only – the repeating flower becomes a leaf. And writing from these diary notes, in the printed text on 'Gothic Palaces' of *Stones*, he praises these 'exquisite mouldings, not cast, but *moulded in the clay by hand*, so that there is not one piece of the arch like another'.[28] The stress on the vitality of hand-work is what Ruskin later encouraged at the Oxford Museum, while in the preceding epochal chapter on the 'Nature of Gothic' he extols the 'characteristic or moral element' of Gothic 'Changefulness' and the 'perpetual variety' evident when the worker is not enslaved: 'Wherever the workman is utterly enslaved, the parts of the building must of course be absolutely like each other.'[29] Having praised the hand-moulding of this arch Ruskin breaks – with the rhetorical effect of the Evangelical preachers he had often heard – to deliver a homily on the contemporary use of brick:

> And here let me pause for a moment, to note … the real use of brick. Our fields of good clay were never given to us to be made into oblong morsels of one size. They were given us that we might play with them, and that men

FIGURE 20.2 John Ruskin, window 'at the Tana'

Source: Worksheet No. 205, February 9th, 1852.

who could not handle a chisel, might knead out of them some expression of human thought. In the ancient architecture of the clay districts of Italy, every possible adaptation of the material is found exemplified.[30]

And, after showing how 'many of the best thoughts of [Italian] architects are expressed in brick', he concludes:

How much more ought it to be so among the fields of England! I believe that the best academy for her architects, for some half century to come, would be the brickfield; for of this they may rest assured, that till they know how to use clay, they will never know how to use marble.[31]

So it proved in many ways, though Ruskin himself fled 'the accursed [polychromatic brick] Frankenstein monsters of ... [his] own making', complaining that 'there is scarcely a public-house near the Crystal Palace but sells its gin and bitters under pseudo-Venetian capitals'.[32] Ruskin's polemic, and inspiring collage-like plates, encouraged the almost manic variety of High Victorian architecture; but the huge spectrum of coloured and glazed brickwork offered by the manufacturers was 'coincident with the transformation of brick making by mechanical processes'.[33] Look at just one provincial example: Ponton and Gough's *The Granary* (Figure 20.3) – the apogee of the so-called 'Bristol Byzantine' style – 'in red, black and yellow brick, a layer-cake of arcaded openings each treated differently. Sienese, Gothic and Venetian motifs are detectable, all coloured by the influence of Ruskin.'[34]

Despite some of the dubious ensuing outcomes, it is obvious that there is already a lot of political economy inscribed in Ruskin's writing and drawing by 1853. And 'How to use clay?' has become a fundamental ethical question in the making of architecture. In Ruskin's typological reading of scripture it was profoundly symbolic that the journey of the Jewish people was away from the slavery of the building site, as Moses led them out of the straw-less brickfields of Egypt and '*labour without hope*'.[35] Later, the post *Unto this Last* (1860) Ruskin, develops this theme of brickmaking in 'Letter 64' (April 1876) of *Fors Clavigera* – his 'Letters to the Workmen and Labourers of Great Britain'. This was at a time when, as noted earlier, his social critique had deepened in its questioning of the servility produced by modern political economy. Against the vital evidence of the Arsenal arches, and in his most bitter-satirical mode he indicts the industrialization that was returning humanity to Egyptian levels of enslavement:

Here is the Grand Junction Canal Brick, Tile, and Sanitary Pipe Company, Limited; Capital £50,000, in 10,000 shares of £5 each; 'formed for the purpose of purchasing and working [a brickfield] estate ... You will sit at home, serene proprietor, not able, still less willing, to lift so much as a spadeful ... yourself; but you will feed a certain number of brickmaking Ethiopian slaves thereon, as cheap as you can; and teach them to make bricks, as basely as they

FIGURE 20.3 Detail of *The Granary*, Bristol

Source: Architects Ponton and Gough.

can; and you will put the meat out of their mouths into your own ... A clerical friend of mine in that neighbourhood has, I hear, been greatly afflicted concerning the degenerate nature of brick-makers. Let him go and make, and burn, a pile or two with his own hands; he will thereby receive apocalyptic visions of a nature novel to his soul. And if he ever succeeds in making one good brick ... he will have done a good deed for his generation.[36]

Conclusion

If Ruskin's sense of freedom is predicated on handcraft and a dislike of the machine, this can be over-stated. Besides, it seems that digital fabrication, 3-D printing and so on, may already be leading us back towards more Ruskinian variety in our possibilities of individual play with material and craft. For Ruskin buildings are made by, and for, men and women, labouring with hope in a certain equality. All are involved in building this world, and we saw how he attacks the 'sit at home' proprietor, expecting everyone 'to work with our hands, and make ourselves hot'. In the Hinksey Road experiment at Oxford in 1874 he sent his students out to make a new country road, to 'let my pupils feel the pleasures of *useful* muscular work' – and even did some stone-breaking himself.[37] Some contemporaries laughed at this project, but Ruskin wanted to foster a shared engagement in building the good polis of Lorenzetti's fresco, based ultimately upon the moral laws of the household. The beauty of the Tana arch is in its play of material, and again it is Ruskin who inspired those 'nasty English' Adolf Loos writes of, who came along and 'spoiled the game for our knights of the drawing board' by saying: 'Don't design, make. Go out in the world and see what is wanted. And when you have fully grasped that, go and work at the forge or the potter's wheel.'[38] In his researches on medieval Venice Ruskin sought a world in which Life is the true Wealth, and whose real value is measured out in the relationship of Play, Art and Work.

Notes

1 E. T. Cook and Alexander Wedderburn (eds), *The Works of John Ruskin* (London: George Allen, 1904–13), vol. 10, p. 98, *Stones of Venice, vol. 2*. Subsequent references in the form *Works*, 10: 98, *Stones of Venice, vol. 2*.
2 Thomas Piketty, *Capital in the Twenty-First Century*, trans. by A. Goldhammer (Cambridge, MA: Belknap Press, 2014). Piketty's figures – contested by some – show the share of the wealth owned by the top decile in the UK declining from a peak in 1910 at over 90 per cent of total wealth to over 60 per cent at around 1980, but then rising again to some 70 per cent in 2010, p. 344. Further points on social progress, p. 350.
3 *Works*, 16: 26, *A Joy for Ever*.
4 See recent discussion in Dinah Birch, 'John Ruskin: Political Economy and the Culture of "Social Affection"', *Ruskin Review and Bulletin*, vol. 10, no. 1 (Spring 2014), pp. 11–18 (p. 14).
5 *Works*, 16: 18, *A Joy for Ever*.
6 *Works*, 16: 19, *A Joy for Ever*.
7 *Works*, 16: 20, *A Joy for Ever* (Proverbs xxxi).
8 *Works*, 16: 54ff., *A Joy for Ever*.
9 *Works*, 35: 13, *Praeterita*.
10 *Works*, 17: 105, *Unto this Last*.
11 *Works*, 17: 46, *Unto this Last*.
12 *Works*, 17: 46, *Unto this Last*.
13 Richard G. Wilkinson and Kate Pickett, *The Spirit Level: Why Equality is Better for Everyone* (London: Penguin, 2010).
14 Richard Sennett, *The Craftsman* (New Haven, CT; London: Yale University Press, 2008).
15 *Works*, 16: 37, *A Joy for Ever*.
16 *Works*, 16: 37–8, *A Joy for Ever*.
17 Frederick O'Dwyer, *The Architecture of Deane and Woodward* (Cork: Cork University Press, 1997), p. 224.
18 O'Dwyer, *The Architecture of Deane and Woodward*, p. 227.
19 Bann quoted in Robert Hewison, *Ruskin on Venice* (New Haven, CT; London: Yale University Press, 2009), p. 120.
20 See Michael W. Brooks, *John Ruskin and Victorian Architecture* (London: Thames & Hudson, 1989), Chapter 8.
21 *Works*, 9: 349–50, *Stones of Venice, vol. 1*. See also J. B. Bullen, *Byzantium Rediscovered* (London: Phaidon, 2003), pp. 108–9. Wild had studied the Islamic architecture of Cairo, and collaborated with his brother-in-law Owen Jones, author of the celebrated *The Grammar of Ornament* (1856).
22 *Works*, 10: 302, *Stones of Venice, vol. 2*.
23 *Works*, 10: 303, *Stones of Venice, vol. 2*. See Stephen Kite, *Building Ruskin's Italy: Watching Architecture* (Farnham, Surrey: Ashgate, 2012), Chapter 4 '"Watchful wandering":

evolving a Gothic taxonomy', for a contextualization of this arch in Ruskin's 'Orders of Venetian Arches'.
24 *Works*, 10: 303, *Stones of Venice, vol. 2*.
25 Worksheets 205 and 206 are held in the Coniston Museum and Ruskin Library respectively.
26 *The Diaries of John Ruskin 1835–1847*, selected and ed. by J. Evans and J. H. Whitehouse (Oxford: Clarendon Press, 1956), p. 476. The editors of the *Diaries* tend to omit the detailed architectural notes as here: 'Then come twenty pages of undated notes: historical, architectural, and biblical', p. 476. The diary manuscript is: 'Diary 1851–52 (MS 08)', Ruskin Foundation (Ruskin Library, Lancaster University).
27 'Diary 1851–52 (MS 08)', p. 36, original emphasis.
28 *Works*, 10: 303, *Stones of Venice, vol. 2*, original emphasis.
29 *Works*, 10: 204, *Stones of Venice, vol. 2*.
30 *Works*, 10: 303, *Stones of Venice, vol. 2*.
31 *Works*, 10: 304, *Stones of Venice, vol. 2*.
32 *Works*, 10: 459, *Stones of Venice, vol. 2, editors' Appendix*.
33 See Brooks, *John Ruskin and Victorian Architecture*, p. 171.
34 Andrew Foyle, *Pevsner Architectural Guides: Bristol* (New Haven, CT; London: Yale University Press, 2004), pp. 31–2.
35 *Works*, 28: 562, *Fors Clavigera*, original emphasis.
36 *Works*, 28: 567–8, *Fors Clavigera*.
37 E. T. Cook, *The Life of John Ruskin, 2 vols, Vol. 2 1860–1900* (London: George Allen, 1911), p. 187, original emphasis.
38 From Adolf Loos, 'Glass and Clay', quoted in David Leatherbarrow, *Architecture Oriented Otherwise* (New York: Princeton Architectural Press, 2009), p. 69.

ILLUSTRATION CREDITS

The authors and publishers gratefully acknowledge the following for permission to reproduce material in the book. Every effort has been made to contact copyright holders for the permission to reprint material in the book. The publishers would be grateful to hear from any copyright holder who is not acknowledged here and will undertake to rectify any errors or omissions in future editions of the book.

0.1 © The Trustees of the British Museum.
1.1 © 'Front of the First Church of Christ, Scientist, in Berkeley, California. Attribution: Coro – Own work, http://commons.wikimedia.org/wiki/File:First_Church_of_Christ_Scientist.jpg. This file is licensed under the Creative Commons Attribution-Share Alike 3.0 Generic license.
1.2 © Simon Sadler.
1.3 © Simon Sadler.
1.4 © 'Apple store fifth avenue'. Attribution: Nk, http://commons.wikimedia.org/wiki/File:Apple_store_fifth_avenue.jpg. This file is licensed under the Creative Commons Attribution-Share Alike 2.5 Generic license.
2.1 No copyright reserved. Author Chris Schulte.
2.2 © Brooklyn Museum Archives. Goodyear Archival Collection. Visual materials [6.1.014].
2.3 No copyright reserved. Author Chris Schulte.
4.1 © Kim Trogal.
4.2 © Kim Trogal.
4.3 © Kim Trogal.
5.1 © The British Library Board, Add. 78628 A.
6.1 © Conway Library, The Courtauld Institute of Art, London. Photograph by Vaughan Hart.
6.2 © *Country Life*.

Illustration credits   **249**

6.3   © Conway Library, The Courtauld Institute of Art, London. Photograph by Vaughan Hart.
6.4   © The Trustees of the British Museum.
7.1   © Agency Spring/CVoA.
8.1   © RIBA Journal, www.ribaj.com.
9.1   © Ralph Doggen, Achim Menges.
9.2   © Pavlos Sideris, Achim Menges.
9.3   © Ralph Doggen, Achim Menges.
12.1 © Emiel Koole.
13.1 © Victoria and Albert Museum, London.
13.2 © Victoria and Albert Museum, London.
14.1 © Silke Ötsch.
14.2 © Silke Ötsch.
14.3 © Silke Ötsch.
15.1 © Cristian Suau.
15.2 © Cristian Suau.
15.3 © Cristian Suau.
15.4 © Cristian Suau.
16.1 © Owen Hatherley.
16.2 © Owen Hatherley.
16.3 © Owen Hatherley.
17.1 © Peter Nicholson.
17.2 © Hannah Lewi and Cameron Logan.
17.3 © Hannah Lewi and Cameron Logan.
18.1 © Kevin Mitchell.
18.2 © Kevin Mitchell.
18.3 © Kevin Mitchell.
19.1 © Witherford Watson Mann.
19.2 © Witherford Watson Mann.
20.1 © Stephen Kite.
20.2 © Courtesy of the Ruskin Museum, Coniston, Cumbria.
20.3 © Stephen Kite.

SELECT BIBLIOGRAPHY

Adorno, Theodor W., 'Cultural Criticism and Society' in *Prisms*, trans. Samuel and Shierry Weber (Cambridge, MA: MIT Press, 1967).
Alexander, Christopher, *The Timeless Way of Building* (New York: Oxford University Press, 1979).
Anderson, Stanford, 'Modern Architecture and Industry: Peter Behrens and the Cultural Policy of Historical Determinism', *Oppositions* (1977), pp. 52–71.
Anglès, Magda, *In Favour of Public Space: Ten Years of the European Prize for Urban Public Space* (Barcelona: Centre de Cultura Contemporània de Barcelona and ACTAR, 2011).
Arendt, Hannah, *The Human Condition* (Chicago, IL: University of Chicago Press, 1958).
Arendt, Hannah, *Between Past and Future* (New York: Penguin Books, 1993).
Aristotle. *Politics*, trans. H. Rackham (London: William Heinemann, 1972).
Ault, Bradley A., '*Oikos* and *Oikonomia*: Greek Houses, Households and the Domestic Economy', in *Building Communities: House, Settlement and Society in the Aegean*, ed. by R. Westgate, N. Fisher, and J. Whitley (*Studies of the British School of Archaeology at Athens*, 15 (2007)), pp. 259–65.
Austin, Norman, *Archery at the Dark of the Moon: Poetic Problems in Homer's Odyssey* (Berkeley: University of California Press, 1975).
Bateson, Gregory, *Steps to an Ecology of Mind* (New York: Ballantine, 1972).
Benoît-Lévy, Georges, *La Cité-Jardin* (Paris: Jouve, 1904, introduction by Charles Gide).
Blau, Judith, *Architects and Firms: A Sociological Perspective on Architectural Practice* (Cambridge, MA: MIT Press, 1988).
Booth, William James, *Households: On the Moral Architecture of the Economy* (Ithaca, NY; London: Cornell University Press, 1993).
Brand, Stewart, *How Buildings Learn: What Happens after They're Built* (New York; London: Viking, 1994).
Brand, Stewart, *Whole Earth Discipline: Why Dense Cities, Nuclear Power, Transgenic Crops, Restored Wildlands, and Geoengineering are Necessary* (New York: Penguin, 2010).
Brooks, Michael W., *John Ruskin and Victorian Architecture* (London: Thames & Hudson, 1989).

Brown, Tim, *Change by Design: How Design Thinking Transforms Organizations and Inspires Innovation* (New York: Harper Business, 2009).
Calvino, Italo, *Invisible Cities* (New York: Harcourt Brace, 1978).
Carlos-Kucharek, Jan, 'One Foot in the Past: Bespoke Prefabrication', *RIBA Journal*, July/August 2010, pp. 47–50.
Carson, Anne, *Economy of the Unlost: Reading Simonides of Keos with Paul Celan* (Princeton, NJ: Princeton University Press, 1999).
Castells, M., Portes, A., and Benton, L., *The Informal Economy* (London: The John Hopkins University Press, 1989).
Champy, Florent, 'Professional Discourses under the Pressure of Economic Values', *Current Sociology*, 54 (2006), pp. 649–61.
Champy, Florent, 'La culture professionnelle des architectes', in *Sociologie des Groupes Professionnels*, ed. by Didier Demazière and Charles Gadéa (Paris: La Découverte, 2010), pp. 152–62.
Chase, John, Crawford, Margaret and Kaliski, John, eds, *Everyday Urbanism* (New York: Monacelli Press, 1999).
Colquhoun, Alan, *Essays in Architectural Criticism* (Cambridge, MA: MIT Press, 1977).
Community Economies Research Network: http://www.communityeconomies.org
Cook, E. T. and Wedderburn, Alexander, eds, *The Works of John Ruskin* (London: George Allen, 1904–13).
Cooney, E. W., 'The Origins of the Victorian Master Builders', *The Economic History Review*, 8 (1955), pp. 167–76.
Cuff, Dana, *Architectural Practice: The Story of Practice* (Cambridge, MA: MIT Press, 1992).
Dallmayr, Fred, 'Exit from Orientalism', in A. L. Macfie (ed.), *Orientalism: A Reader* (Edinburgh: Edinburgh University Press, 2000), pp. 365–8.
Darley, Gillian, *John Evelyn: Living for Ingenuity* (New Haven, CT; London: Yale University Press, 2006).
Davis, Mike, *Planet of Slums* (London: Verso, 2006).
de Angelis, Massimo, 'On the Commons: A Public Interview with Massimo De Angelis and Stavros Stavrides', *E-flux*, vol. 17 (August 2010), http://www.e-flux.com/journal/view/150 (accessed 10.02.2001).
de Angelis, Massimo, 'The Commoner: A web journal for other values', http://www.commoner.org.uk
de Montlibert, Christian, *L'impossible Autonomie de l'Architecte: Sociologie de la Production Architecturale* (Strasbourg: Presses universitaires de Strasbourg, 1995).
Debord, Guy, *Introduction à une Critique de la Géographie Urbaine* (Brussels: Les Lèvres Nues, 1955).
Deleule, Didier and Guéry, François, *Le Corps Productif* (Paris: Mame, 1972).
Deleuze, Gilles and Guattari, Félix, *Mille Plateaux*, 1980, trans. Brian Massumi, *A Thousand Plateaus: Capitalism and Schizophrenia* (London: Continuum, 2002).
Derrida, Jacques, *Given Time 1: Counterfeit Money* (London: University of Chicago Press, 1992).
Donlan, Walter, 'The Homeric Economy', in *A New Companion to Homer*, ed. by Ian Morris and Barry Powell (Leiden: Brill, 1997), pp. 649–67.
Dougherty, Carol, *The Raft of Odysseus: The Ethnographic Imagination of Homer's Odyssey* (Oxford: Oxford University Press, 2001).
Downes, Kerry, *Vanbrugh* (London: Zwemmer, 1977).
Dunleavy, Patrick, *The Politics of Mass Housing in Britain, 1945–1975: A Study of Corporate Power and Professional Influence in the Welfare State* (Oxford: Clarendon Press, 1981).

Dutoit, Allison, Odgers, Juliet, and Sharr, Adam, eds, *Quality out of Control: Standards for Measuring Architecture* (London: Routledge, 2010).

d'Espagnet, Jean, *Enchyridion Physicae Restitutae, or, the Summary of Physicks Recovered Wherein the True Harmony of Nature is Explained … Wherein the True Harmonie of Nature is Explained …* trans. Dr Everard (London: W. Bentley, 1651).

Finnimore, Brian, *Houses from the Factory: System Building and the Welfare State 1942–74* (London: Rivers Oram Press, 1989).

Forty, Adrian, *Words and Buildings: A Vocabulary of Modern Architecture* (London: Thames & Hudson, 2000).

Franklin, Geraint with Harwood, Elain, Taylor, Simon and Whitfield, Matthew, 'England's Schools, 1962–1988: A Thematic Study', *English Heritage, Research Report Series*, No 33-2012 (2012).

Frederick, Christine, *The New Housekeeping: Efficiency Studies in Home Management* (Garden City, NY: Doubleday Page & Company, 1913).

Gadamer, Hans-Georg, *Reason in the Age of Science*, trans. Frederick G. Lawrence (Cambridge MA; London: MIT Press, 1981).

Gibson-Graham, J. K., *A Postcapitalist Politics* (Minneapolis; London: University of Minnesota Press, 2006).

Gide, André, *Fruits of the Earth*, London: Vintage 2002 [*Les Nourritures Terrestres*, Paris: Gallimard, 1917 (1898)].

Gide, Charles, *Exposition Universelle de 1900, Rapports du Jury International, Sixième Section: Economie Sociale* (Paris: Imprimerie Nationale, 1902).

Gide, Charles, *Political Economy*, trans. Constance Archibald, London: George G. Harrap, 1914 [*Cour d'Économie Politique*, 3ème édition, Paris: Recueil Sirey, 1913].

Glendinning, Miles and Stefan Muthesius, *Tower Block: Modern Public Housing in England, Scotland, Wales and Northern Ireland* (New Haven, CT; London: Yale University Press, 1994).

Goodbun, Jon, Iossifova, Deljana, and Till, Jeremy, eds, *Scarcity: Architecture in an Era of Diminishing Resources* (Chichester: Wiley, 2012).

Goodbun, Jon, Klein, Michael, Rumpfhuber, Andreas, and Till, Jeremy, *The Design of Scarcity* (Moscow: Strelka Press, 2014).

Habakkuk, H. J., 'Daniel Finch, 2nd Earl of Nottingham: His House and Estate', in *Studies in Social History: A Tribute to G. M. Trevelyan*, ed. J. H. Plumb (London: Longmans, Green, 1955), pp. 139–78.

Hall, Suzanne, *City, Street and Citizen: The Measure of the Ordinary* (London; New York: Routledge, 2012).

Harris, Frances, *A Passion for Government: The Life of Sarah, Duchess of Marlborough* (Oxford: Clarendon Press, 1991).

Harris, Frances, *Transformations of Love: The Friendship of John Evelyn and Margaret Godolphin* (Oxford: Oxford University Press, 2003).

Harvey, David, *The Condition of Postmodernity: An Enquiry into the Origins of Cultural Change* (London: Blackwell, 1991).

Hatherley, Owen, *Militant Modernism* (Winchester: Zero Books, 2009).

Hatherley, Owen, *A Guide to the New Ruins of Great Britain* (London: Verso, 2010).

Hensel, Michael and Menges, Achim, eds, 'Versatility and Vicissitude: Performance in Morpho-Ecological Design', *AD*, 78(2) (March/April 2008).

Hensel, Michael, Menges, Achim, and Weinstock, Michael, eds, 'Emergence: Morphogenetic Design Strategies', *AD*, 3/74 (May/June 2004).

Hensel, Michael, Menges, Achim, and Weinstock, Michael, eds, 'Techniques and Technologies in Morphogenetic Design', *AD*, 76(2) (March/April 2006).

Homer, see under M for Morris.

Hoskins, Andrew, *Nothing Like a Dame: The Scandals of Shirley Porter* (London: Granta, 2006).

Houghton, Walter E. Jr., 'The English Virtuoso in the Seventeenth Century: Part I', *Journal of the History of Ideas* 3 (1942), pp. 51–73; and 'Part II', *Journal of the History of Ideas* 3 (1942), pp. 190–219.

Howard, Ebenezer, *To-morrow: A Peaceful Path to Real Reform* (London: Swann Sonnenschein, 1898, republished 1902 under the title *Garden Cities of To-morrow*).

Huntington, John, 'Furious Insolence: The Social Meaning of Poetic Inspiration in the 1590s', *Modern Philology*, 94 (1997), pp. 305–26.

Ingold, Tim, 'The Textility of Making', *Cambridge Journal of Economics*, 34 (2010), 91–102.

Ingraham, Catherine, 'Lines and Linearity: Problems in Architectural Theory', in *Drawing/Building/Text: Essays in Architectural Theory*, ed. Kahn, Andrea (New York: Princeton Architectural Press, 1991), pp. 63–84.

Jenkins, Frank, *Architect and Patron: A Survey of Professional Relations and Practice in England from the Sixteenth Century to the Present Day* (London: Oxford University Press, 1961).

Kahn, Andrea, ed., *Drawing/Building/Text: Essays in Architectural Theory* (New York: Princeton Architectural Press, 1991).

Keay, Anna, *The Magnificent Monarch: Charles II and the Ceremonies of Power* (London: Continuum, 2008).

Kira, Alexander, *The Bathroom* (London: Penguin, 1976).

Kirk, Andrew G., *Counterculture Green: The Whole Earth Catalog and American Environmentalism* (Lawrence: University Press of Kansas, 2007).

Klossowski, Pierre, *Sade My Neighbor* (Evanston, IL: Northwestern University Press, 1991). Translation of *Sade mon prochain* (Seuil: Paris, 1947) by Alphonso Lingis.

Koolhaas, Rem, *Delirious New York: A Retroactive Manifesto for Manhattan* (London: Thames & Hudson, 1978).

Koppetsch, Cornelia, *Das Ethos der Kreativen* (Konstanz: UVK, 2006).

Kostof, Spiro, ed., *The Architect: Chapters in the History of the Profession* (Berkeley: University of California Press, 1977; repr. 2000).

Kurke, Leslie, *The Traffic in Praise: Pindar and the Poetics of Social Economy* (Ithaca, NY; London: Cornell University Press, 1991).

Laguerre, Michel S., *The Informal City* (London: Macmillan, 1994).

Lane, Barbara Miller, ed., *Housing and Dwelling: Perspective on Modern Domestic Architecture* (London: Routledge, 2007).

Le Play, Frédéric, *Economie Sociale* (Paris: Guillaumin, n.d., preface by Fernand Auburtin).

Le Play, Frédéric, *Les Ouvriers Européens*, 6 vols (Tours: Alfred Mame et Fils, 2nd edn, 1877–1879).

Lefebvre, Henri, *The Production of Space*, Chapter 5 'Contradictory Space' (Malden: Blackwell Publishing, 1974).

Leighninger, Robert D. Jr., 'Cultural Infrastructure: The Legacy of New Deal Public Space', *Journal of Architectural Education*, 49(4) (May, 1996), pp. 226–36.

Libeskind, Daniel, 'Between the Lines: Extension to the Berlin Museum, with the Jewish Museum', *Assemblage*, 12 (August, 1990), pp. 18–57.

Linebaugh, Peter, *The Magna Carta Manifesto: Liberties and Commons for All* (Berkeley: University of California Press, 2008).

Livingstone, Ken, *You Can't Say That: Memoirs of Ken Livingstone* (London: Faber & Faber, 2011).

Lyotard, Jean François, *Libidinal Economy*, trans. Iain Hamilton Grant (London: Continuum, 2004). Translation of *Economie Libidinale* (Paris: Les Editions De Minuit, 1974).

Mauss, Marcel, *The Gift: The Form and Reason for Exchange in Archaic Societies* (London: Routledge Classics, 2002).
McVicar, Mhairi, 'Specifying Intent at the Museum of Childhood', in *Architectural Research Quarterly*, 16(3) (2012), pp. 218–28.
Meadows, Donella, Meadows, Dennis, Rangers, Jørgen, and Behrens, William, *The Limits to Growth: A Report for the Club of Rome's Project on the Predicament of Mankind* (London: Universe Books, 1972).
Mehta, Lyla, ed., *The Limits to Scarcity: Contesting the Politics of Allocation* (London: Earthscan, 2010).
Mies, Maria and Bennholdt-Thomsen, Veronika, *The Subsistence Perspective: Beyond the Globalised Economy*, trans. Patrick Camiller (London: Zed, 1999).
Moore, Charles, 'You Have to Pay for Public Life', *Perspecta*, 9–10 (1965), pp. 57–106.
Morris, Ian and Powell, Barry, eds, *A New Companion to Homer* (Leiden: Brill, 1997).
Mumford, Lewis, *Technics and Civilization* (New York: Harcourt, Brace and Company, 1934).
Neeson, J. M., *Commoners: Common Right, Enclosure and Social Change in England, 1700–1820* (Cambridge: Cambridge University Press, 1993).
Nietzsche, Friedrich, *On the Use and Abuse of History for Life* (Sioux Falls, SD: NuVision Publications, 2007).
Nussbaum, Martha C., *Political Emotions: Why Love Matters for Justice* (Cambridge, MA: Belknap Press of Harvard University Press, 2013).
O'Dwyer, Frederick, *The Architecture of Deane and Woodward* (Cork: Cork University Press, 1997).
O'Malley, Therese and Wolschke-Bulmahn, Joachim, eds, *John Evelyn's 'Elysium Britannicum' and European Gardening* (Washington, DC: Dumbarton Oaks Research Library and Collection, 1998).
Ötsch, Silke,'The Emperor's New Firm: Inside the Global ¥€$ … and How to Get Out', *Graz Architecture Magazine*, 4 (2007), pp. 108–33.
Ötsch, Silke, 'ArchitektInnen zwischen Paternalismus und Kundenorientierung: Berufsethik', *Momentum Quarterly*, 4 (2013), pp. 183–95.
Parker Morris Committee, Ministry of Housing, and Local Government, *Homes for Today and Tomorrow* (London: Her Majesty's Stationery Office, 1961).
Peck, Jamie, 'Austerity Urbanism', *City*, 16(6) (2012), pp. 626–55.
Perez-Gomez, Alberto, *Architecture and the Crisis of Modern Science* (Cambridge, MA; London: MIT Press, 1983).
Picon, Antoine and Ponte, Alessandra, eds, *Architecture and the Sciences Exchanging Metaphors* (Princeton, NJ: Princeton Papers on Architecture, 2003).
Plato. *Critias*, trans. Rev. R.G. Bury (London: William Heinemann, 1981).
Plumb, J. H., ed., *Studies in Social History: A Tribute to G. M. Trevelyan* (London: Longmans, Green, 1955).
Polanyi, Karl, *The Livelihood of Man*, trans. Harry W. Pearson (New York; London: Academic Press, 1977).
Port, M. H., 'The Office of Works and Building Contracts in Early Nineteenth-Century England', *The Economic History Review*, 20 (1967), pp. 94–111.
Procacci, Giovanna, 'Social Economy and the Government of Poverty', in *The Foucault Effect*, ed. by Burchell, Graham, Gordon, Colin, and Miller, Peter (Chicago, IL: University of Chicago Press, 1991).
Redfield, James M., 'The Economic Man', in *Approaches to Homer*, ed. by Rubino, Carl A. and Shelmerdine, Cynthia W. (Austin: University of Texas Press, 1983), pp. 218–47.
Rogers, Richard and Fisher, Mark, *A New London* (London: Penguin Books, 1992).

Select bibliography **255**

Roy, Ananya, *Slumdog Cities: Rethinking Subaltern Urbanism*, in Angélil, Marc and Hehl, Rainer, *Informalize!* (Berlin: Ruby Press, 2012), pp. 109–21.

Rudofsky, Bernard, *Architecture without Architects: A Short Introduction to Non-Pedigreed Architecture* (New York: Doubleday, 1964).

Russell, Barry, *Building Systems, Industrialisation and Architecture* (London: John Wiley and Sons, 1981).

Saint, Andrew, *Towards a Social Architecture: The Role of School-Building in Post-War England* (New Haven, CT; London: Yale University Press, 1987).

Saint, Andrew, *Architect and Engineer: A Study in Sibling Rivalry* (New Haven, CT; London: Yale University Press, 2007).

Samuel, Flora, Butterworth, Carolyn, Lintonbon, Jo, Awan, Nishat, and Handler, Sophie, 'Cultural Value of Architecture Report' (University of Sheffield/AHRC, 2014), www.culturalvalueofarchitecture.org (accessed 01.09.2014).

Samuel, Flora, Coucill, Laura, Dye, Anne, and Tait, Alex, 'RIBA Home Improvements Report on Research in housing practice' (RIBA, 2013), www.architecture.com/research (accessed 10.02.2011).

Samuel, Raphael, *Theatre of Memory: Past and Present in Contemporary Culture* (London; New York: Verso, 1994).

Saumarez Smith, Charles, *The Building of Castle Howard* (London: Faber & Faber, 1990).

Seaford, Richard, *Money and the Early Greek Mind. Homer, Philosophy, Tragedy* (Cambridge: Cambridge University Press, 2004).

Sennett, Richard, *The Craftsman* (New Haven, CT; London: Yale University Press, 2008).

Sergison Bates architects, *Papers 2*, London 2007.

Sergison Bates architects, *Buildings*, Quart Verlag, Lucerne 2012.

Sharr, Adam, *Reading Architecture and Culture* (London: Routledge, 2012).

Shaw, R. Norman and Jackson, T. G., eds, *Architecture, a Profession or an Art: Thirteen Short Essays on the Qualifications and Training of Architects* (London: John Murray, 1892).

Singer, Kurt, '*Oikonomia*: An Inquiry into Beginnings of Economic Thought and Language', in *Aristotle 384–322 BC (Pioneers in Economics)* ed. by Blaug, Mark (Brookfield, VT: Edward Elgar Publishing Company, 1991).

Sörensen, Christiane and Liedtke, Karoline, eds, *Specifics: Discussing Landscape Approaches* (Hamburg: Jovis Verlag, 2014).

Starr, Kevin, *Golden Dreams: California in an Age of Abundance, 1950–1963* (Oxford; New York: Oxford University Press, 2009).

Stevenson, Christine, *Medicine and Magnificence: British Hospital and Asylum Architecture, 1660–1815* (New Haven, CT; London: Yale University Press for the Paul Mellon Centre for Studies in British Art, 2000).

Suau, Cristian, 'Potential Public Spaces in the Modern Suburbia: Urban Reflections for the Regeneration of Free Spaces', *Nordic Journal of Architectural Research*, (4) (2005), pp. 31–41.

Suau, Cristian, 'Transgressive Urbanism', in *Creativity Game: Theory and Practice of Spatial Planning Journal* (2013), pp. 70–4.

Suau, Cristian, *Climate and Urban Design of Maritime Public Spaces in Mediterranean Arab Cities*, PLEA Conference (Munich: Fraunhofer Verlag, 2014).

Suau, Cristian, 'Transgressive Urbanism: Borderlands and Urban Informality', *Specifics: Discussing Landscape Approaches*, ed. by Sörensen, Christiane and Liedtke, Karoline (Hamburg: Jovis Verlag, 2014), pp. 144–9.

Tapie, Guy, '*Les Architectes: Mutations d'une Profession* (Paris: L'Harmattan, 2000).

Tavenor, Robert, *Smoot's Ear: The Measure of Humanity* (New Haven, CT; London: Yale University Press, 2007).

Teige, Karel, *The Minimum Dwelling* (Cambridge, MA: MIT Press, 2002).

Thirsk, Joan, ed., *The Agrarian History of England and Wales*, vol. IV 1500–1640 (Cambridge: Cambridge University Press, 1967), pp. 396–465.

Todd, Margo, *Christian Humanism and the Puritan Social Order: Ideas in Context* (Cambridge: Cambridge University Press, 1987).

Tonkiss, Fran, 'Austerity Urbanism and the Makeshift City', *City*, 17(3) (2013), pp. 312–24.

Turner, Fred, *From Counterculture to Cyberculture: Stewart Brand, the Whole Earth Network, and the Rise of Digital Utopianism* (Chicago, IL: University of Chicago Press, 2006).

Vanbrugh, John, *The Complete Works*, vol. 4, *The Letters*, ed. by Webb, Geoffrey (London: Nonesuch Press, 1928).

von Reden, Sitta, *Exchange in Ancient Greece* (London: Gerald Duckworth & Co., 1995).

Wall, Christine, *An Architecture of Parts: Architects, Building Workers and Industrialisation in Britain 1940–70* (London: Routledge, 2013).

Westgate, R., Fisher, N., and Whitley J., eds, *Building Communities: House, Settlement and Society in the Aegean* (*Studies of the British School of Archaeology at Athens*, 15, 2007).

Wiener, Norbert, *Cybernetics: Or Control and Communication in the Animal and the Machines* (Cambridge, MA: MIT Press, 1961).

Wiener, Norbert, *The Human Use of Human Beings: Cybernetics and Society* (London: Free Association, 1989, first published 1954).

Xenos, Nicholas, *Scarcity and Modernity* (London; New York: Routledge, 1989).

INDEX

Page numbers in *italics* denotes an illustration/table/figure

Acland, Henry Wentworth 240
AD (journal) 109; 'Versatility and Vicissitude' edition (2008) 111–12
Adam, William 80
Adorno, Theodor W. 105
agriculture, urban 50
Albert, Prince 152
Alberti, Leon Battista 124
Alexander, Christopher 22
All Hallows church (London) 81
allotment gardening 54
Anne, Queen 74
Apple 20, 24
Apple Store (Manhattan) 20, *21*
architects 162–73; in Austria 165, 166, 172; and branding of place 93; clients 166; and co-production approach 94; creating sense of identity and belonging 92; earnings and income 87, 149, 165, 166; economy of skills 88–95; in financialized spaces 164–9; in France 165, 166, 172; impact of financial crisis (2008) on 162; influence on networks and communities 92; link to financial sphere 162–73; and mapping 94–5; marginality of 87; and networking 166; and professional ethics 163; professional image of 163; and proprietors 78–80, 81, 83; public perceptions of in UK 86, 87; role of in nineteenth century 156–7; role of 144, 148; shift from professional to financial criteria 169, 172–3; skillset of commercial 90–1; skillset of cultural 91; skillset of social 89–90; sources of income 165; star 162, 165, 166, 169; strategies and earnings 169, *170–1*; Swiss and UK compared 148–9; transforming mental and physical states 91; in UK 87–8, 147, 149, 164, 165, 172; in United States 88, 165, 166, 172
Architectural Association 109; 'Emergent Technologies and Design Group' 111
architectural education 86, 95, 149
architectural husbandry 73–83; and Blenheim 73–8, *75*, *77*, *79*, 80, 82; gentlemen and players 78–81; St Luke's Hospital for the Insane 81–3, *82*, 83
Architecture Foundation 227, 230
architecture schools 94, 124
Arendt, Hannah: 'The Crisis of Culture' 216; *The Human Condition* 34
Arica (Chile) 182; informal housing beyond 'Zona Urbana' in 182–3, *183*
Arica-Tacna borderland 176, 182–3
Aristippus 124
Aristotle: *Politics* 217
Armitage, Rachel 92
art connoisseurship 105
art-historical criticism: economy of and Libeskind prefabricated house 105–6
Arts and Humanities Research Council (AHRC): Home Improvements project 86

Austen, Jane 114; *Emma* 116; *Pride and Prejudice* 114
austerity urbanism 226–7
Austin, Norman 121
Australian Institute of Architects 213
Australian schools 204–14; Auditor-General's report on BER 212; Building the Education Revolution (BER) 204, 205, 208–14; Light Timber Construction (LTC) system 206–7; and multiplier effect 205–6; non-template solutions 212; objectives of BER programme 206; positive impact of BER 205, 212; response to BER by architects 205–6; South Australian Modular Construction system (SAMCON) 207; standardization aspiration 210–11; template solution 206–12, *209*, 213
Austria: architects in 165, 166, 172
Autarkic House project 138
avant-garde 39

Banham, Reyner 46
Bank of England 134–5
Bankside Open Spaces Trust 230
Bankside Urban Forest project 226, 227–35; challenges 228–9; design framework 232; incremental approach 228–32; maturing of *233*; origins 227; public space conception 229–30; seeds of 230–2, *231*
Bankside Urban Forest report (2007) 227, 228
Bankside Urban Pioneers initiative 230
Bann, Stephen 240
Barbon, Nicholas: *An Apology for the Builder* 79
Barcelona Olympic Village 199
Bateson, Gregory 19, 20, 21
Bauer, Catherine 15
Bay Region/Bay Region Style (California) 13–24; critique of by East Coast 22; and cybernetics 18–21; Eichler houses 16, 20; and equalitarianism 15–17, 24; features of 15, 16–17, 22, 23–4; First Church of Christ Scientist 13–14, *14*; and monumentality 13–15; and Mumford 17–18; People's Park 14, 19; Sea Ranch 16, *16*; and state of mind 17–22; *Whole Earth Catalog* 18, 20
beauty: in the built environment 92–3
bedroom tax 197
behavioural economics 87

Belgium 147
Bennett, Alan 198
Bennholdt-Thomsen, Veronika 49
BER (Building the Education Revolution) 204, 205, 208–14
Bernal, J.D. 43–4
Betham Tower (Manchester) *168*
Bethnal Green Museum of Childhood 151
Better Bankside 230, 232, 234
Bevans, John 82
Bilbao effect 166
Bill Hillier 94
biotechnics 18
Bishop, Peter 228
Blankenberge library project (Belgium) 147
Blau, Judith 163
Blenheim Palace (Oxfordshire) 73–8, *75*, *77*, 79, 80, 82
body: Lyotard on 108
Bohlin Cywinski Jackson practice 22
Bourdieu, Pierre 74, 86, 105
Bourgeois, Victor 136
Boyle, Robert: *Some Motives and Incentives to the Love of God* 65
Brand, Stewart 13, 18, 19, 21–2; *How Buildings Learn* 22
brand-name architecture 107
branding of place 93
BREEAM 138
Britain *see* UK
British Institute of Architects 157–8
Brompton Boilers (Iron Museum) (London) 151–9, *153*, *155*; architectural front 152; conception of 152; critique of by *The Builder* 155–6; design and construction 152, 153; hostile reviews of 156–7; production of 155–6; value of 152–3, 157
Brown, Jerry 18
brownfield land 194
Builder, The (journal) 154, 155
Building Design 191, 195
Building the Education Revolution *see* BER
building industry 143–8
Building Stable Communities programme 194
Burdett, Richard 195
Burj Khalifa (Dubai) 217, 219, 221–3, *222*, *223*, 224
Burley-on-the-Hill (Rutland) 76, *76*, 79
Burroughs, Andrew 20
Business Improvement Districts 234

CABE (Commission for Architecture and the Built Environment) 93–4, 194, 195, 200, 227; *Physical Capital* report 89
Caffentzis, George C. 56
California 13–24, 18–19, 22–3; 'delirium' of 23; design culture 23; East Coast/West Coast dialectic 22–3; Sacramento's Bateston Building 19, *19*; *see also* Bay Region/Bay Region Design
California Water Atlas 19
Calvino, Italo 103
Camden, London Borough of 196–7; gentrification 198—9; municipal housing programmes 198; plan to rehouse families outside of London 196–7
Capita 195
capitalism 162–4, 238; and professional ethics of architects 163
care labour 49; commons and hidden 55–6
carretoneros (Santiago de Chile) 181
casas de carton (cardboard houses) 182–3
Castell, Manuel 177
Castle, Helen 111–12
Cathedral Group 92
Centre Commercial Euralille (Lille) *168*
Chambers, William 74
Champy, Florent 163
'Change We Can See, The' campaign 192
Chatsworth House (Derbyshire) 79
Chicago School 22
Church, Thomas 15
CIAM congress (1929) (Frankfurt) 136
Cité-jardin de Suresnes 28, 35
cités-jardins: and *économie sociale* 27–8; funding of 28–9; as interpretation of Howard's garden city 27; Paris 27–9, *28*
Ciudad Juárez (Mexico) 184 *see also* El Paso-Ciudad Juárez borderland
climate change 138
Club of Rome 137–8, 139; *Limits to Growth* 137
co-production approach 94
Cockerell, C.T. 154
colonais 183, 184
Commission for Architecture and the Built Environment *see* CABE
commons 49–57; and gift community 51–2; hidden care labour of 55–6; and local food production 50–1; and reciprocity 52; *see also* Incredible Edible
Community Economies Collective 57
contractors 147
'Contracts by Gross' 156
Cook, Sydney 198

Cooney, E.W. 156
Copenhagen 87
cost effectiveness analysis 88
council estates/houses: demolition of 199–200; selling off of 47, 194–5, 197
Council of Scientific Management in the Home: *Meals in Modern Homes* 41
crime: design against 92
Crystal Palace 152, 154–5, 158
Cullen, Gordon 40–1, *41*, 43, *43*, 45, 46, *46*
cultural capital 86, 105
cultural syncretism 18
Cultural Value of Architecture in Homes and Neighbourhoods Project (CVoA) 88
cybernetics: and Bay Region (California) 18–21
Cyclopes, land of the 121–2

Dallegret, François 46
Dallmayr, Fred 102
Dance, George 81
Darent Valley Hospital (Dartford) 192, *193*
Davies, Mike 138
De Angelis, Massimo 56
de Botton, Alain 89
Deleule, Didier 115
dematerialised wall 43
Denmark 87
Department for Communities and Local Government (DCLG) 146
Department of the Seine 27, 28
Derrida, Jacques 49; and gift exchange 54–5
design and build contracts 147, 187, 193
Design Council 227
Design for London 200, 201
Design Thinking 13
d'Espagnet, Jean 62
disburbanism, Tory 196–200
Dougherty, Carol 120
Dovey, Kim 87
Dubai 216–25; Burj Khalifa 217, 219, 221–3, *222*, *223*, 224; characteristics of large-scale residential developments 220; economic diversification 219; establishment of the Real Estate Regulatory Agency (RERA) 216–17; International City 217, 219–21, *221*, 224; origins of contemporary economy 218–19; role of architecture 216–17; and scarcity 218, 224
Dudley Report (1944) 40–1
Durand, J.N. 157

Eckbo, Garrett 15, 17
École Polytechnique 157
économie sociale 31–4; and Gide's proposed cathedral 33–4; and Paris' *cités-jardins* 29–34; and Paris Universal Exhibition (1867) 32, 33; and Paris Universal Exhibition (1900) 29–31
economy of means 143–50
Edinburgh 198
Edinburgh Royal Infirmary 80–1
education, architectural 86, 95
Ehrenkratz, Ezra 208
Eichler houses (Bay Region) 16, 20
Eisenman, Peter 22
El Paso (Texas) (US) 183–4; Fox Flea Market 184, *184*
El Paso-Ciudad Juárez borderland 176, 182, 183–4
Emmons, Paul 39
English Heritage 207
English Partnerships 194
environmentalism 137–8
equalitarianism 13–24
equilibrium: and architectural membrane 115
Evans, Martyn 92
Evans, Robin 40
Evelyn, John 59–66; background 59–60; and Christianity 66; expert in collections 63; 'History of Religion' 61; 'Instructions Oeconomique' 59, 60–6; and labour 62–4; literary career 59; and love 64–6; and microcosm metaphor 61–2, 64; *see also* Sayes Court (Deptford)
Evelyn, Mary 59
Everett, Percy 206
existenzminimum 40, 136

famille-souche 32
Federici, Silvia 50
Ferias Libres (Santiago de Chile) 181
fetishism 109
financial crisis (2008) 135, 138, 162, 165, 191, 226, 237
financial sphere: link to architecture 162–73
financialized capitalism 162–4
Fisher, Mark (politician) 199 [? not sure if these two names are the same?]
Fisher, Mark (writer) 195
Ford, Henry 39, 40
Fordist house 38–47
Forrester, Jay 137

Forty, Adrian 45
Foucault, Michel 73
France: architects in 165, 166, 172; *Caisse des Dépôts* 28
Frankfurt bathroom 39–40
Frederick, Christine: *The New Housekeeping* 39
free professions 163
Fry, Maxwell 210
Fujiwara, Daniel 87

Garden Cities 27
Geddes, Patrick 18
Gehl, Jan 94
Geneva 148
gentrification 192; Camden 198—9
Gibson, Lisanne 86
Gibson-Graham, J.K. 57
Gide, Andrew: *Les Nourritues Terrestres* 34–5
Gide, Charles 29, 31–4
Giedion, Siegfried 136
gift community: and commons 51–2
gift economy: and Incredible Edible 52–6
gift exchange: and Derrida 54–5; and Odysseus' stories 119
Godly household 60–1
Godolphin, Margaret 65
Godwin, William 132
Gomez, Alberto Perez 157
Gothic 241, 242
Gottman, Erving 179
Gove, Michael 200, 212, 213
Granary, The (Bristol) 244, *245*
Great Exhibition (1851) 152, 154
Green, Nick 52
Gropius, Walter 39, 44, 209–10
Guéry, François 115

Hall, Peter 93
Halpern, David 92
Halprin, Lawrence 15, 17
Harvey, David 133, 138
Hayball and Gray Puksand Architects 208
Henry, Ken 205
Hensel, Michael 19, 111–14
heritage 93
Holocaust 104, 105
home economics 86–96
home ownership: attitudes to 146–7
Home Sweet Home (film) 199
Homer 217; *Odyssey* 118–25
Homes and Communities Agency 195; *Additionality Guide* 87

Homes for Today and Tomorrow see Parker Morris report
Hood, Walter 17
hospital buildings 80
Housing Act (1980) 47
Housing Associations 146, 197
housing crisis 44, 196, 201
Housing Market Renewal programme 197
Howard, Ebenezer 27
Howard, John Galen 14
Hughes, Francesca 86
human-nature dualism 139

IDEO 13, 20
Incredible Edible, Todmorden UK (2011) 49, 50–7, *50*; activities 50–1; care in giving and taking 51–6; and gift economy 51, 52–3; propaganda gardens 51
incrementalism 234, 235
informal economies 127, 176, 177, 181, 185
informal urbanism: in Latin American border cities 175–85
Ingold, Tim 76
Ingraham, Catherine 83
International City (Dubai) 217, 219–21, *221*, 224
International Style 23
iron 154, 155–6
Iron Museum *see* Brompton Boilers

Jebel Ali (Dubai) 218
Jewish Museum (Berlin) 104
Jobs, Steve 17, 20, 22
Jones, Owen: *Grammar of Ornament* 158

Kerslake, Bob 195
Keynes, John Maynard 44, 205
Kickstart programme 195
King's Cross redevelopment 201, *202*
Klein, Alexander 39
Klingmann, Anna: *Brandscapes* 87
Klossowski, Pierre 109, 110
Koolhas, Rem 23, 158–9
Kucharek, Jan-Carlos 101, 102

labouring classes 31–2, 34
Laguerre, Michel 177
Landor 224
Latin-American border cities: informal urbanism in 175–85
Le Corbusier 157
Le Play, Frédéric 31–2

Leatherbarrow, David 99
LEED 138
Leppla, Heinrich 136
Libeskind, Daniel 99–107
Libeskind prefabricated house 99–107; and economy of art-historical architectural economy 105–6; economy of technical efficiency and commercial profit 101–3, 106; in *RIBA Journal* 99; self-referential economy of shape-forms 104–5, 106; as a thing-unto-itself 103–4, 106
libidinal economy 108–16; and membrane 109, 111–16, *113*, *115*; and Sade 109–10; sexuality and monetary systems 109–10
Light Timber Construction (LTC) system 206–7
Linebaugh, Peter 56
Livingstone, Ken 197, 227
Lloyd Wright, Frank 43
local public space projects 235
Lohmann, Larry 133
Loi Bonnevay (1912) 28–9
Loi Cornudet (1919) 28, 29
Loi Siegfried (1894) 28
London 196–7, 200–1; exodus from 196–7; need for new homes 146; new brick face 201; regeneration 201; rise in house prices 146
London Councils 146
London Metropolitan University 109
Loubert, Emile François 30–1
love: Evelyn on 64–6
Lucretius: *De Rerem Natura* 64
Lyotard, Jean-François 108; on body 108; *Economie Libidinale* 108, 109–11; and political economy 109–10

Maccreanor Lavington 201
MacMillan, Sebastian 88
Macvicar, John 158
Major, John 193
Malthus, Reverend Thomas 31, 132–3; *An Essay on the Principle of Population* 132–3; Marx's critique of 134; *Political Economy* 132; and Soane 133–4
Manchester 196, *196*, 199
Manhattan 23
mapping 94–5, 176
Marcus, Clare Cooper and Sarkissian, Wendy: *Housing as if People Mattered* 92
Marlborough, Duke and Duchess of 74, 75, 76, 78, 79, 80
Martin, Leslie 95

Marx, Karl: critique of Malthus 134
mass housing debate 136
mass-produced house 44
mass production 39, 102
Master Builders 156
Mauss, Marcel 52, 53
Maybeck, Bernard 13, 14
Meades, Jonathan 193
Meals in Modern Homes report (1956) 41, *42*, 45
membrane, architectural 111–12, *112*; and equilibrium 115–16; and libidinal economy 109, 111–16, *113*, *115*
Memorialists 158
Menges, Achim 109, 111, 112–16
Merz, Michael 105
metapolisation 177
microcosm metaphor: and Evelyn 61–2
Mies, Maria 49, 50
Mies van der Rohe, Ludwig 43, 137
Ministry of Housing and Local Government 45 [not sure which one is correct?]
Ministry of Local Government and Housing 44
mixed development 92
MLTW 16
modular coordination 44
Modular Society, The 44
Montlibert, Christian de 163
Moore, Charles 14, 15, 17, 22
Morrison, Kerry 52–3
multiplier effect 205–6
Mulvey, Laura 109
Mumford, Lewis 15, 17–18; *Technics and Civilization* 18

National Planning Policy Framework 200
nemó 217–18
neo-classical economics 132, 134
neo-liberalism 138, 175, 195, 235
Netherlands 93
networking: and architects 166
New Economics Foundation 93, 94
New Labour urbanism 191–6, 200
New York Museum of Modern Art 22
Newham Council 197, 198
Nottingham, 2nd Earl of (Daniel Finch) 79

Ocean 111
Odysseus 118–25; and building a raft 119, 120; economic crisis of 118–19, 124; and exotic travel for architects 124; lessons learned in the land of the Cyclops 121–2; recognition and renewal with Penelope 123; renewing households by recalling founding stories 123; stories of and gift exchange 119; stories of 120, 121; stories of as valuable intellectual goods 121
oikonomia 118, 217–18, 224, 238
Olcayto, Rory 193
Olympic Village (London) 199
open systems building 44–5
Oxford 198
Oxford Museum 239–40, 242

Pan-American cities 175–85; Arica-Tacna borderland 176, 182–3; El Paso-Ciudad Juárez borderland 176, 182, 183–4; and informal economies 176; informal urban dynamics of 177; map *178*; Santiago de Chile 176, 177–81, *180*; tension between formal and informal socio-spatial productions 177, 179; transgressive informality in 176–7
Paris: *cités-jardins* 27–9, *28*; and *économie sociale* 29; School of Advanced Urban Studies 28; Universal Exhibition (1867) 32, 33–4; Universal Exhibition (1900) 29–31, *30*, 32–3
Parker Morris report (1961) 38–45; Cullen's diagrams 40, *41*, 43, 45, 46, *46*; and dematerialised wall 43; 'New Patterns of Living' section 40–1; and open systems building 44–5; setting up of 44; and *Space in the Home* design manuel 45
Pathfinder programme 200
pauperism 31
Paxton, Joseph: and Crystal Palace 152, 154–5
Pelletier, Louise 157
Perelman, M. 133, 134
Pevsner, Nicholas 152
Phooey Architects 212
Picard, Alfred 30
Pike, Alexander 138
Piketty, Thomas: *Capital in the Twenty-First Century* 238
planning permission, securing 146
Plato 124; *Symposium* 64
Policy Exchange 197, 199
political economy 31–2, 115–16, 163; and architectural membrane 114; and Lyotard 109–10; material and craft in Ruskin's 237–46; and social economy 31–2

poor: and Malthus 132–3
Poor Laws 133
Pope, Alexander 75
population: and Malthus 132
Port, M.H. 156
Porter, Shirley 194
Post Occupancy Evaluation 95
poststructuralism 110
poverty 31; and scarcity 133
Power, Anne 195
Power Tower (Linz) *167*
prefabricated construction 99 *see also* Libeskind prefabricated house
Prescott, John 195
Price, Cedric 46
Private Finance Initiative (PFI) 192–6
Procacci, Giovanna 31
project managers 145
Pseudomodernism 193, 195–6
Pugin, Augustus: *True Principles* 158
Punter, John 93
Puritans 60

QinetiQ 195
qualitative value of architecture 158–9

Real Estate Regulatory Agency (RERA) (Dubai) 216–17
Redcross Way project 234
regeneration 194
Regional Development Agencies 200
RIBA Journal 99, *100*; article on Libeskind prefabricated house 99–107
RIBA (Royal Institute of British Architects) 44, 88, 95; Student Destinations survey 86
Ring, Heather 234
risk management 145
Robbins, Lord: *An Essay on the Nature and Significance of Economic Science* 135–6
Rogers, Richard 191, 194, 195, 199
Ronan Point 198
Rosenblatt, Ted 92
Rotterdam Academy of Architecture and Urban Design 109
Rowe, Colin 9
Royal Docks 201
Royal Institute of British Architects *see* RIBA
Ruskin, John 237–46; on brickmaking 244–5; on Crystal Palace 154–5; and Gothic 242; and Hinksey Road experiment (Oxford) 245–6; lectures to Manchester mill-owners 238; on material and craft 239–40; *Praeterita* 238; *Seven Lamps* 158; *Stones of Venice* 237, 240–4; and Tana window 240–5, *241, 243*, 246; *Unto this Last* 237, 238, 239, 244; view of economy 237–9

Sade, Marquis de 109, 110
St John, Caruso 151, 159
St Luke's Hospital for the Insane (London) 73–4, 81–3, *82*
Santiago de Chile 176, 177–81, *180*; *carretoneros* 181; *Ferias Libres* 181; *Vendedores Ambulantes* 181
Sartre, Jean-Paul 131
Saunders, George 156
Sayes Court (Deptford) 59–66; Evelyn's 'Instructions Oeconomique' 59, 60–6; Evelyn's plan of intended improvements 59, *60*, 62–3
scarcity 131–40; and architecture 139–40; and Club of Rome report 137–8; as constructed 139–40; and Dubai 218, 224; and economics 135–6, 140; and existenzminimum 136; and Malthus 132–3, 134, 135; and mass housing debate 136; and neo-liberalism 138; and poverty 133; and Robbins 135–6
Schneider, Tatjana and Till, Jeremy: *Flexible Housing* 45
School Construction Systems Development (SCSD) model 208
Semper, Gottfried 152
Sennett, Richard: *The Craftsman* 239–40
Seraphick friendships 65
service sector 148–50
sexuality: and monetary systems 109–10
Shoreditch Trust 94
Sideris, Pavlos 113
Silicon Valley 18
Simms, Andrew 131
Singer, Kurt 217, 218, 219
Smith, Neil 138
Soane, John 133–4; Bank of England 134–5
social economy *see économie sociale*
Social Function of Science, The 43–4
social Thatcherism 193
Société d'économie sociale 31, 32
South Australian Modular Construction system (SAMCON) 207
South Kensington Museum 151
Southampton 191
Space in the Home 45
Space Syntax 94

Stam, Mart 136
star architects 162, 165, 166, 169
Starr, Kevin 17, 18
Stiglitz, Joseph 205
Studio Libeskind 104
Sunday newspapers: architecture columns 105–6
sustainability 112
Swiss Engineers' and Architects Institute (SIA) 149
Switzerland 148; architects 148–9; architectural schools 149; housing market 146
systems building 44–5

Tacna (Peru) 182 *see also* Arica-Tacna borderland
Tana window (Venice) 240–5, *241*, *243*, 246
Taut, Bruno 40
Taylor, Frederick Winslow: *Principles of Scientific Management* 38–9
Taylor, Jeremy 66
Taylorism 38–9
Teige, Karel: *The Minimum Dwelling* 136
templates 208–9; and school building in Australia 206–12, *209*, 213
Thatcher, Margaret 38, 46
theōria 124
Thompson, D'Arcy Wentworth: *On Growth and Form* 20–1
Todd, Margo 60
Tory disurbanism 196–200
Tuke, William 81–2
typification 209

UK: architects in 87—8, 147, 149 164, 165, 172; architectural education 95; 'Building Schools for the Future' scheme 205, 213; construction industry 148; designing public space in austerity 226–35; home ownership 146; public-private partnerships 187; school building 207–8; service sector 148; and visioning 93

Union Street Urban Orchard 234
United Arab Emirates 219, 223
United States: architects in 88, 165, 166, 172; school building 208
University of Bristol 92
University of California (Berkeley) 14
Urban Renaissance 194, 195–6
Urban Task Force 194, 195
urbanism: austerity 226—7; Latin American border cities and informal 175—85; New Labour 191–6, 200
Urbed 93

value 87, 88; of architecture 157–8
Van den Broek, Johannes 136
van der Ryn, Sim 18–19
Vanbrugh, John 74, 76–8, 79, 80, 82
Vendedores Ambulantes, Santiago de Chile 181
Vila, Joan 136
villa, ancient: and economy 99, 101, 103, 106, 107
visioning 93
Vitruvian Man 62
Vitruvius 157; *On Architecture* 124

Wandsworth project 145–6
Warhurst, Pam 53
Watkin, David 134
Westminster Council 194
Wild, James 151, 240
Wilkinson, Richard G. and Pickett, Kate: *The Spirit Level* 239
window wall 44
Witherford Watson Mann Architects (WWM) 227
Wittman, Richard 73
Wurster, William 20
WWM 230

York Retreat 81–2

Zurich 146